GLOBAL
SOUTH
ASIA

Padma Kaimal
K. Sivaramakrishnan
Anand A. Yang
SERIES EDITORS

New Lives in Anand

Building a Muslim Hub in Western India

Sanderien Verstappen

UNIVERSITY OF WASHINGTON PRESS

Seattle

New Lives in Anand was made possible in part by a grant from the Andrew W. Mellon Foundation, with additional support from the Department of Social and Cultural Anthropology at the University of Vienna.

Copyright © 2022 by the University of Washington Press
Design by Copperline Book Services Inc.
Typeset in Garamond Premier Pro by PageMajik

26 25 24 23 22   5 4 3 2 1
Printed and bound in the United States of America

The digital edition of this book may be downloaded and shared under a Creative Commons Attribution Non-commercial No derivatives 4.0 international license (CC-BY-NC-ND 4.0). For information about this license, see https://creativecommons.org/licenses/by-nc-nd/4.0. To use this book, or parts of this book, in any way not covered by the license, please contact University of Washington Press. This license applies only to content created by the author, not to separately copyrighted material.

UNIVERSITY OF WASHINGTON PRESS
uwapress.uw.edu

LIBRARY OF CONGRESS CATALOGING-IN-PUBLICATION DATA ON FILE
ISBN 978-0-295-74963-1 (hardcover)
ISBN 978-0-295-74964-8 (paperback)
ISBN 978-0-295-74965-5 (ebook)

S|H   **The Sustainable History Monograph Pilot**
M|P   Opening Up the Past, Publishing for the Future

This book is published as part of the Sustainable History Monograph Pilot. With the generous support of the Andrew W. Mellon Foundation, the Pilot uses cutting-edge publishing technology to produce open access digital editions of high-quality, peer-reviewed monographs from leading university presses. Free digital editions can be downloaded from: Books at JSTOR, EBSCO, Internet Archive, OAPEN, Project MUSE, and many other open repositories.

While the digital edition is free to download, read, and share, the book is under copyright and covered by the following Creative Commons License: CC-NC-ND 4.0. Please consult www.creativecommons.org if you have questions about your rights to reuse the material in this book.

When you cite the book, please include the following URL for its Digital Object Identifier (DOI): https://doi.org/10.6069/9780295749655

> We are eager to learn more about how you discovered this title and how you are using it. We hope you will spend a few minutes answering a couple of questions at this URL:
> **https://www.longleafservices.org/shmp-survey/**

More information about the Sustainable History Monograph Pilot can be found at https://www.longleafservices.org.

CONTENTS

Preface: On the Road to Anand ix

Map of Gujarat and Surroundings xiii

Map of Anand Town and Surroundings xiv

Acknowledgments xv

INTRODUCTION
Reorientation in a Post-Violence Landscape 3

CHAPTER 1
Regional Orientations: The Charotar Sunni Vohras 23

CHAPTER 2
Rural-Urban Transitions: From the Village to the Segregated Town 45

CHAPTER 3
Uprooted and at Home: Transnational Routes of (No) Return 70

CHAPTER 4
Getting Around: Middle-Class Muslims in a Regional Town 95

CONCLUSION
New Lives, New Concepts 116

Appendix: Tables 129

List of Characters 137

Glossary 139

Notes 141

Bibliography 153

Index 169

Preface

On the Road to Anand

On a hot day in September 2011, we step into an old and not-so-white car. The day's journey leads to the town of Anand from the nearby city of Ahmedabad. Behind the wheel during the two-hour trip is Amrapali Merchant, Professor of Sociology at the Sardar Patel University in Anand.[1] She takes the "normal" (free) road—not the new expressway that has a toll booth—and in doing so displays her impressive driving skills: she overtakes buses, trucks, two-wheelers, and buffalo-drawn carts, while successfully avoiding bumping into speeding cars, stray dogs, and the occasional cow that strolls onto the road. The rickshaws and buses we pass are packed—elbows stick out from windows. Food stalls and tea shops along the road abound. On either side of the road are the tobacco, ginger, and potato fields of the Charotar region, cold-storage facilities where farmers store their produce, small-scale factories and processing workshops that cater to the agricultural economy, and the occasional air-conditioned restaurant. It has rained and the road is muddy, so we keep the windows closed.

As the hustle and bustle of a rural road unfolds before us, Amrapali points at landmarks, tells stories, and shares her life philosophy inspired by Jainism. Finally, we enter Anand, cross the "overbridge" (an overpass) and head toward the main road that is the pulse of Anand: Anand-Vidyanagar Road. Just before the overpass, as we enter the town, Amrapali suddenly asks me, "What is your religion?" When I mention my Catholic family in the Netherlands, she continues:

> All religions are pathways to God. Now, look outside the car. These houses you see weren't there before. This was just agricultural land. In 2002, there were riots here. Then, there was a lot of killing in the villages around here, and so many Muslims were murdered. After that, Muslims left their village and came here. Maybe 50,000 Muslims are now living in Anand. They occupy the gates of the town. Whenever you enter Anand, you pass Muslims.

As we cross the overpass, I look out the window but do not see much that indicates a Muslim presence (figure P.1). The sights that strike me on that day are the construction along the road, some churches—which stand out from the landscape due to their height and whiteness—and the blue patches of tents

FIGURE P.I. View from the overpass, Anand. (Photo by the author, 2014.)

(which, I learned later, are the temporary homes of temporary laborers—both Hindu and Muslim—working in Anand's thriving construction industry).

As we continue our journey through Anand, into the spaces I learn to perceive later as Hindu areas, Amrapali points out vegetable markets, the town hall, and the Sony store, where she stops to buy a computer cable. We pass the statue of Bhaikaka, the hero-engineer who is credited with designing the spacious and airy campus area of Vallabh Vidyanagar. Vidyanagar, as residents call it, is an educational hub of Gujarat, home to the Sardar Patel University and its many affiliated colleges and schools, and attracts students from all over India and Nepal. This is our destination. At Sardar Patel University I register to start my research. Amrapali makes sure I am assigned housing on campus.

IT WAS INITIALLY through the directions of non-Muslims that I was able to see the Muslim spaces of the town from the outside. Like many other researchers who have studied the Charotar region, my research started with Hindu and Jain contacts. I could have remained in the campus area, which is seen by Muslims as a Hindu area, although Muslims also participate in it as students, staff members, and consumers. I could also have accepted the invitations of Hindu friends,[2] who generously offered to host me during my research. But I had come with the aim of studying lesser-known perspectives. After two months, I found a Vohra family willing to rent out the apartment above their house to me, and I moved into the Muslim area that I had seen from the car window on my first day in Anand.

The stories I tell here stem from my experiences of living in Anand for ten months in 2011–2012, with repeat visits in 2014 and 2017, and from interviews and observations with overseas Gujarati Muslims in the United Kingdom (in 2012 and 2016) and United States (in 2015 and 2018). The aim of this research was to study one of India's Muslim areas in the making, and to see it from the perspective of those who participate in its making. During most of the research period, I lived in a housing society described by its residents as relatively well-to-do within the economically heterogeneous Muslim area. Housing societies (a group of neighboring houses that, like a subdivision, share joint regulations) tend to develop a feeling of commonality, in that residents are broadly aware of who their co-residents are and develop ideas about their shared characteristics. The residents of this housing society, which had twenty-four houses, described it as middle-class territory. They self-identified as middle-class people, and as Muslims. While a few neighboring housing societies consisted of Christians, most of the residents of the surrounding housing societies were also middle-class Muslims.

My encounters with this neighborhood started with my landlady, Shahinben Vahora (a pseudonym), and Minaz Pathan, a young woman who worked with me as a research assistant, both of whom had their own local networks. Shahinben no longer lives in Anand and has since moved to Australia, but at that time she worked as an English teacher in a Catholic school funded by the state government, and her husband ran a small business as a vendor on a pushcart. Her two sons had moved to Australia a few years before I arrived, and their remittances had been used to build an apartment on top of the house, as accommodation during their visits. The apartment became available for rent soon after the younger son's visit had ended. From here, I started participating in the social life of the neighborhood and in the regional and transnational networks of my neighbors.

The neighborhood study was shaped by participation in neighborhood life, interviews, and a survey I conducted in 147 Muslim households (Survey A).[3] Besides walking around with Shahinben and Minaz, I visited organizations in the neighborhood and became a frequent visitor to a nearby primary school and a health clinic. It did not take long for my new neighbors and acquaintances to start inviting me to accompany them to places near and far: a shop, a school, a workplace, or the home of a relative. Through these invitations I became involved in a variety of movements and flows. The neighborhood study grew into a regional study by following my new acquaintances to the places that mattered to them in the surrounding villages and towns, and partly by developing my own contacts with Muslim associations.[4] These journeys—on foot, on two-wheelers, or in cars or shared rickshaws—brought many topics, destinations, and pathways under the scope of conversation.

During these encounters, I also met overseas Indians from the United Kingdom and United States, visiting their region of origin. Some of these visitors were very busy, and they granted my project only a few minutes of their time; others welcomed my company and took me along for several days while they were arranging their affairs. As the transnational life of Muslims in Anand centers mostly on the United Kingdom, the United States, and Australia, I conducted follow-up research in two of these locations, following the leads of the British and American visitors I had met in Gujarat, who supported me in continuing my research among their families and communities abroad.[5] In these ways, I gradually came to see how the neighborhood was embedded in the town, the region, and the transnational networks that surround it.

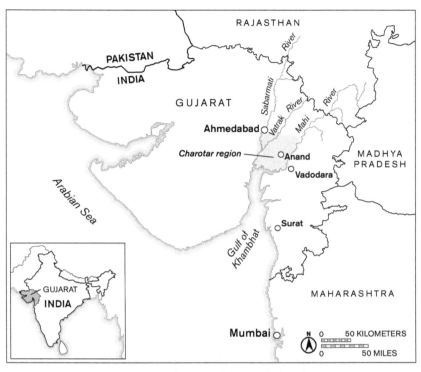

MAP 1. Gujarat and surroundings, with the Charotar region highlighted. (Map by Ben Pease.)

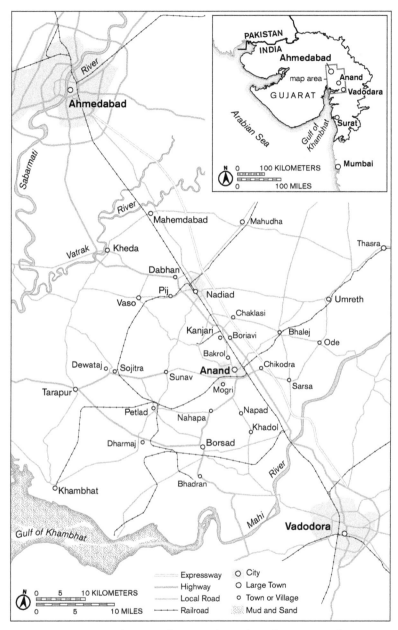

MAP 2. Anand town and surroundings. (Map by Ben Pease.)

ACKNOWLEDGMENTS

This book could be written because of many people in India, the United Kingdom, and the United States, who welcomed me into their lives and shared their stories. I thank all of them, particularly Roshan and Yasin Vahora; Abedaben Vahora; Minaz Pathan; Rahila, Selma, and Bibi Vahora; Suhanna and Rukhsar Pathan; Ilyas Vahora; Mansurisir, Subhan, Sajid, and Tanzima Vahora; Asif Thakor; Ayub and Ishaq Vohra; Hifzur Rehman; Rashid, Salim, and Mohammed Vohra; Dr. Gulamnabi Vahora; Yusuf and Mumtaz Bora; Dr. Parvez Vora; Firoz Vohra; and their families.

The research was conducted in two phases. The first phase (2010–2016) was conducted as a project within the Provincial Globalisation research program, hosted at the Amsterdam Institute for Social Science Research (AISSR) at the University of Amsterdam and the National Institute for Advanced Studies (NIAS) in Bangalore, and funded by the Netherlands Organization for Scientific Research (NWO/WOTRO). The second phase (2017–2019) took place during fellowships at the International Institute for Asian Studies (IIAS) at Leiden University and the University of Tübingen, with travel funding by the Asian Modernities and Traditions fund at Leiden University (AMT) and the Moving Matters research group at the University of Amsterdam. The Open Access publication of the book was made possible by the Mellon Foundation, with additional support from the Department of Social and Cultural Anthropology at the University of Vienna.

The person who introduced me to central Gujarat is Mario Rutten, whose lifelong commitment to regionally rooted yet transnational ethnography proved contagious. Between 2007 and 2011, Mario and I collaborated with Isabelle Makay to make the documentary film *Living Like a Common Man*, about Gujarati youth in London and their parents in Gujarat. After I joined the Provincial Globalisation research program in 2010, I developed my own line of research in Gujarat, with input from Mario, Carol Upadhya, and many other scholars and colleagues. Very sadly, Mario fell ill and died in 2015.

During the second research phase, the IIAS and the University of Tübingen provided a highly supportive academic climate in which I could conduct further fieldwork and write this monograph. At IIAS, I thank Nira Wickramasinghe, Sanjukta Sunderason, Erik de Maaker, Ward Berenschot, Luisa Steur, Tina Harris, Britta Ohm, Priya Swamy, Roshni Sengupta, Bindu Menon, Erica van Bentem, and Philippe Peycam. In Tübingen, I thank all the members of the Anthropology Department, especially Karin Polit and Eva Ambos. My writing buddies included Radhika Gupta, Raheel Dhattiwala, and, especially, Willy Sier.

In the revision phase, Rosanne Rutten was the first to read the entire book. She responded with substantial comments on each chapter. Anand Yang invited me to the book writing workshop of the American Institute of Indian Studies and the American Institute of Pakistan Studies at the South Asia Conference in Madison, where I received further comments on some of the chapters. Chritralekha Manohar and Carole Pearce helped to prepare the manuscript for review, and Lorri Hagman directed the peer review and editorial development process. I thank them all for their generous input.

NEW LIVES IN ANAND

Introduction

Reorientation in a Post-Violence Landscape

2002. A line of trucks traverses a road in central Gujarat from the village of Ode to the small town of Anand, a distance of twenty-five kilometers. They halt at an open piece of land in the northeastern outskirts of Anand. They unload their passengers—refugees who have survived a violent attack on their homes a few hours earlier, when a mob entered their village carrying kerosene and matches, setting fire to houses after locking them from the outside, and burning twenty-three people alive. Ode is one of the villages in which Muslims are targeted during Gujarat's anti-Muslim pogroms, organized by militant Hindu nationalist organizations in the run-up to the Gujarat state elections. Of the Muslims who escape the fire, many seek refuge in Anand, in a hastily set up camp alongside hundreds of other refugees, whose numbers swell into thousands during the following months. All the refugees have arrived from nearby villages. All of them are Muslim. Many of them belong to the regional Muslim community of Charotar Sunni Vohras. Some return to their villages afterward; many stay in Anand. In the fifteen years after 2002, many other Muslims leave their villages and move to Anand, too.

2016. In a living room in London, photographs of Anand's 100 Feet Road appear on a flat-screen TV. The pictures are taken from the balcony of a new flat in Anand, recently purchased by an overseas Gujarati Muslim family for a vacation home. The family has just returned from another trip to Anand, and enthusiastically describe Anand's rapid development and the comfort offered by some of its newly constructed houses. The atmosphere is cheerful, their delight palpable. While the family comments on the new curtains and furniture in their holiday home, I wonder how a neighborhood grown out of violence and displacement has evolved into a vacation destination within the span of a decade. This family has no prior history in Anand—most of their family is in Mumbai, and they trace their roots to a village in Gujarat that did not see violence in 2002.

2017. A middle-aged Vohra woman drives around Anand on her two-wheeler. She talks about how the town has changed since 2002. The 100 Feet Road, she explains, was considered to be the border between Hindus and Muslims in 2002, when the police had stood guard along this road to prevent residents from crossing it. The border is moving, she adds, pointing southward. Hindus and Christians have been selling their houses, and Muslim buyers from the nearby villages are willing to pay high prices for them even now, fifteen years after the pogroms. New housing societies are being constructed on the agricultural land around the town to meet the housing demand. Pointing around her, she says, "This area is very lucky for us [Muslims]. Everybody thinks that. This area is very lucky. This is a good area."

HOW DO PEOPLE get on with their lives after an episode of violence? How, in the process, are new spaces and societies made? This book addresses these questions. It describes the long-term transformations that have occurred in a town where, according to the residents, "nothing happened in 2002," while the surrounding villages were on fire. It shows how this town grew into an important focal point for Muslims in central Gujarat, a "safe" place, a "lucky" place, a regional "center" for the local Muslim community of Charotar Sunni Vohras, and a place to which overseas Gujarati Muslims "return." Just as the villagers found a new home in the town, their relatives living abroad did the same, buying houses and land in a town that previously had little meaning for them. In a rural region undergoing rapid urbanization, these relocations have been accompanied by the creation of new rural-urban imaginaries, in which the rural is seen as primarily a Hindu domain, whereas the urban—or rather the urban outskirts—has come to be seen as a Muslim domain. Amidst this changing landscape, people's sense of direction, of belonging, and prospects has also been reconfigured. These relocations and reimaginings are viewed here through the lens of "center-making" and the broader social implications through the lens of "reorientation."

Representing Indian Muslims

This book can be read as a reconsideration of the available vocabulary with which Muslim spaces and experiences are described, and as an invitation to expand this vocabulary. The public and political stakes in representing Muslims are high, not just in India but around the world, where stereotypical representations dominate. With the growing suppression of minority voices in India in recent years, information about how Muslims understand themselves has been limited even further.

The representation of Muslims as non-Indian and as not belonging in India is crucial to the Hindu nationalist agenda, which consists of a majoritarian and exclusivist interpretation of nationalism. In Hindu nationalist articulations, Muslims are represented as stereotypical outsiders against which the nation has come to be defined. This story has grown in popularity since the 1990s (Hansen 1999) and has consolidated into a political agenda that commentators have compared with fascism (Banaji 2013). In Gujarat, the state that has been described as a testing ground (laboratory) for the Hindu nation, Hindu nationalism been couched in the language of *asmita*, or Gujarati pride—an interpretation that makes Gujarat and Gujaratis synonymous with Hindus and antithetical to Muslims (Chandrani 2013; Ibrahim 2008). While this language resonates with forms of Islamophobia that exist in Europe and the United States, it operates in distinctive registers, for example, when the Gujarati ideal of Hindu vegetarianism is projected against a stereotype of Muslims as (disgustingly) meat-eating (Ghassem-Fachandi 2010, 2012). Stereotypical representations of the supposedly threatening or evil character of Muslims can be used to legitimize anti-Muslim violence during electoral campaigns in order to divide the electorate along religious lines.

Another representation of Muslims highlights their marginalization. The social, political, and spatial marginalization of Muslims has been well recorded in a multitude of research reports, some written by committees that had been established by the Indian government itself (Sachar et al. 2006). Indian Muslims are excluded from holding power in the state apparatus; they are underrepresented in the judiciary, the administration, and the police, marginalized within the formal sector of employment, and are only minimally present among salaried public sector workers (Gayer and Jaffrelot 2012, 4–6, 314). They have also been at the receiving end of violent attacks on their lives and property. A particularly gruesome wave of anti-Muslim violence took place in Gujarat in 2002, during which mobs of men travelled around the state, killing and raping, looting and burning, while police and politicians waited and watched or even supported the attacks.[1] In the aftermath of this violence, many researchers studied the causes (among others, see Berenschot 2011; Dhattiwala 2019; Varshney 2002), including the causes of the sexual violence committed against Muslim women (Kumar 2016). Some studies explored the consequences of the violence: the massive displacements that occurred when Muslims fled their homes (Lokhande 2015), and the loss of trust by Muslims in the Gujarati state (Jasani 2011). These studies have provided important insights and frameworks to understand the position of Muslims in Gujarat and India. Yet the continuous focus on violence and marginalization, in a way, also blinds us to other perspectives. With the best of intentions, these studies may contribute to muting the Muslim experiences that do not neatly fit the narrative of marginalization.

A third way of representing Muslims is found in their own self-representations. Studies show us that Muslims can sidestep their binary representation of villain or victim to assert themselves as human beings in different terms: for example, by defining themselves as educated people, highlighting their achieved over their ascribed status (Jeffrey, Jeffery, and Jeffery 2004); by defining themselves as modern people, cultivating new kinds of religious identities (Osella and Osella 2008a, 2008b); or by articulating alternative viewpoints in oral histories or cultural practices (Ibrahim 2008, 75). Several studies expose situations in which people defy the very idea of the generic categories "Muslims" and "Hindus" (Gottschalk 2000). Muslims and Muslim groups can carve out a different position, for example, by claiming shared characteristics with local Hindus or by claiming a separate identity that is different from other Muslims (Ibrahim 2008, 195; see also Simpson 2006, 87–109). These claims can be regarded as ways of recovering agency and crafting self-representations on their own terms. They testify to the agency of Muslims to shape at least some aspects of their lives—to tell other kinds of stories, about other topics. In many cases, these self-representations are articulated only among themselves, without being formulated in wider public spheres. The space for Muslims to assert their concerns in the political or public arena, or even in the legal sphere, is limited.

The viewpoints and stories that were shared with me in Anand have prompted me to take into account Hindu nationalism and Muslim marginalization, but also to look beyond these themes, to include other aspects. By now there is extensive literature on how "the Muslim" has been crucially positioned an internal "other" against whom the Indian nation has historically been defined (Pandey 1999, 2001), and on the discursive exclusion of Muslims and other minority perspectives from the "idea of Gujarat" (Simpson and Kapadia 2010). My attempt has been to understand how Anand's Muslims themselves interpret what happened to them and their surroundings. I attempt to look at Anand's Muslim area not from the outside in, but from the inside out.

From the Ghetto to the Hub

Urban studies scholarship in India has in recent years paid considerable attention to issues of spatial transformation, particularly residential segregation. Yet, as several authors before me have argued (Gupta 2015; Jamil 2017; Jasani 2010), the terms in which these discussions are couched do not necessarily reflect the experiences of Muslims themselves. The term "ghettoization" has been repeatedly critiqued, yet it continues to dominate scholarly and journalistic discussions about Muslims in Indian cities. It is time to seek ways out of this impasse.

The concept of the ghettoization of Muslims in Indian cities is defined as the regrouping of individuals of different social, class, and caste backgrounds on the basis of the religious (ascribed) identities in response to political and social constraints, the neglect of these areas by state authorities, the estrangement of the locality from the rest of the city, and a sense of closure among its residents (Gayer and Jaffrelot 2012). This concept was developed through research in eleven Indian cities. Ghettoization is understood as a response to anti-Muslim violence and the insecurities that result from this, leading Muslims to seek safety in numbers. The city of Ahmedabad in Gujarat, a few hours' drive from Anand, is presented as an emblematic case of ghettoization (Jaffrelot and Thomas 2012). Other research that has been done on this city[2] confirms that segregation has developed, describes the marginalization and (stereotypical) representation of its Muslim spaces, and explores the ways in which Muslims have coped with or attempted to influence the situation.

Several scholars have followed up on these findings to inquire further into the causes of Hindu-Muslim segregation in India's cities. One approach focuses on how bureaucratic practices produce reified notions of community and space (Punathil 2016), another employs statistical indices as a way of indexing segregation in Indian cities (Susewind 2017), and a contribution inspired by Marxist theory theorizes segregation in India as a process of "accumulation by segregation" in a neoliberal economy (Jamil 2017). These contributions offer insights into the underlying political and economic structures that may contribute to the formation and marginalization of Muslims areas, in addition to the hypothesis that Muslims self-segregate in response to violence. Another line of research does not seek to explain the causes of segregation so much as to describe the heterogeneity of residents' experiences of everyday life in a ghettoized Muslim area (Chatterjee 2017).

These works also offer opportunities for comparing India with instances of segregation elsewhere in the world (e.g., Wacquant 2008). In discussions about Black ghettos in the United States and Jewish ghettos in Europe, a recurrent question has been the extent to which residents of a segregated neighborhood are still integrated into the social and economic life of the rest of the city (e.g., Marcuse 1997). This question has been addressed for the Muslim ghetto in India by Ghazala Jamil (2017) and Raphael Susewind (2015), who have forcefully argued against the idea that the state is absent in such neighborhoods and point to the mechanisms of real estate markets and labor circulation through which Muslims are integrated into the city economy. Anasua Chatterjee (2017) and Nida Kirmani (2013) also discuss the ability to participate in work, education, and consumption in the other spaces of the city, especially for the urban middle class, who can, to some extent, shake off the stigma of living in a Muslim neighborhood due to their class position (Chatterjee 2017, 166).

"Ghettoization" is a central term in all these studies, but several authors have expressed discomfort with it. One critique raised is that the term inadvertently reproduces stereotypes of the "other" and produces the very thing that it describes—creating a "ghetto effect" (R. Gupta 2015). A related critique is the tendency to reiterate the Hindu-Muslim divide and thus to overlook the intermixtures that continue to exist in so-called ghettos (Jasani 2010, 166–67). Moreover, the usage of the word "ghetto" might normalize segregation, and the word can be misleading in the Indian context because of its Euro-American baggage, conjuring associations with Jewish and Black ghettos in European and US history quite different from the situation in contemporary Indian Muslim localities (Jamil 2017). The term nevertheless continues to prevail, and no alternatives have yet been proposed.

I have refrained from ghettoization discourse primarily because it made no sense to my interlocutors.[3] The words used by Muslims in Anand to demarcate the spaces where they live are neutral—they talk about a "Muslim *vistar*" (Muslim area) or "our area," but also often simply use the name of the town, Anand, to refer to their home. When I asked residents what they thought about the term "ghetto" (in 2017),[4] considering its regular use in English-language Indian newspapers, I found that the term was unfamiliar to them. "Ghet-to?": an English teacher tasted the term. She had never heard of it but was eager to learn, so she wrote it down and asked me if she had got the spelling right. "Do you mean, a get-together?" she asked. When I hesitated to answer, she added, "Yes, you can say that; Muslims get together here in Anand!" This was said with a smile, without the negative connotation that the term has in academic and journalistic literature, by a woman who thinks of her family's relocation to Anand as an event that liberated her from the constraints of village life. Such encounters have continually challenged me to reevaluate the terms of the debate and to consider other notions that might better capture developments in Anand from the perspective of its residents.

The Muslims I met in Anand told me different stories about their town—that it was the center of the Vohra community, a good place, a safe place, a lucky place, and our place, a place for Muslims. A board member of the Charotar Sunni Vohra community jokingly referred to Anand as a "Mecca of Vohras"—a telling joke. For Muslims, the city of Mecca (in Saudi Arabia) is not only the direction to look toward during prayer and a site of pilgrimage and religious orientation, but it is a meeting point where one meets other Muslims—a site of community-making. Mecca is also an aspirational site: a place one can visit only if one has the financial capacity to do so. The relocation to Anand, in this analogy, is an experience of geographic mobility paired with a distinctive sense of directionality, connectivity, and social class mobility.

While they are diverse, the descriptions of Anand that I have mapped by talking to Muslims of the town have one common aspect; they use neutral or positive terms for the localities where Muslims live: safe, social, happy, central to the meaning of the town, and a regional center for the rural hinterland. These descriptions contrast with the prevalent discussions about marginalization and completely invert the meanings imposed on Muslim spaces—by the popular media, political discourses, and everyday conversations with non-Muslims in Gujarat—as being dirty, full of crime, alcohol, meat, and possibly rape; in other words, as peripheral to society (Ghassem-Fachandi 2010).

These inversions have led me to describe the town in particular ways. If I describe the dramatic demarcation between Hindu and Muslim areas that was a response to communal violence, I also show that the residents do not understand their move to Anand in exclusively communal or post-violence terms; instead, they describe their translocation as a compound and multifaceted process. Muslims of Anand cannot be reduced to their religious identity, and indeed are often reluctant to be described in this way. Many prefer to speak of themselves and their changing surroundings in terms of other social identities they consider to be important: the regional Vohra community, or the Indian middle class, for example. Conceptualizing Anand's Muslim area as a "center" or "hub," I believe, is a way to do justice to their experiences.

The term "hub" deviates from that of "ghetto" in that it rejects the idea that residential segregation is paired with estrangement and closure. It instead highlights the residents' continued ability to maintain connections with a variety of people and places: urban and rural, local and transnational, as well as Hindu, Christian, and Muslim. It also deviates in that it broadens the scale of the analysis, seeing the neighborhood not only in relation with the rest of the city but also in relation with regional and transnational networks. Not only are the Muslims of Anand making a new home in its Muslim area; Muslims living in nearby villages and towns, and even overseas Gujarati Muslims in the United Kingdom and United States, are discovering Anand as well, and contributing to its meaning as a hub for Muslims in central Gujarat.

Center-Making

"Center" and "hub" are apt terms to describe a neighborhood that has turned into a focal point of urban, rural-urban, and transnational connectivity. This account is based on mobile, multisited and multiscalar research that combines descriptions of one such neighborhood with research into the regional and transnational networks that emanate from it. This approach combines a "neighborhood" lens, as is common in urban studies, with a "diaspora" lens that encompasses the wider regional and overseas networks of the residents. This methodology stems from the theoretical position that places and societies cannot be studied in isolation (Wolf 1982), because the people who dwell in them are both locally and translocally embedded—they are territorial as well as deterritorialized (Appadurai 1996; Inda and Rosaldo 2008, 12). Such translocal understandings of space and society are well established in the field of transnational migration studies (Glick Schiller, Basch, and Blanc-Szanton 1992), and have also been articulated in urban studies (Sassen 2001; and, in Gujarat, Spodek 2013), but they have not often been applied in studies of Muslims in Indian cities. Many scholars have studied how violence against Muslims is legitimized and organized in India, and how Muslims have been relegated to segregated neighborhoods in response to such violence. Some of these works provide us with in-depth descriptions of daily life in India's Muslim-majority neighborhoods (Chatterjee 2017), while other studies have explored the transnational mobility of Indian Muslims across the Indian Ocean (Osella and Osella 2009; Simpson and Kresse 2007). Here, I analyze an urban sphere with respect to its multiple linkages: rural-urban, local-global, and Hindu-Muslim. I describe the networks that emanate from Anand from the perspective of its Muslim residents and show how their experiences of residential segregation are paired with distinctive practices of mobility and exchange.

While existing studies offer insights into the urban experiences of Indian Muslims, and to some extent into their class and gender identities, my contribution is to describe regional orientations. This contributes to a recent set of scholarly attempts to describe Indian Muslims beyond a singular focus on their religious identity (Kirmani 2013). Muslims in Anand continue to be part of the regional economies and networks surrounding India's cities and towns, even under conditions of residential segregation. This reality contrasts with the view presented in discussions of ghettoization, of residential segregation as a process that leads to estrangement or a subjective sense of closure of residents (Gayer and Jaffrelot 2012, 22).

It is possible that the situation in Anand is specific to small towns in rural regions with a dense pattern of rural-urban connectivity. If so, the case study of Anand is also an opportunity to counter the dominant metrocentric focus in the existing literature on Muslims in India, which has often been limited to large and metropolitan cities. The focus on cities in the literature on Indian Muslims has been justified by the idea that the city occupies a central place in the history of Indian Muslims (Gayer and Jaffrelot 2012, 13–18). Lost in these discussions, however, is the fact that many urban residents in India live in small and medium-sized towns (Scrase et al. 2015). In Gujarat, most discussions of the impacts of the 2002 violence on Muslims are focused on the city of Ahmedabad, yet what happened in Gujarat's towns and villages is largely unknown.[5]

The case study of Anand also shows how transnational modes of community organization are entwined with regional politics. My research builds on a particular line of scholarship within the broad field of migration studies, that is, works that focus on the connections that transnational migrants maintain with their regions of origin. Considerable thought has gone into the question of how diaspora communities are formed and conceptualized (R. Cohen 1996; Safran 1991; Brubaker 2005) around ideas of a shared "homeland" as a source of community making under conditions of migration (Axel 2002; Biswas 2010; Clifford 1994). The social, economic, and political relations between transnational migrants and their homeland are further scrutinized in the field of migration and development (de Haas 2010).[6] In this book, the term "migrants" is reserved for cross-border migration, with a focus on overseas Gujaratis in the United Kingdom and the United States. The term "relocation" (rather than "migration") is used for residents who moved to a new house within the vicinity, within the town, or to Anand from nearby villages. The term "displacement" is reserved for situations where people were forced to migrate or relocate.

In the literature about migration and development, migrants have been conceptualized as agents of development (Faist 2008; Levitt and Lamba-Nieves 2010) who can change conditions in their homeland. They are described as senders of remittances and investments, starters of businesses, and intellectual innovators whose overseas education and professional skills can inspire various kinds of transformations in their regions of origin.[7] In studies of conflict regions, the mostly optimistic tone shifts to one of concern, and the question is raised whether transnational migrants should be conceived as promoters of radical viewpoints or as having a role as peacekeepers in their regions of origin (Anderson 1998; Orjuela 2018). Studies in this field have delivered diverse and increasingly nuanced insights into the myriad ways in which mobile actors remain embedded in their home regions (Upadhya, Rutten, and Koskimaki 2018).[8] This book builds on these works, but also asks a less familiar question within the frameworks of migration and development: how do spatial transformations in a migrant-sending region influence migrants' "development" practices? The spatial transformation under discussion in this book is the processes of center-making in Anand in the fifteen years after 2002.

Questions of migration and development resonate directly with everyday experiences in central Gujarat, where overseas Gujaratis have become highly visible as participants in social and economic life. National Indian and state-level Gujarati policies have stimulated overseas Indians to invest, remit, donate, and contribute to various kinds of social initiatives in their regions of origin. Moreover, the vocabulary of "development" is not limited to the policy documents and speeches of state officials. It is commonly used in everyday speech in Gujarat, especially when people talk about new buildings and townships, but also when they talk about broader economic and social transformations signaling "improvement" or "progress."[9] The overseas Gujarati Muslims who appear in this book also use the term in this sense.

While some of the national-level and regional-level politics of migration and development enable overseas Gujarati Muslims to act as agents of development, their activities are also influenced by conditions at the microregional level, such as urbanization and residential segregation in central Gujarat. These affect where migrants can participate in "development," and where they can't. While overseas Hindus have been able to maintain, and to some extent strengthen, their relations with their villages of origin by making contributions to village development, overseas Muslims from these villages are challenged to redirect their mode of spatial anchoring. They have witnessed how their acquaintances back home fled their villages and found refuge in Anand. They have sent remittances and charitable support to help these refugees to find new homes, and, eventually, some made investments of their own in Anand, such as buying a house so that they could participate in the social life of the growing Muslim area during their holidays or retirement. The story of Anand thus shows how transnational migrants respond to, and participate in, a process of center-making in their home region.

Reorientation

To describe the social implications of this move to Anand, I employ the lens of "reorientation," a practice of familiarizing oneself once again, of adjusting to new circumstances after being disoriented. Reorientation is a spatial process when it involves alignment to a new direction or selecting a different path. It is also a social process when it involves an adjustment to new social surroundings or new modalities of sociality. It involves a shift in aim or focus, a turn to new horizons that would otherwise not have been envisioned.

This ethnography of reorientation combines anthropological approaches to place, sociality, and aspiration. Anthropological perspectives of place look at the narratives and "place-making practices" by which people actively shape and understand their surroundings (Harney 2006; Rodman 2003) and formulate their own "theories of dwelling" (Feld and Basso 1996; Basso 1996). In light of the regional community narratives articulated by the Charotar Sunni Vohras, in particular, anthropological approaches to the concept of region are relevant. These look beyond the official formulations of a region by state institutions or as depicted on maps, and conceive of the region as a flexible concept that develops from the ways in which people interact with their surroundings during everyday practices of work, socializing, travel, or going to the market (van Schendel 1982; Skinner 1964; see also Ingold 2005). The Charotar region in central Gujarat has no official existence as an administrative unit, but it is popularly perceived as a region with its own social networks, practices, and histories. Muslims' perspectives of this region are influenced by the watershed episode of 2002, as we can see from their comparisons between the past (in many cases located in the villages) and the present (in the town).

This description of the regional orientations of Muslims is informed by anthropologies of community and caste. Community is a classic theme in anthropology, although it has been neglected somewhat in recent anthropologies of humanity, materiality, and infrastructure. Instead of taking community for granted as a unit of analysis, anthropological approaches seek to capture people's experiences and the meanings they attach to community (A. Cohen 2000, 38). In Gujarat, "community" is a much-used term, the meanings of which are shaped not only by Hindu-Muslim dynamics but also prominently by caste and regional politics, as well as social networks of kinship, neighborliness, and trade.

In Anand, the production of a new space happened in parallel with a reconfiguration of community concepts. Of the multiple changes brought about by the move of Muslims to Anand, a significant one is the reconceptualization of the Vohras' regional community, from a rurally embedded mercantile community to an increasingly urbanized one. Vohra leaders and associations have articulated a regional Charotari community narrative since at least 1926. Now that Vohras are moving to and investing in a segregated Muslim area in Anand, their regional narratives are maintained but acquire new meanings. The term "reorientation" is used in this book to describe these changes in the conceptualization of a regional community.

With the term "reorientation," anthropologies of community can be linked to anthropologies of both class and place. The notion of reorientation resonates with anthropological works that analyze "aspiration" (Appadurai 2004), "anticipation" (Jeffrey 2010), and "dreaming" (Cross 2014), but adds a spatial dimension and, in particular, draws attention to the rural-urban divide as an important aspect of the crafting of aspirations in small-town India (comparable to Jeffrey 2001). Aspiration is a prominent theme in discussions on class in India, as, for example, in studies on the formation of the middle class in neoliberal India (Baas 2020; Dickey 2012; Upadhya 2016). Some studies have specifically addressed the topic of aspiration among middle-class Muslims, describing the strategies by which they can affirm their class status despite marginalization—for example, through a focus on education (Jeffrey, Jeffery, and Jeffery 2008, 147); religion (F. Osella and C. Osella 2008a, 2008b), and modernity (F. Osella and C. Osella 2011). When the topic of aspiration is addressed in a study of a changing regional community, this requires a closer look at aspects of spatial imagination and directionality.

The Muslims' (spatial) move to Anand can be viewed as one aspect of an (aspirational) process of self-transformation: Anand is seen as the direction to move toward in the future. Within Gujarat, Anand is associated with education, urban occupations, and enhanced geographic and social mobility; from the perspective of overseas Gujarati Muslims, Anand is a site to realize aspirations to leisure, retirement, and vacationing. Anand can thus be viewed as a place of hope and promise, even as these hopes are intertwined with anxieties over safety, economic security, and social standing. Relocating to a new space also requires making new relationships with new neighbors and reconfiguring old relationships (for example, with business partners and other acquaintances in the villages of origin), which do not necessarily end after moving into a new space but instead are given new shape and meaning.

A Regional Community

Most of the material I present here is derived from fieldwork among the Charotar Sunni Vohras (Sunni Vohras from Charotar, or, in short: Vohras). As the community name suggests, Charotar Sunni Vohras cultivate a strong sense of belonging to the rural region of Charotar.[10] This is the rural inland region surrounding Anand town (the Anand and Kheda districts), located in between the cities of Ahmedabad and Baroda. The region is considered part of the political and economic "center" of Gujarat, in contrast of the "peripheral" regions of the coast (Spodek 1972), and has attracted much interest from historians, sociologists, and anthropologists. While Vohras regard the region as central to their community, existing books and articles about the region only rarely include the Vohra's perspectives. In Gujarat, where Hindu nationalist concepts have become dominant, the Vohra's regional narratives are a testimony to the subtle yet steadfast ways in which people can uphold a regional orientation even within an ideological environment that marks them as outsiders to the region, and even after moving to a new location away from ancestral villages and lands.

Vohras are the largest Muslim community (*samaj*) in Anand, and residents estimate that they constitute approximately 50 percent of Anand's Muslim population.[11] They are also a relatively wealthy and powerful Muslim community among the Muslims of central Gujarat (in their own view and in those of other Muslims).

While overviews of Muslims in Gujarat briefly mention the Sunni Vohras (Engineer 1989; Misra 1964), most studies have focused not on the inland regions of central Gujarat but on coastal or urban locations. There are considerable differences between Muslims in these localities. For example, Muslim communities on the coasts of Kutch and Baruch have been described as seafaring and trading groups that have long participated in social and economic exchange across the Indian Ocean (Simpson 2006; Koch 2017). Like these groups, Charotar Sunni Vohras have been described as a trading community (Heitmeyer 2009a), but their mercantile practices are quite different. The seafaring Muslim communities of Kutch, for example, traversed the Gulf in small ships to bring back exotic goods from the East African coast and see themselves as having a long history of travel and cosmopolitanism (Simpson 2003). In contrast, the Vohras of Charotar have been oriented toward the agricultural economy. Their narratives of the past describe how they worked as traders in agricultural produce and as small-scale industrialists who processed and stored vegetables and other agricultural products. Some worked as shopkeepers and door-to-door traders, selling everyday goods such as clothing in the villages of the region. International migration has been limited in this community until recently. Vohras consider themselves the most transnational group of all the Gujarati Muslims in the inland Charotar region, but their experience of living overseas remains scarce in comparison with the descriptions of Gujarati Muslim groups on the coast.

Charotar Sunni Vohras are distinguished from other Sunni Vohra communities in Gujarat, such as the Baruchi Vohras in Baruch and Surti Vohras in Surat. These endogamous Sunni Vohra communities must in turn be distinguished from the Shia community of Daudi Bohras, an urban Gujarati Muslim community that is widely known in India because it attracts frequent media coverage. Different from the Charotar Sunni Vohras, Daudi Bohras have a sectarian organization with a clerical hierarchy headed by a central religious leader, who holds exclusive rights to interpret matters of religion and provides authoritative guidance to lower-ranking members (Blank 2001).[12] Charotar Sunni Vohras, in contrast, do not have a central religious leader. They are highly diverse in their religious beliefs and practices. They follow and denounce different maulanas and saints, and this religious diversity exists even among different members of the same household, making the topic of religion fluid as well as contested. While I describe some of this dynamism (in chapter 4), the book does not focus on matters of religious doctrine. Instead, it centers on a theme about which there *is* consensus among the Vohras I have talked to: their belonging to the Charotar region.

The Vohras' claim to regional belonging is discussed in terms of their historical links with land and villages, their endogamous marriage practices and geographically dispersed kinship ties, and their belief that they are descendants of, and culturally similar to, local Hindus. This is a twist to the extended body of literature on the Charotar region. Almost all books and articles about this region have focused almost entirely on the perspectives of the Patidars, a regionally dominant landowning caste group.[13] To this Hindu caste of Patidars (also referred to as "Patels") the reader will find several references here, as the Vohras, too, frequently refer to them in their stories of the Charotar region.

The Patidars' influence over how the region is imagined is remarkable, because they are a numerical minority in many of "their" villages. Many scholars and students are drawn into Patidar networks during their first visit to the region, and while their hosts' generous reception allows them to conduct in-depth studies into the internal dynamics of the Patidar caste, the association of researchers with Patidars can make it harder for them to gain the trust of members of other groups. Several methodological descriptions exist of how researchers have been drawn into influential lineages within the Patidar caste, even if they had set out to study or include other people (e.g., Gidwani 2008, 241; Rutten 2007; Tilche and Simpson 2017, 705).

Since 2015, Patidar groups have been making headlines because of the demonstrations and lobbying activities through which they have put forward their demands to be included in the category of "other backward castes" in order to gain access to positive discrimination schemes. Their demands have prompted commentators to ask if the power of this dominant caste has been waning. On the one hand, several sources point to the continued success of Patidars in reproducing their powerful position in the region. Patidar groups have migrated overseas to East Africa, the United States, and the United Kingdom, and the gains from migration become visible when returning migrants operate as development actors in their villages in Gujarat (Dekkers and Rutten 2018). They thereby articulate a narrative that describes the village as ideologically linked to the caste itself: the village is in their blood and remains so even after they migrate overseas.¹⁴ In urban spaces such as Anand, Patidars have also acquired prominent roles in educational, commercial, and government spheres (Verstappen and Rutten 2015). On the other hand, a deep sense of failure prevails among young Patidar farmers who remain in the village, when they are unable to obtain a visa to migrate overseas (Tilche and Simpson 2018). In the village squares, Patidars still dominate, but some members of other castes are finding ways to challenge their power (Gidwani 2008). These different accounts of success and failure seem to present two true stories, from different sections within the Patidar caste—this is a caste with pronounced internal differences and tremendous socioeconomic diversity (Pocock 1972, 1973).

The internal politics of the Patidar caste have been thoroughly described by other scholars of the Charotar region, but of interest here is the question of what it means to belong to this region. The Vohra community narratives assert belonging to the Charotar region in ways that are similar to those of the Patidars. For both Vohras and Patidars, belonging to the Charotar region is constructed through a shared ethos of agricultural entrepreneurialism, attachment to ancestral land and villages, and intracaste but extralocal marriages. Yet, their narratives of regional belonging hold quite different meanings in a region where Hindu claims to the village are ideologically validated, whereas Muslim claims have been called into question.

Some studies have sought to describe and understand the silences within the Patidar narratives of the Charotar region. An alternative view of the region is offered in a historical account of the peasant community known as the Dharalas, which explores not only the Patidars' consolidation of power, but also the histories of exploitation on which this power has rested (Chaturvedi 2007). The only study that engages specifically with Muslims in the region describes the Charotar Sunni Vohra community in the town of Sultanpur ("Sultanpur" is a pseudonym; Heitmeyer 2009a, 2009b). While this study notes that Vohras see Anand as the regional center of their community, it does not scrutinize further the novelty of this orientation.

The story of the Vohras of Charotar is a story about a rural business community whose relations with the land and villages of the region have changed. These changes include, but are not limited to, the influence of Hindu nationalism and anti-Muslim violence. When comparing the Vohra story to available literature about the Patidars of Charotar and other Gujarati Muslims, it also becomes a way of thinking about a broader set of transformations in rural and small-town India that affect many groups, whether Hindu or Muslim: urbanization, changes in the organization of village spaces, the conversion of agricultural lands into real estate, education, and the search for urban professions and lifestyles, as well as a broadening significance of transnational migration and return, even for groups that traditionally have not been as mobile as others.

Rural-Urban Relocation

To describe the rural-urban relocations of Muslims to Anand, qualitative as well as quantitative data are employed here. Both my interlocutors and the available quantitative data suggest there is a direct link between the violence of 2002 and the urbanization of Muslims in Anand district. The violence can be seen as an accelerator of a longer-term trend of urbanization.

In Anand district, Muslims constitute 12 percent of the population; Hindus constitute 86 percent; Christians (1.4 percent), Jains, and Sikhs (both less than 0.5 percent) are smaller minorities (Census 2011). In the decade after the violence, a remarkable shift in rural-urban residential patterns occurred in this district. In 2001, most of the Muslim population in the district (52 percent) lived in rural areas, while 48 percent lived in urban spaces. By 2011, this rural-urban ratio had almost reversed, with only 44 percent of Muslims remaining in the rural areas and 56 percent now residing in urban areas (Census of India 2001, 2011; see table A.01). The changing ratio can be explained by the fact that many local Muslims living in Hindu-majority villages had moved to an urban locality in the intervening years—most of them having moved to the Anand district's eponymous main town.

The Anand district was among the districts in Gujarat where violence was most intense in 2002 (Dhattiwala and Biggs 2012, 505).[15] Yet the district town of Anand, a Hindu-majority town with a total population of 156,050 (according to the census of 2001; see table A.02), remained relatively calm amidst the violence. Subsequently, the population of the town grew (to 209,410, according to the 2011 census; see table A.02). While this growth can partly be attributed to the general dynamics of urbanization and population growth, the Muslims of Anand estimate that it was the number of Muslims, specifically, that grew, and even doubled, in the decade following 2002.

Data recorded by the Government of India confirm the growth of the Muslim population in the town, almost doubling: from 25,099 in 2001 to 45,932 in 2011 (see tables A.03 and A.04; Census of India 2001, 2011). In 2001, the share of Muslims in the total population of Anand town was 16 percent; in 2011, it was 22 percent. In comparison, in Gujarat state as a whole, 10 percent of the population are Muslim, while 89 percent are Hindu (Census of India 2011; see table A.04).

The possible meanings of these quantitative findings are described here from the perspective of Vohras and other Muslims in Anand.

Multisited, Mobile, and Multiscalar Research

My methodological approach has been multisited and mobile, and it analyzes the Vohras' social networks at multiple scales. It focused on the Muslim area of Anand but did not stay there. Building on the networks of the residents, my research zoomed out, as it were, into the surrounding town, region, and transnational social fields that emanated from the neighborhood. This approach is somewhat different from urban studies scholarship of the everyday (de Certeau 1984), which focuses on daily life in a neighborhood (a strategy followed, for example, by Anasua Chatterjee [2017] in Kolkata and Laura Ring [2006] in Karachi). While my material includes observations of everyday practices and social events, it opens new vistas beyond the space of the neighborhood to show how multiple actors forge relations with it and participate in making it.

Multisited fieldwork is a style of research in anthropology that has emerged in response to concerns about the inadequacy of classic single-site fieldwork methods to studying a mobile, changing, globalizing world (Gupta and Ferguson 1997, 3), in which groups migrate, regroup in new locations, and reconfigure their histories and identities without maintaining tight spatial boundaries (see also Hannerz 2003, 202–3; Wilding 2007, 336). This reflects a conceptualization of societies as enduringly and intricately interwoven, and a departure from methodological approaches that that are predicated upon a "container model" of society, projecting societies as distinct "billiard balls" (Wolf 1982).

Such a perspective fits the experience of life in Indian cities and towns, which is shaped by interactions between disparate and unequal, yet interconnected, people and places (Srivastava 2015). It also aligns with historical descriptions of mobility and exchange in South Asia, which offer important correctives to nationalist and sedentary descriptions of society (Ludden 1994). My research has been inspired by approaches in migration studies that look at the world through a "transnational optic" (Levitt and Khagram 2007) as a way of exploring the processes, networks, and practices by which people "forge and sustain simultaneous multistranded social relations" (Glick Schiller, Basch, and Szanton Blanc 1995, 48). Scholars of "transnationalism" (Kearney 1995; Portes 2001) and "mobility" (Urry 2016; Salazar 2017) have critiqued nationalist models of social research ("methodological nationalism"; Wimmer and Glick Schiller 2002). Based on ideas of globalization and deterritorialization suggested by the anthropologist

Arjun Appadurai (1996) and on the translocality of space by the geographer Doreen Massey (1994, 156), they have attempted to look beyond what is visible in a place to explore how various social networks and systems are present and interrelate: "only with an open, global and progressive idea of these migrant places are we able to observe the various crosscutting social networks in which transmigrants are involved" (Gielis 2009, 278).

As not all the flows that are significant to Anand are transnational, I was encouraged to expand my analysis of mobility beyond the figure of the cross-border migrant to include more localized forms of mobility, especially rural-urban mobility (King and Skeldon 2010; Vullnetari 2020). This approach aligns with recent proposals in the field of mobility studies to include a broader range of mobilities, including rural-urban migration as well as more everyday forms of mobility across small distances (Sheller and Urry 2016). Mobility scholars have also started to experiment with various new methods (Elliot, Norum, and Salazar 2017) such as go-along research combined with conversational strategies guided by nonverbal prompts in the surroundings (Pink 2008). In my travel-along research, it was the journey—and sometimes the possibility of a future journey or the memory of a journey in the past—that became a prompt for further conversations.

My main methodological challenge was how best to combine a neighborhood study with attention to the multistranded and interconnected social fields in which the neighborhood is embedded. Multisited projects run the risk of turning into a "hit-and-run ethnography" if their local embedding becomes too loose (Geertz 1998, 72). It has been argued that anthropological research can still best be accomplished by staying in one place for long time (as advocated in Evans-Pritchard 1976), as that enables immersion, grounding the multisited research in the peculiarities of a well-known place (Wogan 2004). If researchers "spread themselves too thin," meeting many people in many places without staying put anywhere, this may prevent them from understanding and revealing the perspectives of the people under study (Hastrup 2013, 147). Various solutions to deal with this problem have been suggested, such as George E. Marcus's oft-quoted (1995) article on the various "modes of construction" that can function as guides for designing a research project with multiple sites of participant observation. Of the techniques he discusses, I have used that of "following the people." This broad strategy still does not answer the underlying methodological questions, however: which people? How does one choose whom to follow and whom not? How does one construct the field?

My main answer to these questions has been to embed the research in the regional and transnational community networks of the Vohras. In the initial phase, when I was getting to know the neighborhood, I did not focus very strongly on the Vohras, but as the research progressed it gradually turned from a neighborhood study to one of a prominent community within that neighborhood. This mode of selection made sense to my interlocutors, for whom the *samaj* is an important social category. It enabled me to travel together with my interlocutors, from the space of the neighborhood into other spaces that mattered to them: the town, the village, the region, and the homes of overseas Vohras in the United Kingdom. This opened new vistas that remain hidden from view in an urban studies or national project.

The notion of scale, drawn from geography, has been added to anthropological discussions about transnationalism and global connections to think about the scope of a framework or phenomenon. The term has been discussed as a way of developing a layered analysis of global processes that moves beyond the rudimentary local-global dichotomy (Tsing 2005, 58). Scale can be conceptualized as a hierarchy of spatial layers—for example when discussing the levels of governance (municipality, district, nation)—but anthropologists have used the term in somewhat different ways. In approaches that highlight political economy and power hierarchies, scales are discussed as structures of unequal power relations that exist in intersecting institutionalized and informal networks (Cağlar and Glick Schiller 2015; Cağlar and Glick Schiller 2018, 8). In practice-oriented approaches, scale is conceived as an "emergent" category, conceptualized from an actor-centric perspective to delineate how practices are constituted at different scales. In this latter approach, scale is used as an analytical tool of studying "the scope of coordination and mobilization that arises from collective actions" (Xiang 2013, 284) and of investigating how different scale-making projects intersect.

I apply an actor-centric approach to scale to conceptualize different yet intersecting social networks that emanate from a neighborhood. The chapters describe imagined geographic "zones" that are shaped by everyday practices (Osella and Osella 2008). This description follows up as much as possible on the "topographical awareness" (Hastrup 2013, 156) of the interlocutors. Following their leads, the book highlights the region as an important social network but also incorporates urban and transnational networks. "Scaling" or "scale switching" (Hastrup 2013, 145) is used here as an organizing tool to put these different perspectives to work. Regional, urban, and transnational scales are presented in separate chapters and combined in the fourth empirical chapter.

This study of Anand begins with a description of the regional orientations of the Vohras who live in the town: their links to the villages of the Charotar region, their distinctive marriage system that ties them symbolically to these villages, and their notions of social and cultural proximity to local Hindus. These regional orientations are maintained from a position of rupture. Following the longer-term trend of urbanization, paired with residential segregation in the aftermath of the 2002 violence, many residents of the region have relocated in recent decades; their movements combined to enact a new social geography composed of urban and rural spaces that have come to be imagined as Hindu, Muslim, and Christian. The reimagination of spatiality in terms of a Hindu-Muslim divide is paired with a reimagination of the rural-urban divide, and with a reconceptualization of the regional Vohra community from a predominantly rural to an urbanizing one.

Overseas Vohras, who had migrated from the region prior to 2002, have maintained connections with their region of origin. Their ties to the region have increasingly come to be linked to Anand, even among those for whom Anand is not their town of origin. The intersection of regional and transnational arenas in Anand's Muslim area shows that residential segregation does not have to result in isolation, but can be paired with multiple intersecting connections that sustain the segregation process.

CHAPTER 1

Regional Orientations

The Charotar Sunni Vohras

In a community hall on Anand's 100 Feet Road, twelve marriages are taking place. This is a *samuh lagna* (group marriage) of the Charotar Sunni Vohra community. An estimated thousand guests are served lunch—*halwa* (sweets) and a meal of *khichdi* and *dal* (rice with lentils). Afterward, leaders give speeches and distribute gifts to the twelve married couples: a wardrobe, vessel, and pot each, and other kitchen utensils. These gifts have been donated by wealthy members of the community. This *samuh lagna* is organized by the Arsad marriage circle of the Vohra community.

At the front of the hall, a group of elderly men is seated at a table. They are the organizers of the event. They introduce themselves to me as board members of the Charotar Sunni Vohra Samaj. Within this community association they represent the Arsad marriage circle: a sub-set of intermarrying families considered to have originated from sixty-eight villages in the Charotar region (*arsad* is Gujarati for "sixty-eight"). Pointing at the guests, they say that many of them have traveled to Anand from the surrounding villages to be at this event today. They call Anand the headquarters of the Vohra community.

IF CHAROTAR SUNNI VOHRAS articulate a regional identity, what are our resources for studying regional identities? People can construct regions in various ways: spatial, linguistic, economic, cultural, or historical (Cohn 1987). Regions have been thought of as collective mental maps, as geographical areas with social meanings that, depending on historical circumstances, differ between social groups and from issue to issue. There are official regions imagined by administrators and defined by clearly demarcated geographical boundaries, but here I am talking about another kind of region: a microregion (van Schendel 1982)[1] imagined by ordinary people and unknown to outsiders. Charotar is a microregion that does not appear on official maps, but it has had a long existence in popular narratives. Studying such a locally recognized region requires unraveling how people came to think of a set of seemingly unrelated places as an interconnected system. How do Vohras imagine this region and carve out a space for themselves within it?

Charotar Sunni Vohras

> We are the Sunni Vohras from Gujarat. And in Gujarat there are two big rivers: one flows from Ahmedabad, the big city; one from Baroda. Between these two rivers there are 400 villages. These villages have very fertile land and most of our people of the community, those are the Muslims, Gujarati-speaking, they are Vohra—means business people. So, they used to do like farmers, they do breeding for the cattle and cows like that, and they were also doing some small businesses, like grocery stores and stuff like that. So those people, they were from these 400 villages, Charotar. People—Muslims—from that community are called Vohra (interview 2018, USA).

Vohras present themselves as a regional community based in Charotar, and these stories of regional connectivity are told in Gujarat as well as overseas. The fragment above, recorded on video in an interview with an elderly man during a community event of the Vohra Association of North America, in Delaware, is an example of this. The son of a Vohra family of cattle farmers and milk traders, he himself had been raised in Mumbai before he came to the United States; his wife had grown up in Karachi. He nevertheless told the story of his community as one that was located in the distinctive microregion of Charotar.

Charotar land is located between the two rivers of the Mahi and the Vatrak, along the main road and railway tracks that run between the two cities of Ahmedabad and Vadodara (Baroda), with the towns of Anand and Nadiad serving as regional centers. Geographically, it overlaps with the former administrative district of Kheda, which was divided into two separate districts—Anand and Kheda districts—in 1997. Charotar is understood to be a green and relatively affluent land, advantageous for agriculture because of the generous presence of river water. In written descriptions, the Charotar tract is described as a fertile and well-tilled soil, particularly suitable for the cash crops of tobacco and cotton (Rajyagor 1977, 1; Hardiman 1981, 263). *Charo* has been translated as "beautiful" or "pleasant," and *tar* as "land."

Charotar has a productive rural sector. The rural economy has been oriented to commerce since before the early nineteenth century, with tobacco and cotton as important crops, and, since the late nineteenth century, it has exported tobacco, cotton, and dairy products to markets far away (Rutten 1995,

73). Before Independence, irrigation works and the development of small-scale agro-industry raised the productivity of the agricultural economy. After Independence, the government-supported industrialization of agriculture and mechanization of the agricultural process resulted in further increases in productivity. The region became a center of dairy production, engineering companies that manufacture and repair agricultural machinery, industries for irrigation works and the building industry, and mechanical and electrical engineering companies (Rutten 1995, 79–86). Contemporary descriptions of the region's economy suggest that most of the available land is cultivated, although agriculture is no longer considered as important as it once was, with off-farm work emerging in trade, industries, and white-collar jobs, as well as transnational migration (Gidwani 2008; Tilche and Simpson 2018).

Vohras have profiled themselves as a regional community based in this agricultural region of central Gujarat since at least the formation of the Charotar Sunni Vahora Anjuman (an assembly) in 1926 (Vahora n.d., 78–90). Since then, there have been recurrent attempts to organize a Vohra/Vahora[2] community, and this community has been conceptualized as rooted in the Charotar region, as evident from the recurrent addition of the word "Charotar" to the name of the community. Attempts to organize the community included two mini-conferences (1926 and 1928) in Uttarsanda and Anand and two conferences (1938 and 1940) in Anand and Sarsa (Vahora n.d., 177–82). Among the issues discussed were the promotion of education in the community, the benefits of simple weddings and group marriages to counter "wasteful expenditure in the community's weddings," the "menace of divorce in the community," and the "encouragement of community spirit" (Vahora n.d., 78–110). A Charotar Sunni Vahora Young Men's Association[3] was registered in 1936. Concrete results were the establishment, in the early 1940s, of an institute of higher education, the I. J. Kapurwala Commercial School in Anand, and two student hostels (one each in Vadodara and Anand).

The period after Independence and Partition in the late 1940s and 1950s is described as the downfall of the Vohra community. The educational institutions set up by the Vohras were closed, and those in Anand who remember this say the closures were caused by a lack of funding following the migration of wealthy Vohras from Mumbai to Karachi in Pakistan. Other reasons for the decline included conflicts among the leaders, the death of some leaders, and a lack of enthusiasm among the next generation (Vahora n.d., 91–100). Nevertheless, some conferences continued to be organized to discuss community affairs. A Charotar Sunni Vohra Panchayat (village council) was established in Petlad in 1954, and a

Charotar Sunni Vohra Tarahija Mandal (an association of the Tarahija subcommunity) was established in Chaklasi in 1979.

I draw these insights from a rare, unpublished, and undated book titled *Vahora Darshan* (*A Glimpse of Vohra*)[4] by Haji Ismailbhai Sabanbhai Vahora, which describes the origins of the Charotar Sunni Vohra community. The author was a Vohra and writes that he lived in Mumbai, though the locations printed with his name (Borsadwala, Karanchi) indicate he may have moved to the city of Karachi from the town of Borsad in central Gujarat. The book is presented as a history of all Vohras in the world,[5] but the history of the Vohras of Charotar is the most extensively covered, and the information provided in the book indicates that the author was well connected to, and informed by, the Vohra residents of central Gujarat and Mumbai. I stumbled upon the book in London in 2012, and later discovered that a school teacher in Anand also owned a copy.

The book suggests that it was Vohras in colonial Bombay— from the Charotar region—who started to organize themselves specifically as Muslims from Charotar. The Charotar Sunni Vahora Young Men's Association was registered in Bombay in 1936. The events they organized took place mostly in Gujarat, but they appear to have been organized and sponsored from Bombay. Ten years after its registration, the association moved its office to Anand, and a bylaw was introduced in the governing body that "instead of only residents of Bombay, all Vohras from Baroda, Charotar region, Anand and Ahmedabad are permitted as office bearers of the association" (Vahora n.d., 100–10).

Such processes of caste and community formation were not unique at the time—people everywhere were organizing around such tropes in response to the colonial state's politics of classification, description, and entitlement distribution (Pinney 1997, 62–63; Risley 1891; van der Veer 1994, 25–27). Colonial efforts to make Indian society governable included classifying India's people, and the social categories of caste and community were studied, described, and then used by the colonial bureaucracy to distribute entitlements among its colonial subjects. In response, people organized themselves around community identities and then attempted to influence their categorization in colonial schemes. These processes have been described in detail for the Patidar caste (Pocock 1955). The name of the Patidars was first registered in the census of 1931, around the same period when Vohras started to organize. The previous name of this caste was Kanbis, an agricultural caste, but under the British colonial tax collecting regime, some of the Kanbis had acquired the honorary title of "Patel" (tax collector at the village level). The efforts of Kanbis to get registered as Patidars marked an effort to be recognized in a higher status (as merchants rather than farmers).

The Vohra community organization declined after the Partition of 1947, but the *samuh lagna* shows it has been reinvigorated. During an interview in 2011, two leaders said that there were sixty board members of the Charotar Sunni Vohra Samaj in the Charotar region at that time. They explained that the main purpose of the board members is to bring the community together, to encourage endogamous marriages, and to organize group weddings and social gatherings, such as singles events, to facilitate interaction between young unmarried men and women in the community. The interview took place in a small office in Anand where the association kept its files and had installed a computer. In the cupboard were copies of the community's newspaper, *Vahora Sudharak* (Vohra Reformation), subtitled *Charotar Sunni Vahora Sudharak Mandalnu Mukapatr* (Pamphlet for the Reformation of the Charotar Sunni Vohra Community).[6] In 2012, however, this office was raided and the computer was confiscated by one of the board members after a conflict over money, showing that the leadership of the association does not function as a coherent whole.

The circulation of different Vohra community books (at the village level and through the marriage circles) confirms that the Vohra community should not be understood as one integrated social unit, or as a political faction or sect following a single leader. I encountered four books (produced between 1986 and 2006) with detailed demographic information about Vohra families in the region; three other books were found earlier by Carolyn Heitmeyer (2009a). The main purpose of these books—which resemble telephone books, but include detailed information about the marital status of each member of a family, and further details that make it possible to assess a family's socioeconomic position—is to facilitate marriage within the community. None of the books aspires to include all the Vohras in Charotar, however. Instead, they focus on a regional marriage circle within the Vohra community (listing all members in Gujarat of either the Makeriya[7] marriage circle or the Dewataja[8] marriage circle) or on town-specific Vohra groups (listing all Vohras in Mahemdabad in 1998, Thasra in 2000, or Ahmedabad in 2004; described in Heitmeyer 2009a, 211–12).

The idea of a regionally specific Vohra community has been institutionalized overseas in the various places where Vohras have migrated. There is a Mumbai Charotar Sunni Vohra Samaj in Mumbai, and a Charotar Muslim Anjuman (association of Charotar Muslims) with a Vohra community hall in Karachi. A UK Vohra Association was established in 1992. A Muslim Vohra Association was established in the United States in 2002, after having been informally organized since the 1990s, and was renamed as Vohra Association of North America in 2019 to signal the increasing membership of the association in Canada.

These associations are specifically aimed at Vohra families "who are originally from Kheda/Anand Dist[rict] of Gujarat/India".[9] Each of these associations has organized social meetings and maintains an address list with details of known Vohra families in the respective regions. The associations are not united in a transnational umbrella association, and their level of activity and organization varies. Nevertheless, these attempts to institutionalize Vohras show that the idea of a regionally specific Vohra community has persisted and is actively reproduced in India and abroad.

Rural Histories

What is this Charotar Sunni Vohra community, then? Four independent regional sections of Sunni Vohra communities are described in the literature: the Charotar Vohras, the Patani Vohras, the Kadiwal Vohras, and the Surati Vohras (Misra 1964, 122–23). The name "Vohra" translates as "trader," and many Vohras self-identify as traders, but trade is only one of the occupations among Vohras. Asghar Ali Engineer (1989, 30–31) calls Vohras "peasants" and "tillers of the soil"; Carolyn Heitmeyer describes Vohras as a "business community" (2009a, 32), and S. B. Rajyagor (1977, 185) describes them as "engaged in business or employed in Government or semi-Government services," with some of them working as lawyers, doctors, and engineers. Satish Misra (1964, 122) says that "the majority of the Sunni Vohras of all regions are cultivators but an increasing proportion is taking to trade for its livelihood."

Despite the diversity observed by these scholars, they seem to agree broadly on the idea that Sunni Vohras are rural or small-town communities. Their residential concentration in towns and villages, as well as cities, distinguishes them from the Shia Daudi Bohras, who mostly live in cities (Heitmeyer 2009a, 75; Engineer 1989, 30–31). In rural areas of Gujarat, conversion to Sunni Islam is said to have taken place during the rule of Sultan Muzfarshah I in the period 1377–1411 (Rajyagor 1977, 185)—one interpretation is that rural converts took on the name Vohra to signify their conversion to Islam.

Community leaders of the Charotar Sunni Vohras in Anand, and other narrators who took upon themselves the task of explaining the history of their community to me, reinforce that it is a regional and distinctively rural community that has long been embedded in the agricultural economy of the Charotar microregion. The community narratives that were recounted to me construct a regional community through three recurrent themes: a) the indigeneity of the community, as shown in narratives that describe the Vohras as the descendants of local Hindus who converted to Islam, b) links to the land and villages of the region, as shown in narratives of their long embeddedness as farmers, traders, and small-scale industrialists playing a distinctive role in the agricultural economy, and c) a distinctive marriage system of regional marriage circles linked to ancestral villages, which not only marks the Vohras as a distinct (endogamous) community but also reaffirms the importance of the villages *and* their similarities with local Hindus.

The first theme is conversion, and this narrative presents the claim that the community *also* belongs to the region—just as local Hindus do—through its affirmation of local ancestry. Vohras are presented as the descendants of local Hindus who converted to Islam. This claim constitutes an important distinction, as it sets Vohras apart from other local Muslims, who trace their lineage to Muslim saints, Saiyeds, believed to be descendants of the Prophet who came to Gujarat from outside the subcontinent. A distinction often referred to in the literature on caste among Muslims is between Ashraf groups (or nobles) and non-Ashraf groups (or commoners): Ashraf communities are regarded as the descendants of immigrants—Arab traders and saints—while non-Ashraf families are seen as people with an Indian origin, who have turned to Islam through conversion (Dumont 1980, 207). In central Gujarat, these differences are recognized although there is no clear hierarchy among these groups (see chapter 4).

The Vohra narrative of conversion distinguishes them from Ashraf Muslims and aligns them with local Hindus. There are various theories about the specifics of this Hindu ancestry. One theory is that the Vohras from Charotar are Brahmins who migrated south from north Gujarat and converted to Islam in Mahemdabad under the reign of Mahmud Begada (1458–1511), a story told to me in the United States by an overseas Vohra from Mahemdabad. If some think that Vohras are former Brahmins, others suspect that Vohras are converts from lower-caste Hindus, and that their conversion was motivated by a desire to escape caste oppression. A third option some of my interlocutors considered is that Vohras had been Patels. This diversity of ideas of origin is a reflection, possibly, of the status differences that exist within the Vohra community at present. The group marriage I described above, for example, was organized by the Arsad marriage circle of the Vohra community. This Arsad marriage circle is considered lower in status than the Chaud ("fourteen") marriage circle. It can be assumed that the members of the higher-status group came from families of a higher socioeconomic background, and were derived from different castes prior to conversion (Heitmeyer 2009a, 107–8; following Enthoven 1920, 206).

The second theme in the Vohra community narratives is economic: it concerns the Vohras' involvement in the long-term development of the agricultural economy, through trade and various kinds of agro-industrial endeavors, and in some cases through farming. These narratives of trade and agro-industrial activities present Vohras as an economic link between the agricultural sector and the cities, selling imported products such as textiles and consumption items to farmers, and buying produce from farms to sell in Mumbai. Some Vohras were small-scale traders either in shops or door-to-door on *feri* (foot carts) in the villages. These small-scale traders would have sold clothes and textiles, either as ready-made garments or tailor-made to suit specific customers, as many Vohra traders still do today. Others were wholesale traders. During a visit to the auction market of Nadiad with a member of a locally well-known trading family, the man who accompanied me explained how he had been groomed as a child in the family business of trading vegetables. At that time, he claimed, 30 percent of the wholesale traders at the auction market were Muslims. These traders bought the produce of the local farmers (mainly of the Patel and Kshatriya communities), and sent it to Mumbai or elsewhere to sell at a profit. The link with agriculture is reflected in the surnames of some of these Vohra business families, including Limbuwallah (from being in the lemon wholesale business), Chanawallah (processing and trading chickpeas), Dudhwala (in dairy), and Fruitwala. Some of these traders still own the cold-storage facilities that they use to store fruit and vegetables until the prices go up, while others own factories for the industrial production and packaging of agricultural products.

These names, occupations, and narratives link Vohras with the rural economy. Sometimes the link is established through farming or land ownership, as in the example of cattle farming and milk production; in other cases, through commercial and industrial endeavors, as in stories of how the Vohras of their village used to press *ganchi* (oilseed) and process cotton in small-scale workshops. For a community narrative rooted in an agricultural economy, however, it is striking that the question of land ownership is not necessarily a central element in these stories of the past. Once I had started wondering about the question of land, I asked about this repeatedly yet received different answers. This happened, for example, during conversations with two friends, Ganibhai and Gulamnabi—elderly men in Anand who had volunteered to tell me the Vohra community's history. Ganibhai, who came from a relatively privileged landowning family, replied that there have been "many landowners" in the Vohra community. Gulamnabi, however, replied that the Vohras have relatively poor and humble origins; their ancestors were hawkers and small-scale traders without land or property. Among them, he believed, those who became successful merchants or government employees have more recently become landowners because they were able to invest their profits or pensions in land.

This pronounced difference in perspective between the two friends—the first belonging to a landowning family and maintaining a productive farm in his natal village of Napad, the other coming from more humble roots and having moved up in life through education and employment—is another indication of the economic differences that exist in the community. This became clearer when Gulamnabi, the second speaker, showed me the house in the village of Chikhodra that he had lived in as a child. It consisted of one small room without windows and one door. It seemed impossible to me that it had been the home of an entire family. Gulamnabi explained that his parents had rented that house, that they had owned no land, and that his father had merely done some "small business." In his youth, Gulamnabi had walked the ten kilometers to the college where he studied in Anand every day. Later on, he became a school teacher and eventually the headmaster of a government school, working himself up the ladder and now enjoying a government pension in his old age.

These narratives of conversion and economic participation in the regional economy are also narratives of the past that are told in a present of rural–urban relocation. We were traveling to the village of Chikodra from Anand (where Ganibhai, Gulamnabi, and I lived) by rickshaw, and they took the occasion of the journey to clarify some of the matters they had explained to me earlier, during an interview in Anand. As we walked through the village, Gulamnabi estimated that approximately 50 percent of the villagers were Patels. While he estimated that 400 Muslims still remained in the village—working as hawkers, rickshaw drivers, or day laborers—most of the Muslim population had moved to Anand, like him.

Village-Based Marriage Circles

Coming back to Anand after such travels, in the evening, I would normally go home to hang out on the couch of my landlady, Shahinben. At such times, I would be writing out my notes on my laptop. Shahinben herself would be found seated on a sheet on the floor in the company of her niece, reading a book or preparing vegetables for the next day while watching television. One evening, as I put my notebooks aside and tried to assist them, Shahinben turned to me and asked pointedly, "Would you like to do an interview tomorrow? I can come along to introduce you." She had a family in mind that could be interesting for my research, she said. Always willing to get to know new people in the neighborhood, I happily agreed.

The next morning, as we walked over to a nearby housing society where this family lived, she advised me to direct my questions to the son of the family. I could ask him, for example, about his education, his current job, and his future ambitions. I understood she wanted to get to know his credentials and followed her advice, chatting with the young man while Shahinben observed our conversation closely. On the way back, she told me she had been observing his behavior while we talked. She had found him well-mannered and his English was good. I then understood what her purpose had been. Shahinben, who was a teacher with many connections in the neighborhood, had been approached by an acquaintance with a matchmaking request. Her friend had a daughter who could be a potential match for the young man we had just spoken to, and had asked Shahinben for her opinion. As it was considered impolite for the parents of the young woman to approach a young man directly, Shahinben took it upon herself to check him out informally, using my research project as an inoffensive way of approaching an unknown family. She liked the young man and recommended him to her friend.

Intermarriage between members of different Muslim communities is not uncommon in India. Vohras, however, maintain an endogamous marriage system. There is a broad consensus among Vohras that they must marry within the community, and in this way they maintain their separation from other local Muslim groups as well as Hindus, with whom there is no intermarriage. I found only few deviations from this norm (similar to Heitmeyer 2009a, 103). Vohra women play an important role in marriage arrangements (Heitmeyer 2009a, 107–8).

As I spent more time with Shahinben, it became increasingly evident that many of the conversations she had with her female neighbors, friends, and relatives concerned marriage. It was obviously a topic of great difficulty because of the many variables to be considered. When I witnessed her exchange details with other women about a certain young man or woman for matchmaking purposes, they would discuss the education level, religious affiliation, and moral character of the potential spouse, the wealth of their family, and whether it was a "business family" or one with the benefit of a "government job." They would also consider their position within the Vohra marriage system. To this end, they used the terms "Chaud" and "Arsad"—words used routinely as signifiers to demarcate the two main marriage circles in the community. The terms are said to refer, respectively, to fourteen (Chaud) and sixty-eight (Arsad) villages of the Charotar region to which Vohra families trace their origins. While the names of the fourteen subgroups are known (table 1.01), a complete list of the sixty-eight subgroups does not exist, and some of the group names reflect occupations rather than villages (e.g., Dudhwala).

This distinctive marriage system has been described in detail by Carolyn Heitmeyer (2009a, 97–132), and I follow her analysis here, with some small adjustments that stem from my observations in Anand. Heitmeyer's analysis of the Vohra marriage system is concerned with its emphasis on endogamy (marriage within the community). Her observations in Sultanpur, where many Vohras self-identify as traders, suggest this might be because the Vohras are a business community, and their endogamous marriage practices function to keep resources within the community. My focus here is on how the Vohra marriage system establishes a concept of the region—how the marriage practices are "central to encouraging unity within the wider Sunni Vohra regional network and are closely linked to the *samaj's* strong sense of identity within the local landscape" (Heitmeyer 2009a, 32). Marriage alliances contribute to region-making through three elements of the practice: villages, status negotiations, and patrilocality.

A quote from a banker in Anand town is illustrative of the significance of villages within the Vohra marriage system: "All our forefathers were given a name at that time by the *mollah*. Our forefathers were given the names of the village where they happened to live at that time. I am Dewataja, so my forefather probably lived in the small village of Dewataj at the time." This statement suggests that he remembers his forefathers' village, but simultaneously that it has become an abstract code, a memory. He remembers this because of its significance in the making of marriage alliances. Even when families have moved into the town in a previous generation, the village of origin continues to be considered in contemporary marriage negotiations. A young man can live in Anand but be "Nepada" (from the village of Nepad, in Chaud) or "Umretha" (from Umreth town, in Arsad). Even if he has never lived in the named town or village in his life, his ancestry can make a difference in the assessment of his suitability during marriage arrangements.

The Vohra marriage system projects a region through the arrangement of related *ataks* (subgroups, or clans) into a hierarchical system, described in table 1.01. The village-based marriage circles provide the basis for an exchange system of hypergamy (in which a lower-status female is married to a higher-status male). Members of the high-status Chaud marriage circle are known to prefer marriage among themselves, and are seen as *ekla kutumb* (a single family), having established ongoing relations and mutual trust over several generations (Heitmeyer

TABLE 1.1. Marriage circles of the Charotar Sunni Vohra marriage system (names in italics indicate marriage circles that refer to villages and cities in central Gujarat)

	Groups in Chaud circle (14)	Groups in Arsad circle (68)	Groups in Makeriya circle	Groups in Dewataja circle
1	*Audya*	Malavadiya	Makeriya	*Dewataja*
2	*Nepada*	*Mahemdabadi*		
3	Pinjara	Amodiya		
4	*Mogriya*	*Vasoya*		
5	Metrala	*Anandiya*		
6	Piyeja	*Khadola*		
7	Bharja	Munshi		
8	*Ahmdavadi*	Sinhuiya		
9	Musela	Dudhwala		
10	Tarajiya	Nariya		
11	*Dabhaniya*	*Sunijya*		
12	*Tarapuri*	Kahra		
13	Vasaniya	*Umretha*		
14	*Kanjeriya*	Aslaliya		
15		Mankdiya		

SOURCE: This schematic representation of the Vohra marriage system, drawn from Carolyn Heitmeyer (2009a, 106), was modified after consultation with interlocutors of Anand. Names in italics refer to place names. Some names are not included in Heitmeyer's list, but were mentioned by my interlocutors. Those who self-identified as Makeriya, Dewataja, or Kanjeriya disagreed with Heitmeyer on their position in the system—I have followed their suggestions in producing this table.

2009a, 108). Members are seen as relatively powerful, owning land and property, and engaged in relatively capital-intensive businesses. The lower-status Arsad marriage circle members often marry among themselves or may attempt to "marry up"—in the customary system, women of the Arsad family circle may enter into marriage with men of the Chaud family circle, but not vice versa.

A similar village-based marriage system exists among the Patidars.[10] In both the Vohra and Patidar communities an intricate system of village-based marriage circles regulates and promotes marriages within the caste, by outlining groups of villages of similar status and encouraging them to intermarry. Similar to the Vohra marriage circles of "fourteen" and "sixty-eight," Patidars also use numbers to name their marriage circles. For example, in the 1950s a middle-ranging group of seven villages was referred to as simply "the Seven" (Pocock 1972), and since 1968 this circle had developed into the "twenty-two," although it was in fact made up of a total of forty villages (Tilche and Simpson 2018, 1524). Another similarity between the communities is the hierarchical relation that exists between the different circles. For both Vohras and Patidars, a family's status on the marriage market is measured by its village of origin, because each marriage circle stands in a hierarchical relation to the other marriage circles.

The ongoing efforts of families in the lower-ranked circles to marry their daughters up into families of the higher-ranked circles (hypergamy) causes tension in the system. For Patidars, according to David Pocock's description (1972, 66–67; 1973, 1), hierarchy is an ideal, to the extent that the Patidars insist on inequality to be able to appear superior to other caste members. For Vohras, according to Carolyn Heitmeyer's description (2009a, 110), social hierarchies exist, but hierarchical marriage practices of hypergamy and dowry are very strongly discouraged by community leaders. Vohras in Anand confirmed this emphasis on equality and described it as a core value of Islam,[11] projecting themselves as upholders of Islamic values of equality in a caste-based society and in some cases displaying embarrassment about the system. While practices of hypergamy are critiqued among Vohras in Anand, the association of families with hierarchically arranged marriage circles is broadly maintained. For example, Chaud families I saw navigating the marriage market first looked around their own circle, and hesitantly extended their search to Arsad families if no desirable match could be found. The status hierarchies between the Chaud and Arsad families are under negotiation in Anand, and some families of the Arsad group are said to surpass Chaud families in status, wealth, and educational level.

Two groups (Makeriya and Dewataja) claim a separate status within the system, neither Arsad nor Chaud. While Vohras in Sultanpur position the Makeriya in the Arsad marriage circle (Heitmeyer 2009a, 105–6), in Anand the Makeriya regard themselves as a separate group. Through a strong emphasis on education and urbanization, they have carved out a new position, in an attempt to liberate themselves from a former low-status position. During a Makeriya community meeting I attended in Anand, their emphasis on education was very striking, with awards being granted to all the young people who had recently received a degree.

The distinctiveness of the Makeriya as a more educated group was also emphasized during the group wedding described at the beginning of this chapter.

Shahinben had taken me there alongside her uncle, who was visiting Anand from the United States. She and her uncle belong to the Makeriya group, whereas the wedding was organized for the Arsad marriage circle. In the midst of the event, Shahinben suddenly left, whispering that she wished me a nice remainder of the day, but had to leave at once because "there are too many uneducated people here." Afterward, she clarified the event had been a bit noisy and overcrowded for her and linked this experience to the differences in education level between the Makeriya and the Arsad (in her view). These moments show how the Makeriya claim a subtly different (educated) position within the community, and indicate the dynamism as well as the continued significance of these demarcations for those involved.

Finally, to clarify how marriage practices contribute to a regional orientation, it is necessary to clarify how marriage systems in South Asia shape the distinctive, short-distance relocation of women between villages and towns. In central Gujarat, as in other western and northern regions of India (Karve 1994), it is common for a woman to move into her husband's house after marriage (patrilocality). When marriages are forged between villages rather than within a village (a common pattern of village exogamy), this means that women spend the most of their lives in villages in which they did not grow up. These short-distance relocations of women, while grossly overlooked in the migration literature, are significant (Alexander, Chatterji, and Jalais 2016, 128–39), and this significance is evident in the case of Vohras: these women become crucial arbiters in cross-village relations between their own and their husbands' families, and thus become central to the imagination of a regional kinship geography.

All the families I knew in Anand included one or more women who had moved into her husband's household after marriage. These married young women had arrived from nearby villages, and sometimes from within Anand itself, or from Ahmedabad. Of the young married couples, none had formed their own independent household; instead, the women moved in with their husbands' families, where they became responsible for a range of household tasks, including the care of his aging parents. This pattern of patrilocality prevails largely undebated, although the young couples may move out eventually to establish an independent household.

Vohras have no strict rules with regard to village exogamy (Heitmeyer 2009a, 102–3). Vohras in Anand have different opinions on this matter. Some families stated that they preferred their daughters to marry within Anand itself, so that they remain close to home after marriage. The women themselves seemed to have different thoughts on this. On the one hand, there are advantages to having your own family close by; on the other hand, some said, a marriage outside one's own town had the advantage of turning their brother's household into a "holiday" destination, where they could take a break from their responsibilities in their husband's household.

Visiting one's brother's village is indeed a common way in which married women in Anand can take socially accepted breaks, particularly during pregnancy, illness, or summer vacations. They return to their own families for a few weeks or just for a day, and their mothers or sisters-in-law take care of them. I regularly saw a married woman put pressure on her husband to visit her kin, telling him to accompany her there. Some used the occasion of my research to this end, telling their husbands that they should not miss the occasion to introduce the foreign visitor to her family—a strategy that was sometimes successful. Married women simultaneously maintain relations with selected women in their husband's extended family network, and encourage their children to spend time with relatives from both sides. In this way, married women play a key role in the (re)production of the regional community: by maintaining and further developing dispersed kinship networks, encouraging visits to and fro, and passing on knowledge about these different geographical locations and their interconnections to their children.

If the Vohras' marriage practices connect urban residents to the Charotar region in an abstract way, through the names of hierarchically related ancestral villages, they also, in concrete ways, bring about the lived experience of a regional kinship geography, in which the short-distance relocation of married women is valued and functions as a binding force.

Gujarati Muslims

Charotar Sunni Vohras thus imagine a region and carve out a space for themselves within it through their narratives, rural-urban networks, and various kinds of economic and social practices. These descriptions of a regionally embedded Gujarati Muslim community provide a corrective to the ways in which Muslims have predominantly been viewed in India, especially in Gujarat. The significance of the Vohras' challenge to prevalent conceptions becomes clear when we consider the dominant idea of Gujarat that is captured in the notion of *Gujaratni asmita*: Gujarati pride or glory.

Scholars of Gujarat have understood *Gujaratni asmita* as a core concept that underpins the contemporary imagination of Gujarati identity as a regional formulation of Hindu nationalism, which projects the picture of Gujarat and

Gujaratis as being synonymous with Hindus and antithetical to Muslims. The growing currency of the notion of *asmita* in the popular media, in election campaigns, and in the everyday narratives of urban middle-class Hindus has been widely discussed (Chandrani 2013; Ghassem-Fachandi 2012; Ibrahim 2008). Its mobilization seems to have been key to the electoral success of the Bharatiya Janata Party (BJP) in Gujarat since the late 1980s (G. Shah 1998).

This idea of *asmita* has been articulated in novels and poems written in the Gujarati language in the nineteenth and twentieth centuries, as discussed by anthropologists Farhana Ibrahim and Yogesh Rasiklal Chandrani. Different interpretations of *asmita* are possible. The present-day interpretation of *asmita*, promoted in election campaigns, is of a more exclusively Hindu identity than some of the earlier articulations of this notion, as formulated, for example, by the Gujarati poet Narmad in the mid-nineteenth century (Ibrahim 2008, 22–25). In his poem "Gujarat Koni?," Narmad asks, "to whom does Gujarat belong?" In his answer, he includes people of all castes and creed as legitimate members of the social fabric of Gujarat, but he also states that those who follow "other religions" are included only under the condition that they express their love of Gujarat. Due to this ambivalence, the poem has formed a basis of both Hindu nationalist interpretations and more inclusive interpretations that are associated with secular versions of nationalism (Chandrani 2013, 178–79). While these nineteenth-century iterations of *asmita* made the concept available to two different political projects, however, even the secularist interpretation of the poem privileges Hindus as more naturally Gujarati than others, and so "the difference between these two projects of Gujarat should . . . not be overstated" (Chandrani 2013, 178–79).

These readings of a nineteenth-century poem underscore a wider argument about the normalization and sedimentation of Gujarati-ness as identical with Hindu-ness. These discourses that reiterate the Hindu-Muslim binary have become so normalized in India that it is almost impossible, even for those who critique them, to think outside them (Chandrani 2013, 199–201). This was one of the conditions that made the 2002 anti-Muslim pogroms possible. During the pogroms, *Gujaratni asmita* became a legitimizing notion (Ibrahim 2008, 15), which justified the idea that Gujarat needed to be cleansed of Muslims.

Scholars of Gujarat have not stopped there. There has been a keen interest among anthropologists of the region to discover and describe possible alternatives to dominant ideas of Gujarat that continue to be articulated by different groups (Simpson and Kapadia 2010). This work demonstrates that the "idea of Gujarat" has been received in varying ways, not always with enthusiasm, and that different interpretations of this idea are still possible. First, even if the idea of Gujarat has existed for a long time in written poetry and novels, many people were confronted with it only in 1960, when the current state of Gujarat came into existence after a political campaign to divide Bombay State in Gujarat and Maharashtra. In Kutch, a former princely state, the incorporation of Kutch into Gujarat was resisted because local elites would lose their influence with the advance of the Gujarati state over local affairs. Historians in Kutch have resisted the idea that their region is "Gujarati" (Simpson 2010a, 12); local groups instead recount their regional history as one of kingdoms and goddesses that are linked specifically to the lands and seas of Kutch and Sindh (Simpson 2010b, 76–77; see also Ibrahim 2008).

The contemporary conceptions of who are the legitimate citizens of Gujarat through the lens of *asmita* have been challenged by both Hindus and Muslims of Kutch. Among the Muslim groups of Kutch, the pastoralist Daneta Jatts and the agricultural Garasia Jatts (Ibrahim 2008) can be compared with the Charotar Sunni Vohras. The Daneta Jatts' critique of the contemporary notion of Gujarat is expressed indirectly through a narrative of a changed ecology, which endows the past with plentiful grasslands, benevolent rulers, and profitable trade routes between Kutch and Sindh. This mythical past is compared with present experiences of scarcity and destruction (Ibrahim 2008, 51–76), which are attributed to contemporary state interference that has marginalized the pastoralists and censured their cross-border trade with Sindh (now in Pakistan). Farhana Ibrahim regards these community narratives as a "discourse of defiance" (following Abu-Lughod 1986, 185) that contradicts the system from below. These internal narratives are not brought up on a wider political stage but are meaningful in that they allow members of the community to expresses ideas that cannot be expressed in the dominant system (Ibrahim 2008, 75).

Garasia Jatts in Kutch, a former community of pastoralists that has moved into agriculture, also critique the present state of Gujarat through an internal community narrative contrasting a good past with a problematic present. In the nostalgic past, rulers were benevolent, and the Jatts played a central role in state proceedings, while the present state sees the Jatts as "Muslims," and thus as untrustworthy. Nevertheless, the Garasia Jatts, unlike the pastoralist Jatts, continue to seek proximity to the state and to the idea of *Gujaratni asmita*. Having settled into an agrarian lifestyle, they have developed distinctive symbols, shrines, and practices that mark them as different from other Muslims and as culturally close to Hindus. These symbols allow them to carve out a space on the inside, even within state-sanctioned Hindu rituals that celebrate Gujarati pride, by presenting themselves as different from the recurrent representations of the Muslim "outsider" (Ibrahim 2008, 94–99).

Like the narratives of the Jatts in Kutch, Vohra stories conjure a somewhat nostalgic past of agricultural embedding and Hindu-Muslim similarities, which are told in a present of rural-urban relocation and Hindu-Muslim segregation. Instead of criticizing the logic of the prevalent discourse directly, as the pastoralist Daneta Jatts do, Vohras' self-representations are closer to those of the agricultural Garasia Jatts, who seek to carve out a space *within* the dominant framework of Gujarati identity. Their self-representations suggest that Vohras *also* belong.

Vohras and Patidars of Charotar

The Vohra community narrative anchors an idea of "Gujarat" to the microregion of the Charotar. The dense literature about this region has rarely included the perspectives of Muslims; nevertheless, scattered traces of the Vohras can be found in it. This repertoire of regional representations broadly confirms the Vohra story of a rural past shared with the Patidars and reveals several similarities between the two communities, as well as some significant differences.

The similarities between Patidars and Vohras were described in a 1954 history book on the Charotar region. According to this source, Vohra marriage customs were like those of the Patidars, and their clothing was also similar (Mahammad 1954, 8–13). In this period, the anthropologist David Pocock conducted research in Sundarana, a small village with a population of 2,290. His work focused on the Patidars, with only brief descriptions of other groups.[12] Pocock has little to say about Hindu-Muslim relations in the village, which is remarkable because he conducted his research shortly after Partition, and his research assistant, Momad, was a Muslim (Simpson et al. 2018). Nevertheless, this work gives several indications of Vohras' relations with the local Hindus. Pocock observed that the Muslims "were treated much as a Hindu caste by the Patidar," and that a Muslim boy was a keen participant in a Hindu hymn-singing association. He even suggests that the Muslims of the village were ignorant of the basic tenets of Islam (Pocock 1972, 44). These descriptions suggest that Hindu-Muslim identities were considered almost irrelevant at the time.

There are, broadly, two views on how this situation of similarity and alliance developed after the 1950s. When the anthropologist Alice Tilche studied Sundarana in 2013 to revisit David Pocock's research findings from the 1950s, she found that the relationship between Hindus and Muslims had changed. In 2013, as a result of the advance of Hindu nationalist discourses, the figure of the Muslim had become a recurrent topic of conversation among the Patidars. In 2002, the minaret of Sundarana's mosque had been destroyed, and it was never rebuilt. By 2013, suspicion had hardened, and the Muslims of Sundarana and other villages had moved to Anand (Tilche and Simpson 2017). Interest in Islam had also grown among Muslims themselves, partly as a result of Islamic institutions undertaking missionary activities (Simpson et al. 2018). Overall, separate Hindu and Muslim identities had become more important.

Another description of Vohras in the nearby town of Sultanpur, however, offers a different analysis. Based on research in the period 2005–2006, Carolyn Heitmeyer writes that in Sultanpur, Vohras continue to live close to Hindus in and around the markets of the town, even if other Muslims live in separate parts of the town. Not only do Vohras share business alliances with Hindus, they also align themselves as culturally close with local Hindus (2009a, 84), cultivate amicable relations and socialize with the Patidars and other local Hindus, and are seen (by other Muslims) as remaining aloof from other local Muslim groups (Heitmeyer 2009a, 92). This is reflected in clothing styles, referencing Hindu businesses in Vohra publications, and the shared use of the Gujarati language (a regional language Vohras share with Gujarati Hindus, Christians, and other Gujarati-speaking Muslim groups, which is different from the use of Hindi in many other Muslim households).

Patidars and Muslims in Sundarana have been torn apart, while alliances continue to exist in Sultanpur; in the case of Anand, themes of rupture and alliance both exist. Ruptures resulted from the 2002 anti-Muslim violence and the displacement of Muslims from the villages. Yet stories of continuity are also articulated within the town, even if they are expressed from a tenuous position.

In the regional stories Vohras in Anand told me, several interlocutors drew explicit comparisons between the Vohras and the Patidars—for example, explaining that both are merchants (bania) or that they are "the two dominant communities" in the region. The Patidars appeared in the Vohra stories as business partners, neighbors, and friends, and as role models whose success the Vohras would like to emulate, especially in the field of overseas migration. Their regional narratives highlight the centrality of the Patidar caste to the Charotar region, and delineate the Patidars as the most successful and influential community in the region. For example, a Vohra resident of Anand, an older man, said:

> See, all the development that you see here in Charotar is because of the Patels. They are getting lots of donations. They have many NRIs

[nonresident Indians]. If it was not for Patels, Charotar would still be like Saurasthra ... where dust goes on in the sky ... [He continued the conversation by explaining how Muslims are "lagging behind."]

If the Vohras tell stories about the Charotar region, and if the Patidars frequently appear in these stories, how, then, do Vohra and Patidar conceptions of the region compare? The differences in their spatial conceptions, I suggest, reflect their position in the region as either a dominant Hindu caste or a displaced Muslim community.

Books, oral histories, and websites of Patidar communities[13] establish ideological links between villages, land ownership, and the Patidar community (Hardiman 1981, 43). Despite the increasing importance of overseas migration and a devaluation of agriculture, the village continues to hold importance for both local and transnational members of the Patidar caste. Even after migrating abroad, Patidars maintain village associations and support the development of their home village financially (Rutten and Patel 2004; Dekkers and Rutten 2018).[14] These initiatives are supported in the village by political and cultural institutions that are also dominated by local Patidars. These village-based transnational caste bonds result, for example, in events such as an annual Village Day, during which donations are gathered for the development of the village, and in which the participants tend to be almost entirely from the Patidar community (Dekkers and Rutten 2018, 13). Such transnational caste claims over village spaces are not unique to the Patidars; comparable trends have been described in the coastal villages of Andhra Pradesh, where highly educated transnational migrants belonging to the agrarian landowning elite accumulate economic and cultural capital through migration to the United States, and cultivate philanthropic relations with the home region through diasporic associations, in which caste becomes a principle axis of community formation and assertion (Roohi 2016).

The central point in the Patidars' spatial imagination is the village, and its global caste networks have become the platforms on which internal caste hierarchies are enacted and renegotiated. The remittances and investments in village development sustain the Patidars' economic and political power in the village, and reinforce a symbolic link between a specific subsection of the Patidar community and its home village. In the Patidars' regional imagination, the village is central, while the links with the broader region beyond the village appear natural. This reflects the Patidars' position as the dominant Hindu community in the region.

For Vohras, on the other hand, as a displaced Muslim community in Gujarat their relation with the villages and the region does not appear as natural, and has to be narrated in order to be remembered. The dominance of Patidars in many of the Vohras' villages of origin makes it unlikely that Vohras have ever claimed these village spaces as their own in the same way that Patidars could. Following the displacement of Muslims over the last decades, Hindu claims over village spaces have been reinforced. In Anand, Vohra families continue to cultivate economic and social ties with these villages, yet in many families the village is decreasing in relevance, and for some, it has become an abstract code to assess the suitability of a spouse during marriage arrangements.

Online representations illustrate these different ways of imagining the region. On websites representing sections of the Patidar community, village names are usually specified, and sometimes further highlighted in illustrated maps. On websites and Facebook pages created by members of the Charotar Vohra community, villages names are usually not specified, or not as prominently, yet the community is projected a regional one—for example, through the inclusion of a generic state map of Gujarat.

Besides villages of origin, Anand town has acquired a special position in the Vohras' regional imagination as an arrival point that has also become a meeting point for the dispersed community members. During the group wedding in Anand, a man, a big smile on his face, declared good-humoredly that "Anand is the *Makka* of the Vohras!" At my puzzlement, he got serious and explained: "Previously, Vohras were happy in their villages. They had some small business there. But since the riots in 2002, Vohras want to be in Anand."

Conclusion

To the question "Can a Gujarati be Muslim?" (Chandrani 2013, 193), the Vohras' answer is clearly "Yes." Vohra affirmations of regional belonging call into question the dominant view that Muslims are outsiders in Gujarat. This is a subtle yet substantial inversion of prevalent discourses. Their affirmations do not fundamentally attack the logic of local ancestry and belonging utilized by exclusivist Hindu political discourses, but redress this logic with the claim that Vohras *also* belong.

Vohras' positioning in the Charotar microregion is highlighted in their consistent inclusion of the word "Charotar" when they name and describe their community and community associations. It is also narrated through histories of local ancestry and village-based marriage circles, and in stories of a longstanding social and economic embeddedness in the Charotar's fertile agricultural economy. Mobility and exchange between geographically dispersed households in the region is shaped by patrilocal joint-family living arrangements, and married women play a key role in smoothing kinship linkages between Vohras in different villages and towns.

A recurrent theme in the narratives of Charotar Sunni Vohras is their similarities to the local Hindus, especially the Patidars. The regional articulations of Vohras are similar to those of the Patidars, but the differences between them are also telling. While both communities arrange their marriages through distinctive village-based marriage circles, the relations they maintain with the designated villages have nevertheless evolved differently: while Patels can claim dominance in "their" villages, for Vohras the link with the village is less self-evident after the expulsion of Muslims from these villages. While continuities exist between past and present, village and town, Hindu and Muslim, they are explicated from a position of rupture.

CHAPTER 2

Rural-Urban Transitions

From the Village to the Segregated Town

During the popular Uttarayan kite festival, the sky is filled with kites and snatches of disco music coming from different directions. On Anand's rooftops, young men frenetically pull ropes while their friends shout encouragement; their wives and sisters patiently stand by to reel in the kite line; and elderly people hang around to enjoy the sights. Every now and then there is a scream—"Cut!"—and then the loud cheering of "Aiaiai!" when a kite is lost in air battle. At dusk, Chinese lanterns go up in the sky. In the kitchens, *undhiyu*, a Gujarati vegetable dish, is prepared.

On the occasion of this kite festival in January 2012, I went from rooftop to rooftop to visit acquaintances in Anand's Muslim area. If beforehand some maulanas had announced that Uttarayan would be an unnecessary or even objectionable celebration (by declaring it "Hindu"), evidently none of the Muslims I visited that day would take this advice seriously. "Who are the first to play kites? Muslims! They already start in November!" a father smiled, looking at the sky. A mother added, "The maulanas don't understand. How can I tell my kids not to play?"

Standing on the rooftop that day, my hosts and I looked at the kites in the sky and then naturally, as time passed, also turned our gaze to the surrounding streets below. The elevated view became an occasion to tell stories of the neighborhood. The same mother, pointing at a neighboring block, said, "You see, that whole housing society used to be Hindu before the riots. After 2002, all the Hindus left very quickly. They sold their houses at very low prices, and all sold to Muslims. Our house also belonged to Hindus." Her own family arrived in Anand in 2004, from a nearby town. "We came to Anand because of education, for the future of our children. The housing society we now live in was a Hindu society before. Most residents were Patel. Now, only one Patel family remains. We don't know exactly what happened, but we know that this housing society was attacked during the riots. Some stones were thrown. To be honest, it is only because of this that we could afford to buy this big house at a relatively cheap price. The residents were in a hurry to get out. They moved to another part of town."[1]

THE STORIES TOLD in the previous chapter about the regional orientations of Vohras contrast with the contemporary reality of rural-urban relocation and post-violence residential segregation. That day, standing on the rooftop, this contrast was manifested in the affirmations of Hindu-Muslim cultural similarity on the one hand, and the stories of Hindu-Muslim segregation on the other. In Anand, these themes appear together.

Some of the residents talk about Anand's residential segregation as a "partition"—in a reference to the historic partition of British India into two states, India and Pakistan, on the grounds of separating Hindus and Muslims. This "partition" is also discussed by Hindus and Christians in Anand, who decided to move out of the spaces into which Muslims relocated after 2002, and by Muslims in nearby villages. I asked them why they moved. Despite the variations in their narratives, they all point in the same direction. The violence has led to a reimagining of spatiality in terms of a Hindu-Muslim divide, which can also be perceived as a rural-urban divide. The moves express and consolidate this division.

Memories of the Violence

Gujarat, March 1, 2002. On the rooftop of a three-story house in the village of Ode, a group of neighbors gathers after being chased out of their own houses minutes before. A mob of an estimated 1,500 men roam the village carrying sticks, knives, and kerosene bottles, setting properties on fire. The village has a population of 18,459 people, of whom 16,707 are Hindus, 1,131 are Muslims, and 466 are Christians,[2] but only the houses of Muslims are targeted by the mob. Slogans fill the air: "Kill the Muslims!" The rooftop where the escaped Muslims have been gathering turns into a trap when the attackers lock the house from the outside and throw burning rags, kerosene, and gasoline into it. Twenty-three people die in the resulting fire, including nine women and nine children.[3] Six escape by jumping off the roof.[4]

On another rooftop in Anand, approximately twenty-five kilometers away from the village of Ode, a twelve-year-old Muslim girl tries to calm herself. She has heard about Ode. In Anand, there is a curfew; schools and shops are closed, and her whole family has gathered at home. In front of their housing society, her father and uncles stand guard with the other men. On the rooftop, the women are preparing buckets of *marchi* water (water boiled with chilies). If mobs will come to their house, the buckets will be thrown at them from the roof.

In 2002, the rooftops of Gujarati houses became watchtowers and places for sociality and security. Some rooftops, however, became death traps. What differentiated a watchtower from a death trap was its location. In Ode, people jumped from the roof to escape the fire. In Anand, the *marchi* water was prepared but never thrown—the expected mobs didn't come. Eventually, the residents of Anand and Ode met at Anand, where the refugees were housed in makeshift camps in the community grounds of residential neighborhoods (spaces normally used for weddings and games of cricket).

In the years after 2002, people came to terms with the knowledge that some places had been safer than others during the violence. Some villages now appeared as potentially dangerous places for their Muslim residents, while parts of Anand seemed relatively safe and desirable places to live. These spatial reimaginations, in terms of a safe/unsafe division, were enacted and consolidated in the years after 2002. With the reasonable expectation that the mobs could return, in the knowledge that neither fences nor locks would withstand fire, and having learned the hard way that the state would not protect them against communal violence, many Muslims asked themselves, "Where will we be safe if the mobs come again?" For many, answering that question involved moving. Some Muslims moved within Anand, shifting from a Hindu-majority area to a part of Anand where Muslims were in a majority; others came to Anand from nearby towns and villages. Hindus and Christians also moved within the town, away from the spaces that were now becoming marked as "Muslim," and into housing societies where the majority of residents were Hindu or Christian.

Residents estimate that between 2002 and 2012, the number of Muslims in Anand town doubled, which is confirmed by the Census of India (25,099 in 2001; 45,932 in 2011). In the Anand district as a whole, there was a striking transformation in the ratios of Hindus and Muslims between 2001 and 2011 (according to the census records; see table A.01). In 2001, the majority of the Muslim population in the district (52 percent) lived in rural areas; by 2011, however, the majority (56 percent) resided in urban areas, while only 44 percent of Muslims remained in rural areas. This change in the rural-urban distribution of the Muslim population within a decade cannot be explained by general urbanization patterns alone. (By comparison, the percentage of Hindus living in rural areas of the district during the same decade decreased by 2 percent). The change can be attributed to the fact that many local Muslims living in nearby villages moved to Muslim-majority areas in Anand town in the intervening years.

Through countless relocations, often only over a few kilometers, Hindu-rural and Muslim-urban spaces had been demarcated.

Anand's northeastern outskirts, where many Muslims settled, expanded in these years; new housing societies, schools, roads—and, increasingly, also shopping centers, restaurants, and a cinema—were built. Land prices rose, and a flurry of real-estate developers arrived to build new housing societies on formerly agricultural land. The number of mosques in the town doubled. Before 2002, there were twenty-five mosques; in 2012, there were fifty-one. The extended stretch of new housing societies and mosques that emerged from this is referred to by Muslims as *amara vistar* (our area). A Muslim shopkeeper jokingly referred to it as New Anand.

The residents attribute the spectacular expansion of the built environment since 2002 primarily to the arrival of Muslims from nearby villages. This was confirmed in a survey of respondents' prior locations of residence and dates of arrival (part of Survey A, in a housing society of fifty households). The majority (twenty-nine) of these households had moved to Anand in the previous ten years. Ten had resided in Anand between eleven and twenty years, and eleven for more than twenty years. Respondents provided the name of the hometown (*vatan*) of the male head of household and also the hometown (*pir*) of his wife, revealing that the vast majority of towns and villages in which husbands and wives had lived prior to coming to Anand were located within Anand or Kheda district.

Anand has been a key site of arrival for Muslims in central Gujarat for two reasons: first, to seek safety in the aftermath of the 2002 violence; and second, to achieve upward mobility through urban livelihoods and lifestyles. The first process has been prominently discussed in existing scholarship in Gujarat. My data confirm the existing analysis of segregation in the aftermath of violence and show that residential segregation occurs not in only cities, but in rural settings as well.

Pogroms

Countless books and reports describe how anti-Muslim violence spread across the state of Gujarat between February and May 2002, with occasional killings taking place until December of that year. The violence resulted in the estimated death of 2,000 people, most of whom were Muslims.[5] An estimated 20,000 Muslim homes and businesses were destroyed through targeted burning and looting, and an estimated 360 places of worship were demolished. At least 150 to 200 Muslim women were raped, gang-raped, or mutilated, and many of them were burnt afterward in order to obliterate the evidence (Kumar 2016). The violence displaced more than 200,000 people.[6] A distinct feature of the violence—as compared with earlier instances of violence in the state in 1969 and 1985, which had been mostly restricted to the city of Ahmedabad—was that it had been widespread in rural parts of the state, affecting a total of 151 towns and 993 villages.[7] The Ode massacre was one of nineteen violent events that were recorded in the rural district of Anand (table A.06).

Anti-Muslim violence has a distinct history in India. In 1947, when colonial British India was granted independence, and the subcontinent was partitioned into India and Pakistan, large-scale violence against religious minorities broke out in both countries—against Hindus in the new territory of Pakistan, and against Muslims in the newly independent India—with an estimated death toll of between two hundred thousand and two million. After independence, communal violence recurrently surfaced, with a major episode in Ahmedabad in Gujarat in 1969, and rising violence on the basis of religious identity after the 1980s (Wilkinson 2008). In the context of Gujarat's 2002 violence, scholars use the term "pogroms" to highlight the organized and one-sided nature of the violence targeting Muslims. The reports of journalists, nongovernmental organization (NGO) workers, and scholarly researchers who have interviewed perpetrators, victims, and eyewitnesses[8] demonstrate that the violence was well organized, and that those responsible for law and order instructed the police not to intervene. The police stood by, or sometimes even provided assistance, when well-armed mobs attacked (Human Rights Watch 2002).[9]

The violence was organized and legitimized by organizations directly or indirectly affiliated with the Sangh Parivar, a group of organizations that includes the BJP (the political party that was in power during the 2002 violence), the VHP, the RSS, and Bajrang Dal. The Sangh Parivar organizations promote the Hindutva ideology—Hindutva is translated by some as "Hindu fascism," and by others, more euphemistically, as "Hindu nationalism."[10] According to Hindutva ideology, there is one, unified version of Hinduism, which is linked to specific understandings of nation (India as "Hindu nation"), race ("Hindu blood" as superior to others), land ("Bharat Mata," the embodiment of "Mother India" as a Hindu goddess) and culture (promoting cultural practices associated with the upper castes). The ideology was developed in the 1920s by Vinayak Damodar Savarkar and has been propagated through Sangh Parivar organizations through campaigns, speeches, and pamphlets (Bhatt 2001).

Whether the attackers of 2002 actually believed in the Hindutva ideology is debatable. No doubt some did, but scholars of Gujarat have also explored other explanations. In particular, the growing economic insecurities resulting from Gujarat's (neo)liberal economic policies made people greatly dependent on political organizations, such as those associated with the Sangh Parivar, for access to state services and other forms of security (Berenschot 2011). As these organizations had the capacity to help citizens gain access to state services such as health care and education, they could ask for something in return, including the citizen's participation in violence to divide the electorate along religious lines. The 2002 violence occurred in the run-up to the Gujarat state election and targeted only those voting localities or wards where the BJP party faced the greatest electoral competition. The BJP won the state elections with an absolute majority, and its vote share increased the most in the districts where the violence was worst (Dhattiwala and Biggs 2012, 504).

THESE DESCRIPTIONS AND EXPLANATIONS are by now well established in the corpus of academic literature; however, they are not accepted by the politicians under whose watch the violence unfolded. Although police officers, prosecutors, and leaders of violent groups have unapologetically admitted to their complicity, some even to the point of boasting about it, the political rationale for the violence has not been formally admitted. In public statements, leading BJP politicians have denied that the violence occurred, framed it as trivial, or justified it as a natural and inevitable expression of innate and inherently antagonistic cultural identities.[11] They describe the events of 2002 as two opposing religious communities clashing, rather than as an organized attack on a minority. They continue to prefer the term "riots" to "anti-Muslim pogroms" to describe the violence, and have invested a great deal of effort in writing histories to legitimize their version of the events. According to the "riot" narrative, the attacks on Muslims were a "reaction" to an "action"—as suggested, for example, in an interview with Zee TV by the then chief minister of Gujarat, Narendra Modi.[12] The "action" was setting a train on fire at Godhra Station on February 27, in which fifty-nine Hindus died.[13]

In the years following 2002, NGOs, lawyers, victims, and eyewitnesses have worked to bring cases of violence to court. Convictions and charges have been rare, however, because investigators and prosecutors have stalled or obstructed legal processes through acts of nonrecording, intimidation, and bribery, and even by destroying evidence. Some investigators have justified these strategies by suggesting that it is natural for them to protect the state government by preventing convictions. By 2008, when only a handful of attackers had been prosecuted, the judges of the Supreme Court warned that "the [state] court was acting merely as an onlooker and there is no fair trial at all," so that "justice becomes the victim."[14] To reduce the influence of Gujarati state institutions[15] it installed a new legal body, the Special Investigation Team (SIT), to rule on eight cases.

The massacre in the village of Ode was one of the cases brought to court through the SIT. On April 9, 2012, ten years after the attack, a verdict was reached in the Anand District Court. Of the forty-six people accused, twenty-three were found guilty,[16] and of these, eighteen were sentenced to life imprisonment, and five were sentenced to seven years in prison. In 2018, the High Court of Gujarat acquitted three of those sentenced to life imprisonment; a fourth convict died in prison during the pendency of the appeal. Considering that, according to testimonies, the mob consisted of an estimated one thousand to two thousand attackers, the eventual conviction of nineteen attackers can hardly be regarded as the delivery of justice. Moreover, those convicted were only those who were identified by eyewitnesses as perpetrators;[17] they were not the masterminds in the background who planned the events, sent in the mobs, or organized the weapons and logistics.

In the meantime, Narendra Modi, who had been chief minister of Gujarat in 2002 and thus was politically responsible for law and order at the time, moved to the national stage and became the prime minister of India in 2014.[18] His election campaign focused on development and he promised to implement Gujarat's neoliberal model of development on a national scale. This economic agenda won broad popular support, and the political party he represented (the BJP) won enough seats to form a single-party government. In the years after 2014, the BJP carried out its development agenda. It also appointed members of boards and committees that revise history books and restructure educational curricula so that they were aligned with its majoritarian Hindu nationalist agenda, and designed new policies of direct and indirect censorship to curb opposition. Soon, the promise of development became overshadowed by news reports on mob lynchings around the country, mostly directed at Muslims and Dalits involved in the meat trade and conducted in the name of Hindu vegetarianism and the protection of cows.

Many Indians were shocked by the targeted attacks on Muslims and Dalits in these years, and citizens groups in cities such as Mumbai and Bangalore expressed their concern through #NotInMyName protests. Politicians, however, attributed them to "spontaneous emotional outbursts," and the individual perpetrators and the groups directly or indirectly associated with them (such as holy cow protection committees) have rarely been convicted or prosecuted, signaling that the ruling government tacitly approved of the attacks.[19] In 2019, Modi's BJP government was re-elected with an absolute majority. If debates about Indian democracy have long centered on the emergence of "Hindu nationalist" ideologies,[20] since 2014 a growing number of commentators have preferred the term "fascism" (Banaji 2013) to explain developments in the country—although some of those who have dared to do this have been arrested.

These developments and discussions form an important context for the developments in Anand in the years after 2002. Considering the wealth of eyewitness accounts that are available in the research reports, newspaper articles, and legal proceedings quoted above, I have not focused this study specifically on individuals who witnessed or survived violence in 2002. I conducted the research several years afterward (between 2010 and 2017), and I did not think it was necessary to seek out traumatized individuals and ask them to relive their experiences (similar to Kumar 2016). The research focused on a town where very little violence happened in 2002, and included many people who never saw this violence. Yet even they considered 2002 a watershed moment.

The Mobs That Didn't Come

In 2002, most of Anand's Muslims waited for a mob that never came. As a result, their memories of the period were mostly uneventful yet anxious, narrated to me in terms like this: "All the people in our neighborhood locked their houses from the inside and went to the rooftop. All the women in my family were on the terrace." Or: "Everybody did not sleep. They were waiting in their houses. If something would happen, they were ready to fight." And: "We were in our houses, awake all night. Sometimes we [the women of different families] would gather in one house together." And even: "We had fun, that time," smiling at the surprise on my face, sketching a lively scene of women chatting, men staying nearby the house, and children playing till late at night.

Some mobs did come to Anand. They attacked Muslims in the Hindu-majority parts of the town, in the Vallabh Vidyanagar campus area, where a Muslim student hostel was ransacked, and on some of the main roads and markets, where Muslim-owned shops and garages were looted. One stabbing on March 27 in Anand was recorded (in *The Times of India;* table A.05)—insofar as residents recognized this incident when I asked about it, they thought the person stabbed was probably a Hindu.

My research did not investigate why Anand remained relatively safe in comparison with other places in the vicinity. In this, it is different from the majority of studies on communal violence in Gujarat, which have focused on explaining its causes.[21] Yet, to understand how Muslims of the region responded to the violence in the way they did—by relocating to Anand—I did ask them how they themselves explained Anand's relative safety. The most common answer linked numerical strength to physical strength. One man explained, "Anand is safe because so many Muslims are in Anand. We are one group, a big group. The railway station and bus stop are ours. If there are any difficulties, we are safe here." A woman added, "We are strong here. Hindus know that Muslims will fight back if they are attacked." A young woman said, "We are safe here. Because on that side [pointing left] there are the butchers. On the other side [pointing right] there is Ismail Nagar. So nothing can harm us." When I asked why the presence of a butcher street made the area safe, she clarified: "They have knives. People don't dare to pass."

The reference to Ismail Nagar was not clarified in this conversation because the narrator assumed it was evident. Indeed, the story goes that Ismail Nagar is a dangerous place where people have sticks, possibly knives, and are ready to pick a fight if so required. A young man residing in the adjacent housing society of Nutan Nagar explained how, in 2002, he saw Muslim men of Ismail Nagar patrol the area. They were angry, because "Hindu people were beating Muslim people at the village." When the police arrived on this scene, the residents prevented them from entering Ismail Nagar by throwing stones. When the police used tear gas to disperse them, the residents retaliated by attacking the police van. The police, so the story goes, withdrew. According to this local narrator, the resistance put up by the residents made Ismail Nagar notorious even among the "people in Delhi," referring to the government. Its notorious character was confirmed in some of my encounters with local Hindus, who did not know the exact whereabouts of the Ismail Nagar housing society and had never seen it, yet were horror-struck with the idea that I would visit it: "Even the police don't dare to enter Ismail Nagar!" For Muslims, on the other hand, it is precisely because outsiders fear entering it that it has become a possible source of protection in the absence of state protection against violence.

These local explanations why Anand was safe, as put forward by the residents, align with a hypothesis suggested by Laurent Gayer and Christophe Jaffrelot (2012), that there was "safety in numbers," and by Raheel Dhattiwala (2019), that the mobs of 2002 avoided areas where they would be at risk of being outnumbered in the case of a possible counterattack. Some residents also spoke of the alliances between Muslims and Hindus that had existed in the town (for example, between Vohra and Sindhi traders in the marketplace)—an explanation along the lines proposed by Ashutosh Varshney (2002), that cross-community civic relations were a peacekeeping mechanism. These assertions that there were good relations do not contest the notion that Muslims were protected by their numerical dominance in certain parts of Anand.

Muslims in Anand live with the knowledge that there were remarkable differences in the spatial patterning of the violence against them, and they explain these differences in terms of their numerical strength in certain localities. The logical consequence of this has been relocation: relocation from Hindu-majority into Muslim-majority areas of the town, and from Hindu-majority villages into the parts of Anand where Muslims are in a majority.

The Arrival of the Refugees

In 2002, hundreds of refugees arrived in Anand, swelling into the thousands. The refugees were Muslims from forty-six villages[22] in the surrounding region. Some found shelter on the rooftops of relatives' homes, others were accommodated in mosques, community halls, and the three refugee camps that were set up on the community grounds around the housing societies of Nutan Nagar and Ismail Nagar.

When the state government announced the closure of refugee camps in Gujarat in July and October 2002 (Human Rights Watch 2003), Muslim leaders in Anand started rehabilitation plans that aimed to rebuild and repair the damaged houses in the refugees' villages of origin.[23] Besides material support in the form of housing and to (re)start businesses, they tried to mediate between refugees and village leaders to help guarantee them a safe return and to help Muslims reclaim the village as a shared space. Despite these efforts, however, many refugees stayed on in the now-closed camps (see also Habitat International Coalition 2014).

To accommodate the refugees who remained, eight relief societies were built in Anand.[24] They contained 205 houses for approximately one thousand people.[25] One of these housing colonies was named Mogri-Sisva—as a way of remembering the stories of the refugees from the villages of Mogri and Sisva, who were not able to return in safety. In the village of Mogri, just south of Anand's Vallabh Vidyanagar, signs had appeared in 2002 announcing that Mogri was a "Hindu village" in a "Hindu *rashtra*" (country).[26]

The relocation of Muslims into Anand was not over when the refugees had been settled. In the decade after 2002, people kept arriving. The assumption that drove much of these rural-urban relocations was the idea that the urban neighborhood, and the people who inhabit it, were a protection against violence. People who faced financial loss after (part of) their properties in the villages were destroyed waited until they gathered enough financial resources to invest in a house in Anand. Some villagers moved to Anand by living with relatives for a few years, then finding their own houses in the town. In the initial years, people were able to buy houses at discount prices because Hindus, in their hurry to move out of the areas where Muslims arrived, sold their houses below the market value. As time moved on, land and housing prices rose. As a result, many people took loans, some sold their properties in their home villages, and others pooled their income to buy or rent a house in Anand. The violence, however, does not fully explain the overall long-term trend of Muslim settlement in Anand; there were additional reasons for these moves.

Urbanization

Some newly arriving families were not directly affected by the pogroms, but were interested in moving to town for other reasons—for example, because they were tempted to invest in the newly developing housing societies, with their spacious, freestanding two- or three-story houses (figure 2.01) in the vicinity of desirable facilities. To explain these arrivals, it is necessary to also take into account the broader history of urban development in Anand, its distinctive role as a regional center for education and the urban professions, and the economic opportunities for Muslims in the town. Consider the following statements collected from a 2012 interview with three elderly Muslim men, all long-term residents of Anand town. The question I had posed was: "Why did Muslims come to Anand?"

> The main reason why people came to Anand is that they suffered lots in riots. That's why the people can't live in villages; so they transferred here to Anand.
>
> They came [here] because they can easily go to work, easily travel, and easily get religious education.
>
> Education. That's what Anand was selected for. Education and business purpose, no other. And for our religion. How are you going to get religious education in the village?

The pursuit of better employment, business, and education opportunities are additional reasons for the relocations of Muslims, beyond the safety concerns that followed the 2002 violence. These rural-urban relocations are also associated with the adoption of suburban lifestyles, enhanced mobility, and religious education of an incipient middle class of Muslims.

Anand has long been a market town and a regional hub for manufacturing and secondary education. It has recently become an administrative center to

FIGURE 2.1. Sprawling outskirts of Anand, with newly constructed houses, plots waiting for development, and mostly unpaved roads. (Photo by the author, 2012.)

which residents of the wider Anand district travel to visit offices and attend court. Its growth has been gradual but significant. In the 1950s, Anand was still the size of a village, with a population of 25,767 residents (Thakar 1954). By 1962, the town had grown to an estimated 40,000 residents. Thereafter, according to census data, the population kept growing gradually, to 83,936 in 1981 and to 198,282 in 2011. As the town grew, it turned into a sprawling urban conglomerate that now includes several adjoining villages and various newly developed residential and commercial areas. This "Urban Agglomerate Anand," as it is referred to in the census, had a population of 288,095 in 2011. (For an overview of the town's growth since 1991, see table A.06).

By the 1950s, some Muslim families were living in Anand (Thakar 1954). Some lived in the old town among Brahmins, Patidars, Ksatryas, Rabari, and artisans; others lived in a small area called Azad Chowk; and in western Anand, there was a mosque. From the 1960s, more Muslims began to settle in the town. Two housing societies were established specifically for Muslims in the 1960s: Nutan Nagar and Ismail Nagar. These housing societies were established by local Muslim entrepreneurs (Nutan Nagar between 1959 and 1963;[27] Ismail Nagar after 1969) near a large madrassa that had been established in the 1920s, on the northeastern outskirts of Anand, between Anand town and the adjacent village of Gamdi. In the period between 1991 and 2001, the percentage of Muslims in the town's population rose from 13 to 16 percent (Census of India 1991, 2001). After 2002, the area surrounding Nutan Nagar and Ismail Nagar developed further and is a still-growing Muslim area.

Besides the violence, five additional factors contributed to the relocation of Muslims and Anand's urban growth: commerce, industrialization, education, the arrival of government offices, and transportation infrastructure. First, towns like Anand, Nadiad, and Borsad are typical examples of market towns where traders sell produce from local markets and villagers do their shopping. Anand has many shopping centers, and Muslims are quite visible across the town in their roles as shopkeepers, businessmen, tailors, and mechanics. In a survey in Anand's commercial center near the railway station (referred to by townspeople as "Supermarket"), it was established that sixty-five of a sample of a hundred shopkeepers on the ground floor were Muslim (most of them Vohra; the Hindu shopkeepers were Sindhi and Punjabi; see table A.07). Muslims are also prominent in the blossoming textile trade in the town. They are particularly busy in December, when many overseas Indians visit the region to stock up on dresses and kurtas.

Second, Anand saw the arrival of industries with the establishment of the Amul Dairy Co-Operative in 1946, the large-scale industrial enterprise Elecon in 1960, and the Vitthal Udyognagar Industrial Estate in 1965. These and other industries have been established mostly by entrepreneurs from Hindu castes, but they have also attracted Muslims to Anand for employment as mechanics, welders, electricians, and managers, and a few are factory owners themselves. Beside offering employment, these industries also attract related services such as financial services, shops and workshops, and transport companies.

Third, an important reason why Anand gained prominence in the region, and certainly also for Muslims, is its role as a regional center for education. The township of Vallabh Vidyanagar, connected to Anand by the Anand-Vidyanagar Road, is an education town. It started with the establishment of Sardar Patel University in 1955 (Merchant 1999). The oft-narrated history of this university highlights the role of the farmers of Karamsad village, who donated the land on which the university campus was built, and memorializes engineer Bhaikaka as the mastermind behind the planning of the campus. Following the establishment of this university, thousands of rural youth started commuting to Vallabh Vidyanagar by local bus or sought residence in its multiple student hostels. Since 2000, following the privatization of education, Gujarat has seen a rapid increase in the number of private educational institutions across the state (Iyengar 2012), and the public Sardar Patel University is now complemented by schools and colleges managed by commercial enterprises or community-based associations. As of 2014, more than 125 secondary and high schools were located in Anand-Vidyanagar and its surrounding villages, and Sardar Patel University alone had more than 25,000 students spread over twenty-six departments and eighty-seven affiliated colleges.[28] The educational institutes of Vallabh Vidyanagar were a big pull for Muslims who wished to send their children for higher education. Some Muslims also work as teachers in educational institutions.

Fourth, the town's growth has been shaped by a 1997 administrative reshuffling, when Kheda was divided into two separate districts—Anand and Kheda districts—and Anand town became the capital of the newly established Anand district. Government offices arrived, as well as a host of private businesses catering to the expanding public sector. For educated rural youth, the prospect of obtaining jobs in this public sector has great appeal. In the early 1990s, when the Gujarat state economy underwent a process of liberalization, privatization, and deregulation (Hirway 2012a, 2012b), secure employment became rare in the region overall.

Finally, Muslims in Anand have an occupational niche in the transportation sector, as evidenced by the trucks, taxis, and rickshaws that are parked in front of their houses. Anand's position as a central transportation hub in the region has a long history, starting with the colonial government's decision to create a train station in Anand. In the 1990s and 2000s, the Gujarat state invested in infrastructure development, which brought a new city-to-city expressway connecting Anand to Vadodara and Ahmedabad, a national highway linking Anand to Mumbai and Delhi, and a rural road network linking the town to the villages. Buses provide public transportation along these roads. What is more, a fine-grained network of shared auto-rickshaws provides affordable connections within the town and to the surrounding villages, plying back and forth along the same route with four or five passengers at a time, and are a very common mode of local transportation here. Muslims operate in this blossoming transportation sector as auto drivers, taxi drivers, truck drivers, mechanics, garage owners, and driving teachers, and by building and trading vehicles.

In comparison with descriptions of Vohras in the smaller town of Sultanpur (Heitmeyer 2009a, 2009b), my findings point toward a shift in occupational orientation, in which the rural-urban transition was paired with a new emphasis on education and white-collar employment. In Sultanpur, Vohras have regarded themselves as a trading community, strongly oriented toward commerce and self-employment and placing less emphasis on formal education. While business is also important in Anand, the interest in formal education is high, and some families derive their income and status from employment in government offices. In the housing society in which I lived, six of twenty-two heads of household indicated that they were employed as professionals in white-collar work (as a bank employee, tax officer, clerk, advocate, teacher, and professor at a government-funded school). There were also six businessmen, two engineers, two drivers, a mechanic, an electrician, and a farmer (table A.08). Many young people aspired to "service," indicating salaried and secure (i.e., white-collar) employment in offices, and their parents encouraged them to study so that they could pursue these aspirations.

The Makeriya marriage circle in the Vohra community, for example, places much emphasis on this trajectory of education. In Anand, the Makeriya members are described as families without traditional capital, who have made economic progress through education and government employment in the town. In conversations about them, some of my neighbors pointed toward a competition between the families of the Makeriya and Arsad marriage circles on the one hand, and the traditionally more privileged Chaud marriage circle on the other. The less-privileged sections of the Vohra community have been surpassing Chaud families in status and wealth, which could be an impetus for Chaud families to follow their example and start investing in education, too. Business-oriented Chaud families in Anand may hold onto family-owned land and property in their villages of origin, but they also use facilities in town to access education and new kinds of urban occupations, and potentially, international migration.

Leaving the Village

The trend of leaving the village is not limited to Muslims. Throughout rural India, scholars have observed a process of cultural alienation from the village as a result of the rural economy's relative stagnation (D. Gupta 2009). Available statistics point to a dramatic disparity in earnings between urban and rural households (Pradhan et al. 2000), showing that urban earnings are on average twice as high as rural earnings. Besides declining incomes from farming, there are stark disparities between rural and urban India in terms of basic public facilities such as drinking water, health care services, and education. Even the land-owning elites of the villages, who are able to protect their vested interests through their political leverage, are turning toward non-farm enterprises and see their futures outside the village, in urban or international spaces (D. Gupta 2009, chap. 7).

Nationwide trends of agricultural decline also occur in central Gujarat, as described from the perspective of Patidars. In the 1950s, the Patidars were an agriculture-oriented community. Land, farming, and agricultural knowledge were important sources of capital, even if some had already migrated to East Africa at that time (Pocock 1972). In the years that followed, when state investment in agriculture and industrialization was still generous, Patidar farmers developed into an entrepreneurial landowning group by diversifying their economic practices: for example, by starting factories and other ventures alongside their agricultural activities (Rutten 1995). By 2013, however, farming was considered an undesirable occupation; Patidar farmers experienced decline and failure as a result of falling profits; the focus had shifted to education, off-farm occupations, and white-collar work (Tilche and Simpson 2017, 700; Tilche and Simpson 2018).

Elsewhere in India, too, the decline of the rural economy is associated with a rural-urban reorientation. Groups of Dalits and Muslims have followed the pathways of urbanization and education as a strategy to escape marginalization in the village and gain respect, even if this does little to change the overall power balance, as powerful landed elites invest in urbanization at the same time to reproduce their privileged status (Jeffrey, Jeffery, and Jeffery 2004). Considering these dynamics, we can reconsider the relocation of Muslims to Anand as a process of urbanization, which accelerated dramatically as a result of the 2002 violence.

These urbanization strategies are tied to certain hierarchies, as not everyone has the required economic and social capital to obtain this desired urban footing. As the economists Amitabh Kundu and Lopamudra Ray Saraswati argue, it is as if rural-urban migration in India "has an inbuilt screening system, which is picking up people from relatively higher economic and social strata"—this is because India's urban centers welcome private capital but have become "less accommodating to the poor, restricting their entry" (2012, 219). Considering the growing rural-urban disparities and the unequal opportunities for mobility in India described by economists, sociologists, and anthropologists, we can start to appreciate the descriptions of Anand by its residents as a lucky place, a place of privilege—an understanding that derives meaning from comparisons with relatives in villages with less "mobility capital" (Alexander, Chatterji, and Jalais 2016, introduction). These are important contexts in which to understand the narratives of rural-urban mobility in Anand.

Reports of the post-violence developments in Gujarat have used the word "displacement" to emphasize the coerced nature of the movements of Muslims. This term is defined in the United Nations category of internally displaced persons as "persons . . . who have been *forced or obliged* to flee or to leave their homes or places of habitual residence, in particular as a result of or in order to avoid the effects of armed conflict, situations of generalized violence . . ." (United Nations 1998, Principles 3 (25), 2; cited in Lokhande 2015, 15; emphasis mine). With this choice of the word "displacement," scholars and NGOs contest the claims made by the Government of Gujarat, namely, that the individuals staying in relief colonies after the violence of February 2002 had moved there out of their own volition, and out of personal choice—in other words, that their relocation was just another "migration" (Lokhande 2015, 14–16, 90).[29] In these enduring struggles about truth and justice in Gujarat, both the words "displacement" and "migration" have acquired a political meaning.

In Anand, however, the conceptual distinction between forced and voluntary movement is not easy to make. The themes of political marginalization and economic opportunity are both important aspects in the relocation narratives of the residents. Feelings of both being expelled and being privileged surface, sometimes simultaneously. While the existence of the initial refugee camps was directly prompted by the pogroms and can be straightforwardly categorized as displacement, motivations become harder to distinguish in the fifteen years thereafter, when Muslims continued to move to Anand. Concerns over safety and marginalization continue to be discussed throughout these years, but merge with other concerns. These findings provide support for an argument made by Claire Alexander, Joya Chatterji, and Annu Jalais that the conceptual distinction between forced and economic migration in the literature is problematic—the first term erases agency, while the second risks erasing the coercive nature of social structures (2016, chap. 1). To recognize the variety of considerations that drove the moves of Muslims to Anand after 2002, the term "relocation" is used in this book—a term that includes but is not limited to displacement.

If the distinction between involuntary and voluntary is hard to make (see also Kirmani 2013, 61–63), the underlying question of what constitutes choice of residence (Jamil 2019, 301) remains when people are confronted with such dramatic residential segregation. The residential patterns in Anand clearly point to a limitation in peoples' residential choices, and to an imposition of new normative frameworks of what constitutes a "good" and a "bad" place in which to live. These new norms are felt not only by Muslims in Anand but also by Hindus and Christians, and by Muslims who continue to live in Hindu-majority villages.

Urban Segregation

The rural-urban relocation of Muslims to Anand was paired with residential segregation within the town. The perspectives of Christians and Hindus who inhabited the spaces where Muslims settled illuminate how they saw their neighborhood change after 2002. Their narratives highlight considerations of class status and comfort. The issue of safety is not absent from their accounts, but they discuss the problems of residence among Muslims mostly in terms of Muslims' social unacceptability, and in terms of the residential area's lack of "development" due to limited access to state services in these parts of the town.

Gamdi was formerly a village and has now become one of the eastern suburbs of Anand. In the late nineteenth century, Gamdi was a hub of missionary activity by Jesuit Catholics and other competing churches, all of which started convents, schools, and housing compounds in and around Gamdi.[30] The Christian influence is evident in Gamdi through establishments such as St. Xavier's High School, Vimal Miriam High School, and the Jesuit-run Anand Press office. Many Christian teachers and clerks work in the schools and offices of Anand and Vidyanagar.[31]

Mr. Parmar is a teacher, a Catholic, and a long-term resident of Gamdi. His family converted to Christianity from the Hindu community of Vankars, a name that nobody likes to use any more because of its lower-caste status. Vankars, Parmar and others explain, moved from the villages to Anand to escape caste oppression in the villages. The Jesuit church in Gamdi offered Vankars a way out of (caste) oppression via education and urbanization. By moving away from their villages, resettling in housing colonies in Gamdi, and sending their children to Christian schools, many found employment as teachers.

Mr. Parmar traces his roots to the small town of Petlad but grew up in Gamdi. He married and had a daughter. In 2001, when his older brother sold his portion of the family property in Gamdi to him, he decided to improve and expand his house, and air-condition it for his young family, investing an estimated ₹ 16,00,000 in the property (more than US$34,000).[32] Afterward, he saw how the neighborhood changed. Many Christians moved out of Gamdi after 2002. Muslims moved in.

Mr. Parmar shared his views about what happened in 2002: Muslims were forced to move to Anand because "the RSS was slaughtering them in the villages." He said, "These people [Muslims] . . . I feel for them, they have suffered a lot. I pray for them." In the rose garden behind the house in Gamdi, in 2011, he and his elderly mother further commented on the arrival of Muslims. They spoke about the "noise pollution" of the new mosques in Gamdi, which called for prayer five times a day. They were surprised by the remarkably large size of some of the new Muslim houses in the vicinity, because they had previously assumed that Muslims were "poor" and "illiterate." When I asked if they feel safe in Gujarat, considering what happened to the Muslims in 2002, Mr. Parmar said he expected no violence against Christians: "RSS people will kill the Muslims first, and then, Christians will perish by themselves. They hate us equally but we are so small in numbers, they don't bother about us."

Rather than the neighbors, however, his primary concern about Gamdi was the way the neighborhood was classified and treated by the municipality—as a minority area. On one of our encounters, in 2011, he took me on his motorbike from Vidyanagar to Gamdi, pointing out the differences in the neighborhoods along the way. "You see," he shouted when we crossed the overpass and took a sharp turn to enter a small road through Nutan Nagar to Gamdi, "the roads are very bad here. Nobody is maintaining . . . Actually, the municipality should do that. But the municipality is only maintaining the roads in places where Hindus live."

When a Muslim man came to their house in Gamdi expressing an interest in buying it, Parmar was tempted to sell it. Other Christians in the neighborhood were moving to the new Christian townships that were constructed outside Anand, or moving abroad, and some had managed to sell their houses to Muslims at good prices. But Parmar's housing society does not allow sales to non-Christians. What he did instead was to arrange a professional caregiver for his elderly mother, who remained in Gamdi, attending to the large house and rose garden, while he, his wife, and daughter moved to a small flat in Vidyanagar, a Hindu-majority locality (where 95 percent of the population was Hindu in 2001, and 96 percent in 2011; see tables A.03 and A.04). This move was fueled by practical reasons: his daughter went to school and his wife worked as a teacher in Vidyanagar, a commute of eight kilometers from Gamdi, while Mr. Parmar's own job was equidistant from both locations.

After his daughter moved to Ahmedabad for further studies, Mr. Parmar moved back to the big house in Gamdi to reunite with his mother. On the phone in 2021, he commented that many homes in his housing society were now vacant and unlit because many Christian residents had left, some now living abroad. He softened his earlier comments about noise pollution ("noise is everywhere in India, whether you live next to a temple or a mosque") but reiterated his complaints about infrastructural problems: "In Vidyanagar, town planning is good. But in Gamdi, roads are narrow, garbage is not taken care of properly, electricity can suddenly go away, and if we complain [to the municipality] they don't listen, or they listen but don't do anything." Nevertheless, he was planning to stay in Gamdi at least until his retirement.

Hindus, too, left the area after 2002—some very quickly, some a few years later. Vinod Bhatt,[33] who was a boy at the time of the pogroms, was one of the Hindus who lived near the 100 Feet Road in a compound that was a diverse neighborhood at the time. His family lived in the staff quarters of the district's government hospital along the railway line. During the curfew weeks of 2002, they moved to different houses within Anand. Initially, they remained in their own house; fifteen days later, they moved to a nearby housing society of Hindus from Sindh on the "Hindu" side of the 100 Feet Road; fourteen days later, they moved again, seeking shelter in the house of an uncle on the western outskirts of Anand. When the situation became calm, at the end of March, they returned to their house in the staff quarters.

They had intended to stay there. Vinod regrets eventually moving out, and thinks that his parents did so only because of social pressure from relatives. It was not before 2014 that his family finally decided to give in to this pressure and gave up their house in the hospital staff quarters, where they had lived without costs. They took a substantial loan to build a house near Anand's Ganesh Chokdi. Drawing a map of the staff quarters while he talked, Vinod reflected on this decision as follows:

> There was no discomfort . . . in my family, my nuclear family, we did not have much problem . . . many times in our new home also, I used to miss. . . . Here I had ground. Here I had trees. I was used to seeing the snakes . . . or every time . . . there were huge trees there, mango trees and all. I remember my cousins also used to come there and we used to go out and have mangos from the trees and all. . . . So I used to love staying there. . . . Even my mother liked staying in the quarters. . . . Eight, nine years I had already spent in that area. . . . Before riots we could never think that something like this could have happened.

Vinod never went back to his former neighborhood, not even for a visit. If some Hindus do still live in Muslim-majority areas, he thinks these are less-affluent people, who have no choice:

> The Hindus that stay in this community, they are not much affluent, I think. They are doing small things like ironing clothes, selling things, financial constraints are also there. I don't think any rich Hindu families stay in this area.

Like Mr. Parmar, Vinod also highlighted the lack of development in the parts of the town where Muslims live. Before 2002, Anand's municipality was dominated by the Congress party; after 2002, the BJP won the municipal elections in the town. The BJP didn't win in the electoral locations where Muslim live, however, and so their neighborhoods lack powerful representatives and receive little attention from the municipality:

> I think the BJP has much to cover. They are not concerned about this Muslim area. They will hardly go and campaign in this area. They focus on the area where they can win.... [This is why] ... if you compare this Muslim area with the other areas of Anand, you will see a drastic difference in development, infrastructure, and everything.

The stories of the Christians and Hindus who lived in the parts of Anand that have now become Muslim-majority neighborhoods illustrate how the post-violence segregation of Anand town constitutes a shared memory for Anand's residents. Anand has been, and remains, a Hindu-majority town with a sizeable Muslim and Christian population (table A.04). In the neighborhoods into which Muslims moved after 2002, both Hindu and Christian residents moved out. Their moves often entailed traversing only a few kilometers, but expressed a radical transformation of the town's social geography. Neighborhoods with diverse caste, class, and religious groupings were redefined as either Hindu or Muslim. Christians felt caught in the middle and some sought newer grounds of their own. In 2017, residents pointed out that the 100 Feet Road was no longer the "border," as it had been in 2002, as Hindus and Jains who lived close to it on the "Hindu" side had started to sell their houses to Muslims.

The Last Muslims in the Village?

In west London, on a quiet morning in March 2015, Salma Vohra beckons me to sit down on the couch with her. She opens a photo album with pictures of a wedding that has recently taken place in Gujarat. As we go through the book, she names all the people in the pictures—photographs taken in the village where she grew up, and which she left after her marriage in the late 1990s, when she moved to London. Suddenly, she starts crying, seeing a picture of her father. He has died recently, and his image has been edited into a photo in the album. Her sadness, however, goes beyond that felt for the death of a parent—something else is going on. Salma is also concerned about the safety of her living relatives. Of the sixty Muslim families in her village, she explains, thirty have moved to

Anand. Her own family is among the thirty families who stayed in the village. She exclaims, "They don't want to move out. We keep telling them to get away, but they won't. They say they are happy in the village. Many [Muslim] families in the village have already moved to Anand, the rest is planning on moving out too, soon they will be the only ones left!"

Anthropologists hear a lot of stories in the field, but sometimes a story lingers on, repeating itself in the mind. This was one of them. "They are happy in the village," Salma had said about her relatives. The story seemed to offer a counter-perspective—a Muslim family that stayed put in the village when others had left, even against the advice of relatives in London.

In 2017, while planning a trip to India, I asked Salma if I could visit her family in Gujarat. Our conversations on this question—which occurred over Facebook Messenger and were mediated by her husband, Ibrahim—are themselves revealing of the anxieties involved. I explained that my writing would be anonymous, and that in my book a pseudonym would be used for both the family and the village. Ibrahim replied that "the locals would know exactly who said what given the numbers involved," but still said, "in any case, let's see what they say. I will put you in touch . . . if it is likely." The second time we talked, I was told that the family had agreed. Ibrahim then specified certain conditions for my visit: that it needed to be discreet and "preferably without any involvement of local Patel [Hindu]" families. If their story was to leak to the local Patels, this might negatively affect the family's position in the village. I agreed not to talk to anyone in the village about the purpose of my visit and not to bring anyone else with me.

Once in India, I made arrangements with Salma's twenty-two-year-old cousin, Farhan (through WhatsApp), and took a rickshaw from Anand to the village. Farhan was waiting for me on the corner of a small, quiet alley and told the rickshaw driver to stop there, as the alley was accessible only by foot. A man watched us curiously, but we quietly passed by and did not stop to talk to him, as agreed. Farhan led me into an old farmhouse with thick wooden beams. In the cool, quiet interior, his parents and grandmother were waiting for me, along with other relatives.

In London, I was told that the family wanted to stay in the village because "they are happy there." In the village, I encountered a different story. In fact, soon after we started talking, the family mentioned fear: *"Bikh lage che"* ("There is fear"), they said. They wanted to sell the house and move to Anand; however, this was not possible because one family member—an elderly uncle who lived upstairs but was not present at the meeting—wanted to stay. While he was alive it would not be possible to sell the house without his permission. So, in polite terms, they were "waiting for the right moment." Other Muslims in the village were also waiting for the right moment, they said, planning to move to Anand as soon as they could.

The main speaker was Farida. She was the oldest member of the household, Farhan's grandmother, Salma's mother. Soon the conversation turned to the pogroms of 2002. At this time, her children and grandchildren had gone to Anand to live in a camp for several weeks, while Farida and her husband, Mohammed, remained in their house in the village:

> Our village is good. In our village we have never had any problems. In other villages, there was violence. In the neighboring village there was violence too, but not here. Still, even here, people got scared. During the riots, all Vohras in our village fled their homes and went to Anand. Our family went to Anand, too. Everyone stayed in Anand for two months, except me and my husband. We stayed in our house the entire period. Afterwards, many Muslims left the village. There is fear. They all go. Many people go to that side, to Anand. They are scared.
>
> [I asked Farida if she was scared, too.]
>
> No. We are not scared. We have good relations with our neighbors.

Here the conversation got messy and the message more complex: *"Bikh to lage"* ("There is fear"), but *"Apne bikh na lage"* ("We are not scared"). I asked them about the difficulties they confronted. Farhan replied, and spoke about rising tensions in the village. He said that "everyone in the village speaks bad about Muslims," and that even Muslims in the village join in gossiping about other Muslims. Trust between neighbors had been lost. Some had stopped talking with each other. Furthermore, the recent death of Mohammed, the patriarch of the family, had generated new insecurities. He had been a well-known and widely respected elder of the village. He had maintained friendships as well as financial relations with Hindu families in the village, offering loans and gifts to neighbors in need. With Mohammed gone, what would happen now? Wasn't it his reputation in the village that had earned the family protection in 2002?

Ibrahim, who was listening in on the conversation by phone from London, offered further explanations from his point of view:

> It's not a specific difficulty that is actually occurring. It's more a fear of repetition. Knowing what happened in the surrounding villages in 2002, they fear that they will be at risk in the future if it occurs again. The second time there will be no respite.

He continued:

Look at that alley. It's like Amsterdam, yeah. It's like one little street leads to another street. And inside this street . . . they are cornered in. If somebody blocks the way . . . you are stuck, you can't go anywhere.

After adding, "This street is predominantly Hindu, all Hindu," Ibrahim said that in the past few years, he and his wife have been repeatedly telling their family in the village to "get away, get away, get away." He also urged *me* to reinforce this message. "You should maybe reinforce that with them as well, because so far they haven't listened to us." At that moment, I turned back to the family to ask what they thought of this advice. Farida smiled and said that she had heard it many times, and not only from her relatives in London. Similar advice had been given by their acquaintances in Anand. "Do you feel social pressure to move?" I asked. "No pressure," Farhan replied, "only advice."

"And what do you think, Farhan?" I asked. "Will your future be in the city? Or will you also still be in the village?" After all, I thought, this family has land and properties here that might be worth holding onto. Farhan, a student of engineering, replied decidedly, "I want to be in the town. . . . People are a problem, and no facilities available. No facilities. Like, if you want to move anywhere, in Anand, you can go easily. Here, it is a problem."

What I learned that day in 2017 is that, even fifteen years after the violence, the threat of recurrence continued to prompt relocation. Gujarati Muslim families such as Salma's continue to move from their villages to Anand to this day, or aspire to do so, despite continuously rising housing prices in Anand that make the move difficult and, for many, even unaffordable. These reorientations toward Anand, moreover, do not occur only in villages that were directly affected by the violence, but also in those that remained relatively safe. The fact that there has not been any large-scale violence in Gujarat since 2002 is not considered an indication that peace has been restored and the violence is over. At present, anti-Muslim violence seems to be concentrated in other parts of India, but it might return to Gujarat. Those who were waiting for the mobs in 2002 are, in that sense, still waiting.

Conclusion

If communal violence is a strategy to reshape space (Deshpande 1998), then the violence of 2002 has been highly successful in achieving this aim. After 2002, novel understandings of space as either Hindu, Muslim, or Christian prompted many people to change localities. In the years thereafter, the divisions consolidated, and Muslims kept moving into Anand's Muslim area.

Existing research in Gujarat has shown that considerable residential segregation along religious lines has taken place in response to communal violence, even if some of the smaller towns in central Gujarat seem to have escaped such developments. In the city of Ahmedabad, where violent episodes had been occurring since 1985, before culminating in the 2002 pogroms, studies point to the demarcation of Hindu and Muslim spaces—physical landmarks that differentiate these spaces from one another—and to Muslims seeking residence among people of their own religious community in search of safety.[34] The case of Anand shows that such residential segregation occurs not only within the spaces of the city, but also at the regional scale. It points toward a shift in how rural-urban spatiality is perceived, in terms of a Hindu-Muslim division. The interviews, observations, and household surveys presented here, substantiated with census data, all confirm this.

The violence influenced the broad and long-term process of urbanization in the region. Beyond the moment of the flight and the political controversies that surround it, this chapter has discussed the slow, cautious, and thoughtful ways in which people relocate, consider relocating, advise others to relocate, or stay put while looking ahead toward new places. These considerations involve issues of violence and safety (as outlined by other scholars), but also desires to move out of the village and up the social ladder. On one hand, Muslims in the village look toward Anand in hopes of a better future for themselves and their children. On the other hand, non-Muslims who had resided in the urban Muslim area express their concerns over development, access to services, and social status as their reasons for moving out. Rural-urban migrants who have assets in the village may hold onto them while they carve out a new position in the town.

The urban experience of life in a segregated Muslim area is also one of sustaining and forging connections with the realms beyond it. A hint about the importance of mobility is revealed in the chance remark by Farhan, the engineering student, that "if you want to move anywhere, in Anand, you can go easily."

CHAPTER 3

Uprooted and at Home

Transnational Routes of (No) Return

On walks through Anand, my neighbors sometimes directed my gaze to what they called the "closed houses"—houses that were temporarily shuttered while the owners lived abroad. When these overseas owners visited their houses, my neighbors introduced me to them.[1] What struck me about the elderly people among these visitors was that many of them did not have prior histories in Anand. They traced their roots to surrounding villages, and some had grown up in Mumbai or in East Africa before moving to the United Kingdom or United States. Their families had moved to Anand from their villages of origin, and now, after settling overseas, they were spending their retirement days in Anand.

ANAND'S POST-2002 EMERGENCE as a new center for local Muslims has also turned the town into a new home base for Muslims from the region who have emigrated overseas. This development results from a combination of opportunity and constraint. Implementing ideas about migration and development, the Indian and Gujarati state governments have set up structures to encourage overseas Indians to reconnect with India and send their financial resources back to it. Like many overseas Indians, overseas Gujarati Muslims also participate in this economy of migration and development by sending remittances, investing in real estate, and, in some cases, starting or supporting charitable organizations in Gujarat. The rural-urban relocations of Muslims within their region of origin shape the destination of these financial flows. Those whose families left the village do not think of investing in their villages of origin. The parentheses in the chapter title—"Transnational Routes of (No) Return"—reflect this adaption: when overseas Vohras talk about going "back home," they are not returning to their villages of origin; instead, they are carving out a new home in Anand and finding opportunities to invest in the town. As most of these villages of origin are close to Anand, this is not a huge leap in a geographical sense, yet it is a significant one.

This chapter's journey starts in London, with some of the owners of the closed houses in Anand, and then describes the different considerations that influence their investment patterns: histories of transnational migration and overseas organization, neoliberal regimes of migration and development, and the migrants' ambivalent relation to their rapidly transforming regions of origin. Despite their critique of Hindutva, overseas Vohras maintain relations with India, or even build new ones, making practical and symbolic use of the opportunities offered to them by the Indian government. While they can be regarded as "agents of development" (Faist 2008), they see themselves more as followers than influencers of development: small players in a small town, with little influence over local affairs. Their agency lies in adapting to local affairs to the best of their abilities.

Our House on 100 Feet Road

We return, now, to an opening vignette on the first page of this book—an overseas Vohra family in the United Kingdom with a recently acquired flat in Anand. In a living room in West London, on a flat-screen TV, pictures of Indian streets and food stalls flash. "This is Mumbai," Ahmad clarifies. Then, "This is our flat in Anand." The conversation takes place on a Friday evening in 2016, at the weekly gathering of his (extended) family. Surrounded by his brothers, their wives, and his elderly mother, with children playing on the floor in front of the TV, Ahmad uses the occasion of my presence to take another look at the pictures of his recent trip to India. Lately, he has been going every year.

Ahmad bought the flat as a vacation home. A video taken from its balcony shows a wedding passing by on the street below. "You can just sit there, and the entire life of Anand passes by: it's wonderful," he comments. From the image, I recognize it as 100 Feet Road. Calculating the flat's proximity to this street, I react, "We are neighbors!" I clarify which housing society I lived in during my stays in Anand. We spend some time discussing our shared knowledge of the people and places in the area.

Ahmad is so pleased with his new flat that I struggle to raise the question of the town's painful history. When I finally find the words, I ask how he perceives the post-violence trends of displacement and residential segregation. Ahmad briefly responds, "Well . . . yes, but this is not our fault, is it?" For a moment we both fall silent, unsure of what to say. Then, the conversation is back to food stalls and restaurants. "The town is developing fast," he says. His brother and mother nod appreciatively, commenting that it could be developed even more. Ahmad continues, "There are hardly any eateries within walking distance of our flat. People could make great business on that street. You could have a pizza place; why doesn't anyone start that up?"

Ahmad's was one of the sixteen Vohra households in the United Kingdom that I had interviewed in 2012 about their investments in India. Ten households had invested in land or houses in Anand town, while others were considering buying property in Anand in the future. Only a few had ties with Anand prior to 2002, so I asked them why they chose the town. Ahmad's situation made me particularly curious—he had grown up in Mumbai, married in Mumbai, and raised his children in London. Now he had invested in Anand, a one-day train ride away from Mumbai. In 2012, he explained:

> We've invested some money. Basically we bought land [thinking], "We will build a house" or whatever. In Anand.... We bought quite a big plot; we wanted to build a house like this one over here [in the United Kingdom]. Huge plot.
>
> [I ask, "Why Anand?"]
>
> Because that's where the family is. If we go there on holiday, we go to Anand.

In 2016, when I returned to this family in London, they'd sold the plot at a profit, and had just purchased a new flat. When I asked again, why in Anand, Ahmad replied that it was conveniently located within six kilometers of his natal village, Boriavi, so they could easily visit relatives in the village. Moreover, many of the Muslims from this village had moved to Anand in the previous fifteen years, and some of them had bought houses close to the flat. Ahmad reflected:

> I can walk down the street there [in Anand], I can bet you, there will always be someone who will be related to me.... We have good contacts there and [whenever we need anything] someone would mention a name: "Oh so-and-so is doing good work, I know him, he is so-and-so's son, and I was on the phone with him yesterday." That's how it goes.

Anand is a convenient vacation location: the shops, restaurants, and services that are available there provide all that the family needs. Another advantage of investing in Anand, suggested Ahmad and others, was the price differential between Anand and Mumbai. Land prices in Mumbai make land there accessible only to the hyper-rich. In Anand, land was more affordable, at least in the decade after 2002 (prices have risen dramatically since then). Relatives in Anand, moreover, have more time than those in Mumbai to help arrange buying, guarding, and maintaining a house in the absence of the owners, and dealing with bureaucracy.

Mumbai, in contrast (it was suggested), is an expensive city, and its residents work around the clock, with very little time available for helping their overseas relatives.

Of the overseas Vohras in the United Kingdom who had bought flats in Anand, two more examples demonstrate how reorientation works in this transnational social field. Yousuf and his wife bought a flat within walking distance of the relief colony where her family had resettled after 2002. Like Ahmad, Yousuf and his wife had no prior history in Anand. He had moved to Tanzania (then called Tanganyika) from the village of Sunav in Gujarat at the age of four or five. He spent most of his childhood in Tanganyika and moved to the United Kingdom after he turned eighteen. His wife came from a small village in the vicinity of Dharmaj and had relatives in the nearby city of Ahmedabad. Their visits to Gujarat prior to 2002 were mostly spent in his village, his wife's village, or Ahmedabad. It was in 2002 that both his own and his wife's family suddenly left their villages and moved to Anand. At this time, Yousuf became very active in the United Kingdom, organizing charitable relief for Anand (more below), and supported these relatives in finding a home in a relief society in Anand. He and his wife bought their own flat in Anand a few years later. "I am from the village of Sunav," he clarifies. But "now, nobody from my family lives in Sunav. So obviously, I don't have any feelings about Sunav, even though it is my birthplace. Because there is nobody there now! They all have shifted to Anand!"

The investors I interviewed had bought houses within walking distance of their recently relocated relatives; in one case, a new house doubled as a resettlement house for a locally displaced family and a vacation home for their overseas relatives. This house, a third and last example, was bought by an elderly man in London to help his younger brother resettle in 2002. It is big enough to serve two purposes simultaneously: the younger brother is both caretaker and main occupant, with his nuclear family, while the older brother overseas uses part of it as a vacation home. When the older brother and his wife visit from London—which they try to do once a year—they are, as his wife says, "visitors in our own house." She explains:

> We stay there for four weeks, maximum five weeks. They [the relatives in Gujarat] won't let us do anything. . . . OK, I cook once in a while, something different . . . but clothes washing, everything, they won't let me do it. So, I just relax.

Anand has emerged not only as a safety zone and a destination point from the villages, but also as a new base for overseas investment, social connections, and belonging. Referring to the 2002 displacements, Yousuf states, "We [Vohras] have been uprooted!" But when I ask him how he feels when he visits Anand, he nevertheless answers, "I feel at home when I go to Anand . . . I feel at home."[2] These findings conjure a regionally produced meaning of transnational real estate investment, which adds another layer to Vohra stories of rural-urban transformation. Other aspects that shape the overseas Vohras' transnational experiences include their histories of migration and settlement, the community organizations they have formed in their countries of arrival, and the political developments in India that influence their homeland relations.

Overseas Migration

For many young people in central Gujarat, going abroad (or *bahar*—outside) is a key aspiration. Cross-border migrations have so far mostly been described in the regional literature from the perspective of the local Patidars (Tambs-Lyche 1980; Rutten and Patel 2003). When Vohra interlocutors compared their own migration with that of the Patidars, they said that Vohras went abroad later and in fewer numbers. In this, Vohras of central Gujarat are different not only from the Patidars but also from the Gujarati Muslim communities on the coasts of Baruch and Kutch, with their long histories of overseas mobility and exchange across the Indian Ocean.

The story of the Patidars' overseas migration is well known among the Vohras, as illustrated by the middle-class Vohra family whose apartment I lived in during my research in Anand. From my first encounters with this family (in 2011), they made clear that the migration of Muslims was not an ordinary affair here. At the time, one of the overseas sons of the family happened to be visiting from Australia with his wife, and she told me that there were fifteen Vohras from Anand in Sydney. When I told her that some of the neighbors had estimated that there are about 400 Vohras living abroad in total, she considered this an optimistic estimation:

> That may be true, I don't know, but they are not well settled. They are just starting. They have no old links, like Patels. That is why all the Patels go to the United States and United Kingdom: they have connections there so it is more easy for them to start their lives there. We [Vohras] don't have those old links; this is why we go to Australia.

At the same time, the family history did illustrate that an earlier line of migration existed. An elderly uncle of Shahinben was also visiting Anand in the winter of 2011–2012. He had moved to the United States in 1993, in his late forties, to join his son, who had migrated earlier. According to him and other Vohras I talked to in the United States, the overseas migration of Vohras had started in the 1960s. Nevertheless, they agreed that the number of Vohra migrants has remained very limited compared to the number of Patels.

To assess the volume of migration in the neighborhood, I conducted a household survey in six housing societies (Survey A). The residents of these housing societies described themselves as middle-class Muslims, and some indicated that they were more transnationally connected than other housing societies in Anand's Muslim area. Even so, only a third of the surveyed households turned out to have transnational connections—42 of 147 households (see table A.09). Of these forty-two households, thirty-six had one or more family members living abroad. This family member was a child of the family in twenty-six households, with a total of thirty-five children (twenty-seven sons and eight daughters) living abroad.[3] Of these thirty-five children, ten were in the United States, ten in Australia, and eight in the United Kingdom. A few were in the Middle East or South Africa, and one was living in mainland Europe. Four houses were closed at the time of the survey, and neighbors indicated that the owners were abroad (see table A.09).

The locations that figure prominently in these findings are the United Kingdom, the United States, and Australia (and, more recently, Canada)—not Africa, the Gulf, or Sindh in Pakistan, which are destinations that appear more frequently in travel descriptions of Gujarati Muslims on the coast (Ibrahim 2008; Simpson and Kresse 2007). The United Kingdom, the United States, and Australia are important destinations in the Charotar region (Guha and Dhak 2013) and figure prominently in the literature on the Patidars. The Patidars are described as "twice migrants" (Bhachu 1986) because they migrated to East Africa first, and then onward to other destinations, such as the United Kingdom and the United States. The migration of Patidars to East Africa began in the late nineteenth and early twentieth centuries, when the (British) colonial state encouraged Indian merchants and workers to migrate to its other colonies (Jain 1993; Makrand Mehta 2001). These migrants took up jobs on the railways or in the civil service, and some started their own businesses. After the British colonies became independent in the 1960s, Indians were confronted with anti-Indian sentiments and, in Uganda, with forced expulsion. In 1999, Parvin Patel and Mario Rutten wrote that "there may not be a single village from about one thousand villages of Charotar" from which at least one Patel family had not migrated. In some villages, more than half of the Patel families had emigrated (952). To this day, the surname Patel is one of the best-known Indian surnames in the United Kingdom.

Some Vohras of these villages joined the Patidar trails to East Africa, the United Kingdom, and the United States. Vohras report that migration was rare in their community during the colonial period, and, in some cases, was strongly discouraged by relatives. The Gujarati Muslim communities who settled in eastern and southern Africa are mostly from urban or coastal mercantile trading groups, not from the Charotar region. By 1956, when the Patidars from Charotar and Gujarati Muslim groups from the coast had become a prominent presence in East Africa, only a handful of Charotar Sunni Vohra families were living there. This was recollected by an elderly Vohra man who moved to Tanzania (then Tanganyika) from his village, Kanjari, in 1956. He remembered approximately four Charotar Sunni Vohra families living in Uganda, three in Tanganyika, and a few in Kenya. He himself had migrated against the will of his family when a (Muslim) friend from Surat helped arrange a job for him as a teacher in a school in Tanganyika. He moved back to India in 1967, and then migrated to the United Kingdom in 1986, where I interviewed him in Leicester in 2012. This is what he said about the migration history of Vohras:

> From Charotar, when the British government started to build a railway from Mombasa to Nairobi, most of the Patels sold off their land and went as laborers to Kenya. And in Kenya, after the railway was finished, they settled there; they did not come back to Charotar. And in that way, the Patel community started migrating to other parts. But in our community [Vohras], there was no support for that. . . . In Uganda, it so happened that three to four [Vohra] families [migrated], but they were taken there by Patels. In the village, the Hindu-Muslim relations were very cordial at that time, nothing of this riot. So, to his neighbor, a Muslim and a Vohra, he [the Patel] said: "You send your son with me; I'll give him employment there." So, four or five people [Vohras] were there [in Uganda] in this way.

The suggestion that Vohra migration from Charotar was less dense than the migrations of the Patidars is also confirmed in the *Charotar Sarvasangra* (*Chronicles of Charotar* (P. C. Shah and C. F. Shah 1954): a book containing almost 200 pages on the history of migration from the Charotar region and listing overseas migrants from Charotar by name. From its telephone-book-style list of names, it is possible to confirm that only a few Vohras migrated to East Africa in the colonial period. The book mentions 347 migrants from Charotar living in Kampala, Uganda, for example. Most of them (301 out of 347) were Patidars: 287 had the surname Patel and 14 had the surname Amin (who are also considered Patidars). Of the other names mentioned in this list, only two were Vohra. This suggests that caste networks had been important in shaping migration from the region. Only recently have migration networks been broadening, with new groups embarking on overseas study and work, and new destinations emerging.

Among the Vohras who did migrate overseas earlier, and who now have the financial capacity to participate in Anand's real estate markets, approximately ten Vohra men arrived in the United States as early as the 1960s and 1970s. This group of highly educated young immigrants then brought over their wives, relatives, and acquaintances from India, through the US system of family-sponsored immigration.[4] Others came independently on business or work visas, or as students. In 2018, the total number of Vohra individuals in the United States and Canada was estimated (by members of the Vohra Association of North America) to be up to 1,000.[5] Most of them live on the East Coast and in Illinois.

Some Vohras also migrated to the United Kingdom in the 1960s and 1980s. Abdullahmia Hassan Vohra is remembered as the first Vohra in the United Kingdom. He is said to have migrated from Mumbai[6] to the United Kingdom in 1959, and to have then helped his relatives and friends make the move as well. The first Vohra migrants to the United Kingdom arrived on visitor, work, or business visas; some migrated on a special visa for religious leaders. Some worked as taxi drivers, factory workers, or shop personnel; others started businesses of their own. Vohra families who had lived in East Africa also moved onward to the United Kingdom. In 2012, the total number of Vohra households in the United Kingdom was between 110 and 120 (according to the Vohra list maintained by the UK Vohra Association).[7] In addition to these settled families with British passports, an estimated sixty Vohras constituted a floating population of singletons and young couples having arrived recently on temporary (student) visas.[8]

Overseas Organization

For the UK Vohra Association in London and the Muslim Vohra Association in the United States,[9] the events of 2002 in Gujarat were a trigger, a "compelling moment," as one interlocutor said. Their histories of self-organization confirm an idea advanced by political scientists (Koinova 2011, 348) that pogroms, ethnic cleansing, and human rights violations in the homeland can be a trigger for collective action among formerly inactive diaspora members. This collective action was short-lived in the case of the Vohras. But something else also happened in the process: a spatial reorientation within the homeland.

The UK Vohra Association had been started in 1992 for social purposes. After two initial events, however, the association had been mostly inactive. In 2002, the community association and its bank account were suddenly relevant again and became a vehicle for collective fundraising in the United Kingdom, to support the victims in Gujarat. In the United States, the Vohras had organized informal social meetings since the 1990s, to maintain familiar relations between ten to twelve dispersed families who had migrated from Gujarat and Mumbai to different US cities in the late 1960s and 1970s. Initially, reunions were organized in the homes of one of the migrants; since 1991, a space has been rented to accommodate the growing number of new arrivals. Activities during these reunions included Gujarati cooking and *garbah* (a folk dance), communal prayers, cricket and volleyball games, and other social activities. In 2002, for the first time, it was an emergency that triggered the heads of households of these families to meet. At this time, a formal Vohra association was established in the United States, so that collective funds could be gathered for affected relatives in Gujarat.

Yousuf Vohra from Sunav (one of the Anand homeowners mentioned earlier) shared his memories of the 2002 episode in detail during a 2012 group interview with him and two of his friends in East London. An elderly man who had grown up in Tanzania and lived in London since he was a student, Yousuf had traveled to Gujarat many times since he was a child, always as a visitor. This is what he remembers from 2002:

> At the time of those riots [. . .] my wife was in India. I was supposed to go there after two weeks, via Bahrain. My relatives rang me, [saying], "Please don't come. How are you going to come home from the airport? Vehicles are burning on the roadway; houses are burning on the roadway. How are you going to go? Cancel your ticket!" I said, "No, my wife is there; I have to come there. I am not going to cancel."
>
> Then my wife called me. She said, "You can come now; it's a little quieter." Then I saw with my own eyes . . . I heard with my own ears what was happening there. How people suffered. How my wife's family suffered. [. . .] We had been going regularly. I had seen the town [where the family lived, a few kilometers away from Anand], how happily they were living; they had spent a lot of money; they had made a nice bungalow. All ruined. All looted.
>
> What happened? A lot of Vohras came together in Anand at the time and made camps because all the people were fleeing from the smaller villages. Relief camp. There were so many relief camps over there. And I went

to visit them. Personally. In each camp. Had a word with them. Find out what their grievances were. What they suffered. How they suffered.

[I remarked, "That was daring of you, as a tourist, a visitor!"]

Because it is *my* community. I am a Vohra. This is *my* community.

Among the refugees in Anand were members of Yousuf's own family and that of his wife. They never returned to the village afterward. Yousuf returned to London:

> Then I came to the airport [in London]. I talked to my brother-in-law and to other people of my community. I gave them all the reports. What I've seen with my own eyes. Businesses burning. I can still see the flames coming out.

In the following months, Yousuf became active as one of the committee members of the UK Vohra Association. He traveled from London to Leicester to attend the Vohra meeting that had been organized there, in the middle of the country, so that "nobody should [have to] travel so far." The meeting in Leicester was attended by members of eighty-five Vohra households: "The heads of each family, all of us were there," he remembered. They exchanged information and decided to form a relief committee and organize a fundraising event. Yousuf explains:

> As I said, I visited the camps and asked the people what suffering they had.... This man was telling me his experience, what he saw with his own naked eyes. He was telling me that a heavily pregnant woman was knifed, and the child was taken out from her womb and killed—the child died instantly. Another saw a burning tire put on a couple of men; they were burned to death. Young girls were raped by these people [the attackers] in front of their own parents and relatives. I did not see anything, but I heard, in the relief camps. And when I came back here [to London], I told them [pointing at his two friends in the room] and we decided that we should bring all the Vohras in this country together and discuss about this. Make a contribution. Every family should contribute an amount and it send back to India for those people. We did. A couple of meetings were held. Everybody decided, pledged a lot of things. And we liaised with the relief committee in Anand, because nobody could be there (in Gujarat) personally to oversee. We sent twenty-seven to twenty-eight thousand pounds.

[His friend interrupts: "That was the first installment."]

First installment, twenty-eight thousand pounds.

The UK Vohra Association organized collections in mosques in Southall, Leicester, Birmingham, and Coventry. In Leicester, they also organized a *mela* (fair) to raise money. It sold homemade samosas and cakes, and there were speeches, information stalls, and a jumble sale (flea market). The money collected was sent to the relief committee in Anand. It was used to build a housing society for some of the refugees, consisting of thirteen small houses, each with one room and a kitchen, and a communal water pump. Yousuf visited this housing society later "because my wife's family is over there.... They are living there as well, in the relief committee houses. They were displaced."

This collective organization of charitable activities proved short-lived. If the collection of the funds had brought Vohras together, the distribution of the money was accompanied by disagreements, and some disappointment. Some felt that the committee in Anand had not distributed the funds evenly among the victims. In London, one woman said:

> Lot of ladies did, like, you know, in the *mela* they had a stand, dress, clothes, food . . . some did go around collecting, [and] a lot of us donated money straight away. But then, we felt . . . obviously things didn't work out properly back home.... We felt bad. Because all his family [pointing at her husband] is back home. They were all in Anand, well, *now* they are all in Anand, before they weren't.... We sent enough money for people to like . . . clothes, food, money, saucepans, all the necessities for a house. And they didn't get anything. And it upset us, because we were part of the management team here as well. . . . Lot of people [were] homeless; lot of people didn't have places to go . . .

Many of the participants continue to support families in India individually, through household remittances or charitable donations, as they had done before 2002. Many provide support to their own relatives; some have supported schools, hospitals, or social welfare initiatives with donations; and a few have even established their own foundations.[10] But there is not much enthusiasm left for collective donations. The UK Vohra Association still exists but has reverted to being dormant, with occasional social events only. While in 2002, Leicester had been a good location so that nobody would have to travel very far, in 2010, people in East London found a planned community event in West London to be too far from their homes, and the event was eventually cancelled.

If these narratives of 2002 highlight how the violence was a trigger for temporary collective organization in the diaspora, they also show that the collective action drew on an older register of community with which the migrants had been familiar in Gujarat—the Charotar Sunni Vohra Association. In contrast to the broad umbrella organizations of Indian Muslims that also exist in the United Kingdom, the Vohras directed their collected funds specifically to the town where their own relatives had gone after they had fled. The Vohras in the United Kingdom had come from the villages of Sunav, Boriavi, Kanjari, Borsad, Malataj, Mogri, Vaso, Kathalal, Bakrol, Narsanda, Umreth, Petlad, Tarapur, Vera, and Vododla (as indicated in their own records or in the interviews), with some having lived in the cities of Baroda, Ahmedabad, or Mumbai. The events of 2002 marked a turn toward Anand as a new, additional, and collective site of significance in India ("well, *now* they are all in Anand; before they weren't").

An Ambivalent Relationship

When the interviews turned to the relationship with India, ambivalent feelings were exposed, with different tones depending on which aspect of the homeland was at stake. When the discussion centered on politics, a dark narrative emerged, characterized by concerns about the mistreatment of religious minorities in India. When the conversation shifted to the register of personal and economic relations, the tone was much lighter. These ambivalences are a reflection of simultaneous inclusion in and exclusion from contemporary concepts of nationalism in India.

Simultaneous with the exclusion of Muslims at home and abroad from the national imagination, India has gone through a process of economic liberalization and globalization, with an increasing emphasis on policies that include the Indian diaspora in the economic development of the nation. The overseas Vohras I talked to considered themselves in this light. They included themselves in the category of "overseas Indians." To a large extent, this inclusion was a lived experience, not wishful thinking. For example, their real estate investments were facilitated by the arrangement of Overseas Citizenship of India (OCI), which makes it legally possible to invest in land in India, to travel back and forth easily without a visa, and to stay for long periods of time without the hassle of bureaucratic procedures.

India is not the only country that has developed policies to demarcate a diaspora (a transnational community of co-nationals) and incorporate this diaspora within the nation in cultural, economic, and political terms. This has occurred in parallel with the neoliberal economic policies globally propagated by Bretton Woods organizations such as the World Bank. Neoliberalism, in a nutshell, is the idea that basic social welfare services such as health care and education are most efficient and of best quality when they are organized by private actors rather than the state. In countries with a sizable volume of outmigration, one such private actor is the transnational migrant.

In India, where a protectionist and more socialist economic policy has been replaced by economic liberalization policies since the 1990s, migrants and their remittances have come to be recognized as a source of foreign direct investment and as an asset to economic development (Xavier 2011, 34–35). In the 1990s, financial schemes were introduced to attract remittances and encourage overseas Indians to deposit their money in Indian banks. This was accompanied by the cultural project of internationalizing Indian nationalism, as shown, for example, in the shift in Hindi cinema from ridiculing or ignoring overseas Indians to incorporating them as natural and heroic elements in storylines.[11] Overseas Indians responded by demanding specific rights and regulations. In 2003, in response to these demands, the OCI scheme was launched. The Indian government has invited overseas Indian citizens to promote Indian national interests on Indian soil and in their countries of settlement.[12] In the state of Gujarat, government initiatives for nonresident Gujaratis (NRGs) include an official bureaucratic cell started specifically to encourage NRGs to invest and participate in development projects in the state (M. G. Mehta 2015, 329).

This process has occurred predominantly under BJP governments, who have promoted an understanding that India is a Hindu nation. As a result, these governments have also tended to address overseas Indian citizens in nationalist Hindu terms and as a particular kind of Hindu.[13] For example, organizations that aim to advance the welfare of minorities are not treated as being overseas Indian but rather as "foreign," and on these grounds these organizations can be prohibited from receiving "foreign" funds.[14] There has thus been a two-sided reconfiguration of the nation. On the one hand, overseas Indians are encouraged to share their resources and ideas with India; on the other, Indian Muslims at home and abroad are defined as "outsiders" or "foreigners" (van der Veer 2002; Bal and Sinha-Kerkhoff 2005). These political configurations influence how the overseas Vohras describe their relation with the homeland—as shaped by experiences of both exclusion and inclusion.

The Discriminatory Homeland

During interviews, the overseas Vohras drew a stark distinction between India and their place of residence in terms of how religious minorities were treated. They juxtaposed their discriminatory homeland with a tolerant host society, where there is freedom for Muslims to practice their religion and go about their lives without fear or shame. Considering the wide media coverage of Islamophobia and xenophobia in the United Kingdom, the United States, and Europe, I was initially surprised to find such unwavering confidence in the host society's tolerance toward Muslims. The following is a comment by a middle-aged resident of London, whom I interviewed in Anand. During our conversation, I asked him about the differences between India and the United Kingdom. He replied:

> People are given more freedom in those countries [in the United Kingdom], as compared to India. When I went to uni [university], the first thing I noted was that every religion was allocated a separate space for prayer. I was really surprised! This is really good; there is a mosque in the university! And not only in the uni. Even if you go to the workplace, and if you tell them you want to pray, they say fine; they will even think of a way to make it easy for you.

This man, who had moved to the United Kingdom after his marriage, contrasted his experiences as a practicing Muslim in a British university and as a student in Anand:

> Muslims are a minority in Gujarat. It happens a lot in schools that they gang up on you. When I was in primary school, one of my teachers was always making bad statements about Islam. I don't think it was needed. . . . I had a very bad experience [in college in Anand]. I had an exam; on that day it was *Jumma* [Friday], so I wanted to do my prayer, and then I went to my exam. I was fifteen minutes late. I didn't expect my lecturer would have an issue with that. But when I arrived, he asked me, "Why are you late?" I told him I was doing prayer, and he sent me off. I was not very religious, only in college I became a little more religious and I started praying. Then I realized: this is not easy, if you want to practice anything that goes against . . . [long silence] ehhhhh . . . which probably doesn't synchronize with their way of doing things, you know. I experienced communalism a lot.

A younger man, who had lived in the United Kingdom for two years when I interviewed him in Anand, shared what he had heard about the United Kingdom before he moved there (on a student visa), and what he thought after he arrived:

> My uncle had told me that the position of Muslims was very bad in London after 9/11. He had not been to London himself, but he had heard about it. But when I landed at the airport, immediately I saw three or four men with beards in a high position: they were stamping passports and working

as security guards. So immediately I realized: what my uncle said is not true... in London, I can go around dressed in my white clothes even in the center of the city, and nobody turns to look. In East London, the Muslim drivers, six out of seven wear a beard, and they feel safe! In Gujarat, it's different.

Members of the first generation of immigrants, who were highly aware of the political developments in India, also described differences in the way religious minorities were accommodated at the national and the state level in India. For example, several interviewees described the peculiarity of Gujarat as a violence-prone state, more hateful of Muslims than India as a whole. This differentiation between the two layers of state was articulated during 2012 interviews, but evaporated after 2014,[15] when the central government, led by the Congress Party (considered to be more secularist than the BJP), was voted out of power, and the BJP achieved an absolute majority in the national Parliament.

Reports of a discriminatory homeland are similar between the United Kingdom and United States. To illustrate, I share a remark from an interview I recorded in the United States in 2018, two years after President Donald Trump had claimed that "Islam hates us"[16] and called to bar all Muslims from entering the United States, while announcing his love for Hindus ("I am a big fan of Hindu, and I am a big fan of India. Big, big fan"[17]). The interviewee knew about incidents of violence against Muslims in the United States but thought these were relatively contained in comparison with India. He was an elderly Vohra man, a resident of Illinois, and a former resident of Anand who had migrated to the United States thirty-two years earlier:

> I know this ... 9/11. That happened. Right now, some people think that "Muslim is not good." ... Trump, his culture, he no like it. That's OK. But ... I tell you. Law and order is controlled.... Supreme law.... Nobody is scared here [in the United States]. Nobody touches me. Nobody broke the car. We are not scared.... Look at this, I tell you.... I read lots of things, some people broke mosques, threw stones, broke the glass. [But] government controls immediately, in the United States. I know Trump ministry is not good for Muslims, but no! Law and order!... Law and order is good in the United States.... That's why everybody is safe.... That's why everybody says, "America is a superpower."

These optimistic viewpoints about the position of Muslims in the United Kingdom and United States surprised me initially, and when I presented them at research seminars in India and Europe, audiences also responded with surprise, and at times even disbelief. This reaction seems to reveal the success of consecutive Indian governments in maintaining an image of India as being "a pluralistic society with a longstanding commitment to tolerance and inclusion,"[18] even when faced with criticism on its treatment of minorities. The comparative narratives shared here, however, were consistent in interviews with the first generation of migrants. They were presented as part of a wider understanding of migration as a life-changing endeavour that has generated improvement in comparison with prior lives in India. It is likely that second and later generations will more prominently describe experiences of exclusion and violence in their cities of residence.[19]

The Welcoming Homeland

Despite their alienation from Hindu nationalist politics in India, the overseas Vohras I spoke to still used the term "back home" when they talked about India. They continued to project the Charotar region as their homeland and maintained contact with people in the region on an everyday basis.[20] Moreover, India's OCI scheme offers them an opening to cultivate and further develop these personal and financial relations. Their inclusion in the category of "overseas Indians" also becomes a resource that, to some extent, enables them to overcome their marginalized position as Muslims in India.

In the survey I conducted in the United Kingdom in 2012, I asked about transnational practices of exchange with India. Phone calls with friends and relatives in Gujarat turned out to be frequent: every other week on average and, in some cases, every day. Family visits to and from Gujarat were also common.[21] Individual visits to Gujarat were particularly common among elderly men, some of whom have visited at least once a year since they retired, and with airline tickets now more affordable than in the past. Some had invested in business ventures or were involved in charitable organizations in Gujarat. As shown above, some families had also bought land or a house.

In Anand itself, I frequently encountered visiting migrants, staying during a work break for two or three weeks, or longer, in cases of retirement. Some of them stayed with relatives; others had bought houses of their own for these occasions. Shahinben's elderly uncle from the United States, for example, had bought a plot in Anand on which two neighboring houses had been constructed: one for his own use during his annual winter visits, and the other rented out to a Muslim (Pathan) family. Since 2010, he has escaped the harsh American winters by spending several months a year in Anand. His renters operated as caretakers for both houses, cleaned the houses, and even cooked his breakfast and lunch during his stay. These were new houses, which had been constructed shortly after 2002, and were likely a good investment, as land prices had already risen considerably since then.

Formal registration with the Indian state as OCI makes these ongoing personal and financial attachments possible. Besides its practical advantages for ease of movement and investment, the OCI category has also become a marker of status that commands respect in India. For Muslims, this marker seems to work, at least to some extent, to neutralize the "minority" identity, and can be activated to reshape their relations on terms that are not dictated by Hindu and Muslim categories.

One of the visiting migrants who made this point very explicit was Samir Vahora (a pseudonym). A middle-aged man from Nadiad residing in Baltimore, Samir visited Anand twice during my research period in Gujarat (in 2011 and 2012). The aim of his visits was to start up a new business in Anand, a transport company. "I am here for fifteen days, for business, and for fun as well," he said during his visit in summer 2012. "I work from ten to five, or ten to six, and after that I stop and I tell everybody not to call me. . . . I am enjoying every minute of my life. Over there [in the United States] I work all the time; here I can enjoy as well."

Many of the overseas Indian visitors I met in Gujarat were very busy during their stays and were often highly mobile, constantly on the way to their next appointment. I was not always able to see much of what they were doing during these stays. But Samir reined me into his business immediately after meeting me, by inviting me to the formal opening ceremony for his new company. During this spectacular event in a luxurious hotel in Ahmedabad, he presented "the first limousine in India" to the public, and I dressed up in my best blouse to give a brief speech about this remarkable "palace on wheels." Because of my participation, I became part of his crew. For a few days, I accompanied him, traveling around the region in an air-conditioned car, meeting his relatives as well as some of his lifelong friends, and his employees at his new office in Anand. Surrounded by his friends, full of plans for new business ventures, and temporarily relieved from the burdens of work and living in the United States, Samir had an optimism that was contagious.

What struck me during every encounter with him—in contrast to the sorrowful narratives of a discriminatory homeland discussed earlier—was his unambivalent delight in being in India. When I asked him if he had ever faced any difficulties as a Muslim in India, he answered, "In India yes, definitely. Not in the United States," but then immediately continued to add another layer to this story:

> But this is also a matter of how you are dealing with a situation. The problem with the people here [in India] is that they lack confidence. They think oh... this is a Hindu and that is a Muslim. They make these distinctions in their minds. I don't do that. I have never faced any difficulties myself. There is a resistance in here against Muslims in general, but I don't get delayed by that. It's all a matter of how you handle a situation. When I was in trouble, I called Modi myself! And he helped me out.

In the story that followed, Samir claimed that he decided to call up Gujarat's chief minister Narendra Modi to help his family out with a personal matter, and that he had been able to do this because he is an overseas Indian. As the story was long and detailed, I share only its happy ending:

> I didn't know him [Modi]. I looked up his phone number on the website and got his secretary. I told him, "I am a Muslim and I am an NRI [nonresident Indian]. And I am contributing to your economy. Now the chief minister has said that he wants NRIs to contribute to the country... and I am going to be very disappointed if he doesn't help me only because I am a Muslim. I will not make any trouble, but I am going to be very disappointed." Then the secretary said, "Just hold on, sir." Very polite. Then I got Modi on the phone.

Samir's optimistic stories suggest that overseas Indians can present themselves on different terms than the Hindu-Muslim binary and can in this way consolidate their relations with Gujarat, and even with high-ranking representatives of the Gujarati state. This self-presentation includes explicit mention of the communal hurdle that needs to be overcome— "because I am a Muslim." Samir's remark that his confidence is not shared by his relatives in Gujarat is an indication of his privileged position—with his implied financial capacity to invest, and the recognized option to claim inclusion in the celebrated NRI category.

A question for the future is whether overseas Vohras and other overseas Indian Muslims will be able to maintain these relations and financial interests in India, and under what conditions. The exclusion of Muslims from concepts of citizenship has reached a new level in the controversial Citizenship Amendment Act, which was passed in December 2019 by the Indian Parliament and caused widespread protests in India. The act not only introduces religious criteria for emigrants from three neighboring countries (who can become Indian citizens provided they are non-Muslims), but also introduces new provisions for the OCI scheme. Since 2019, OCI cardholders can lose their OCI status if they violate Indian laws. It has become possible for a US citizen to lose OCI status for an act that is criminal in India but not in the United States—including, for example, expression of free speech, which is more limited in India.[22] While such OCI cardholders will have a right to a hearing, they will have no right to a full trial. These new stipulations are expected to be used to mute dissenting voices.[23]

In June 2020, I asked a Vohra interlocutor in the United States what this might lead to in the future. He said that he and other Vohras in his home city of Chicago are deeply worried about the new laws. They had already been concerned about their properties in Gujarat, following the recent violation of the property of an absentee (Hindu) homeowner in Anand, which seemed to signal increasing lawlessness. The new OCI regulations introduce further risks, now that an overseas Indian can be deported after being falsely accused of a small crime. I asked him if houses, businesses, and other financial involvements in Gujarat would be sustainable with the new regulations. He himself runs an import-export business between Gujarat and the United States. He answered, "The short answer is yes, it will stay. The long answer is that yes, maybe people will shrink their portfolio in India, but still they will find their ways around." On the phone from Chicago, having just participated in a Black Lives Matter demonstration, he shared his optimism about the emerging "Muslim Lives Matter" campaign on India's social media platforms, and his hope that the people of India would see through "this fascist government with its draconian laws,... and rise to the occasion." Because "governments come and go," and "at the end of the day, I love India."

Real Estate Business and Rural-Urban Land Conversions

The ambivalent relationship of Vohras to their homeland does not at all resemble classic descriptions of a "myth of the homeland" formulated in diaspora studies (R. Cohen 1996; Safran 1991), as a romantic or nostalgic notion of an ideal place to return to. Instead of romanticizing the homeland or portraying it as fixed in time, Vohras' concepts of the homeland are dynamic and respond to changing opportunities and limitations in Gujarat.

The dynamism of Anand town, as a central site of transnational investment in a changing homeland is shown in the story of investor Idris Vohra. A British citizen, he is different from the investors introduced earlier in that he operates as a land broker, buying and selling land for speculative purposes in a variety of locations in central Gujarat. He is also different in that he grew up in Anand and thus has seen the town's transformation from the perspective of an insider. His interpretations not only confirm how Anand has expanded and segregated at the same time, but also suggest that land on the edges of the town is transferred from one community to another—from Patel farmers to Vohra land brokers and builders. Cross-community friendships play a crucial role in his story of his hometown's transformation. The Patel-dominated town he remembers from his childhood is transformed to a place of Vohra arrival, in which he continues to feel at home.

I first met Idris in Anand in 2011.[24] A schoolteacher I was out walking with commented on a particularly large house we were passing. It belonged to a locally famous businessman, a vegetable trader. He had recently died, and now his son, Idris, had returned from the United Kingdom. After a few minutes of observing the house, we were invited inside and were soon drinking tea with Idris, his wife, their two young daughters, and his recently widowed mother.

At that time, Idris explained that he had taken a sabbatical and was staying in Anand with his wife and children for six months to get more involved with the family business in Gujarat. He had lived in the United Kingdom since 1999, where he worked in the production department of a pharmaceutical company and sometimes as a driver. His father, the vegetable trader, had become active in the speculative land conversion business in recent decades. It was co-managing this land with his mother that brought Idris back to his hometown, Anand.

One of the things that Idris said immediately in that first meeting was that his Gujarati friends in the United Kingdom measured each other's status by the amount of land and investments they owned in Gujarat. Later, I learned that these friends were all Hindus—Patels from the Charotar region, whom he met at a men's club every weekend in his town of residence in Sussex. He was the only Muslim in the club. Idris had grown up in a Patel-majority neighborhood in Anand and had gone to school with mostly Patel students, at a time when segregation was not as pronounced as it is today. His father also had many Patel business partners and friends, he emphasized. After marrying a Vohra woman in the United Kingdom, Idris migrated and maintained contact with his Patel friends, many of whom had also migrated to the United Kingdom. These contacts were important for him personally, but he also felt that they contributed to the success of the family business in Gujarat. Recognizing the powerful position of Patels in the region, he said, "Whoever is in the system is our friend," adding, "Our family has lived and worked with Hindus for four generations . . . so they are very familiar with us." Further, "Some of our lifelong family acquaintances are now high up in the BJP. This is why they support us when we want to get our work done."

In migration scholarship, many have argued that informal social networks of friends from "home" are a crucial channel of help for migrants. Such networks facilitate the process of migration and settlement, but also ensure continued access to resources in the region of origin (e.g., F. Osella 2014). In this light, Idris's extended networks can be seen as a form of social capital—a resource that he can mobilize to realize his own aspirations and to secure access to economic resources in Gujarat. His hope is, as he explained to me later, that the profits from the family business will not only provide for his widowed mother in her old age, but will also help him and his wife support their children in the future. Higher education is expensive in the United Kingdom, but he hoped that the profits from land speculation in Gujarat would help pay for it.

In April 2012, Idris visited Anand again. This time, he took me around in a car for a day to show me what he was doing during his extended stays in the region. He stopped in several villages to show me the parcels of land that were currently, or had been, in possession of the family. Some had already been sold, while others were awaiting development. As he drove me around from plot to plot, he explained about the phenomenon of rural-urban land conversion, on which much of this speculative land business is built. Land conversion is a bureaucratic procedure. An investor buys land that is registered as fit for agricultural use, then tries to convert the legal status of this land to nonagricultural, and finally sells the land at a higher price. Conversion of land from agricultural to nonagricultural use increases its value and can be highly profitable, but it is a complex and lengthy legal process. Contacts, information, and recurrent payments are crucial to its success.

A spatial shift had occurred in the family's investment pattern over the years. The lands of his father had been dispersed throughout the region but, in the period after 2002, he had bought land at the peri-urban outskirts of Anand, in the stretch now known as the Muslim area of the town. They were agricultural lands that were now in various stages of conversion. At one of these plots, Idris and I got out of the car to walk around. He showed me how the land had been divided into smaller plots, which had been sold to 142 individual owners. On each plot, there was a house at a different stage of construction. Idris contextualized the construction:

> Nowadays, Anand has become the center of Vohras in India. When I was three years old, there were about seventy Vohras in Anand! All our neighbors were Patels. During the riots in 2002, *so* many people came to Anand.

Especially Vohras. At the time, my father and I thought we had to do something for these people. So, we started a housing society. It was his vision, and I agreed with it. He wanted to do something for all the displaced people who came here.

Idris presented the project as a contribution to resettling Vohras in Anand after the 2002 displacements. In this narrative, his father was a generous patron. When I asked (Muslim) residents in Anand about this interpretation, they, too, described his father as generous. They were not so sure about Idris's philanthropic intentions, however. They thought, rather, that Idris had come back for "making business" out of Anand's rapid growth. Idris agreed that his actions had been mostly strategic but suggested that he had not made a profit from this particular housing society—or perhaps not enough. He further clarified:

This whole area was a jungle ten years ago. We bought this land at that time. We could acquire it from a farmer because we have good relations with Hindus: a friend of my father owned this land. We bought it and sold it in smaller plots. After we sold the plots, people have been buying and selling with their plots and they have made some money out of that. We also encouraged them to do so; we told them, "Buy two plots, sell one plot after a few years, and with the profit build your house on the second plot!" In the past five years, some plots have been sold five times. Now slowly, slowly, people are starting to build houses . . .

An interview with a (Vohra) friend of Idris in London shed further light on how this real estate business might be related to community politics. He drew a map of the area where Idris's property was located, and explained:

This area is located in Anand now, although part of it is still registered as agricultural land. Before, in this area, Patels were the landowners. Now, Vohras are becoming the landowners. Patels have gone abroad, and they have lost their interest in agriculture; they close the house, and nobody is there to take care of the farm. So, Vohras have bought some of their land, and they try to convert it to nonagricultural purposes.

This suggestion—of a shift in ownership—implies that the business of land conversion does not just convert agricultural land into nonagricultural land, but also Patel land into Vohra land.

Here, the Patidars have again made an appearance in the Vohras' stories, this time as the most prominent landowning community in the region, which has started to sell off its farmland on the expanding urban peripheries so that it, too, becomes available for urbanization. The Vohra story of rural-urban reorientation here also becomes a story about a transfer of land from one community to another—a story of land conversion, linked with transnational migration, infused with regional meanings of caste and community. It is within this narrative of land conversion that Idris can present himself as a transnational broker between Hindu farmers, who have reoriented themselves from agriculture to transnational migration, and Vohra residents of the villages, who seek new homes on Anand's urban outskirts.

Idris grew up in an older part of Anand with mainly Patel neighbors and talks affectionately about how the town used to be. Throughout our interactions, he talked about these long-term friendships with Patels and repeated, "I am good at networking. I can feel comfortable with anybody." He affirmed that "it is politicians that divide the community, nothing else," and made it clear that, in his view, the "community" encompasses both Hindus and Muslims. During his extended stays in Anand, he now lives in the house his father built in the developing Muslim area, together with his mother, using it as a base from which to transact. Rather than lamenting Anand's residential segregation, he has adjusted to it and tries to make the most of recent developments, buying and selling properties where profits can be made.

Idris's interpretations have further implications for the study of residential segregation in India. They add a new perspective to an emerging literature in India that has started to address the influence of real estate markets on segregated residential developments, particularly in Muslim areas (Jamil 2017; Susewind 2015). Drawing on socioeconomic explanatory frameworks, these authors argue that the segregation of Muslims should be explained not only by the dynamics of discrimination, violence, and insecurity, but also by the logics of capitalist accumulation in neoliberal India. While Raphael Susewind (2015) describes some of the conditions that create positive incentives for Muslims to invest in Muslim areas, Ghazala Jamil's analysis (2017) draws on Marxist theories of accumulation to suggest that these neighborhoods function as sources of capital extraction, the profits of which are often reaped elsewhere. In her analysis of Jamia Nagar in Delhi, she points to the consistent flow of rural-urban migrants into the city. Because the Muslims among the newly arrived residents are unable to rent or buy accommodation in other parts of the city, builders and developers are doing a roaring business in Muslim areas; here, they can sell houses to a niche market that has little choice to buy or rent elsewhere (Jamil, chap. 2).

More research is needed to substantiate and refine these arguments. Idris's narratives highlight the importance of a transnational perspective. They open up further questions about how practices of real estate speculation in a city might be co-produced by regionally distinctive patterns of migration and return, as well as by national regimes of migration and development. There are some studies on the real estate investments of transnational migrants in India (Upadhya 2018; Varrel 2012), and on the centrality of land as a crucial yet contested resource (Sud 2014; Upadhya 2017).[25] These show that land investments are also entangled with regional identity politics—e.g., when migrant investors are globally dispersed and "deterritorialized," but still identify strongly with their region of origin and reterritorialize it through their investments (Upadhya 2017, 181).

The case of Anand is an invitation to start looking at the missing links between these two lines of inquiry: one on the political economy of segregation, and another on the transnational politics of regional belonging. Idris's interpretations confirm Ghazala Jamil's idea that the paired developments of rural-urban relocation and segregation create a speculative business with a profit-generating potential. Nevertheless, the meanings Idris ascribes to the themes of community, land, and migration do not seem to be fully captured in the Marxist frameworks of accumulation she uses (Jamil 2019; see also Hansen 2019). Disentangling these dynamics would require further research.

Conclusion

The Muslim area of Anand can be seen as a "zone of awkward engagement" (Tsing 2005, x–xi) that draws different actors together. The different actors have their own goals and interests, and there is no specific overlapping agenda. Through their combined efforts, however, they contribute to the creation of a new home base for local and overseas Gujarati Muslims.

In response to the 2002 violence, overseas Vohras collected funds for the riot victims and directed these to Anand, where their relatives had fled. Thereafter, confronted with changes in their homeland while trying to maintain a relationship with it, they themselves followed their relatives to the town. When Anand became a center for the local Vohra community, it also gained relevance for the transnational migrants among the Vohras—alongside other places of Vohra settlement, like Mumbai, Ahmedabad, or London. Some overseas Vohras describe Anand as a new home, after having been uprooted from their villages of origin.

Reorientation in a post-violence landscape, then, is a process of re-anchoring both local and transnational relations. It is a shared experience of the town's residents and its transnational visitors. The transnational routes of (no) return described in this chapter are made possible by the overseas Indian citizenship scheme, which offers legal and symbolic frameworks for keeping connected, and by the regional developments that shape the spatial contours of their engagement. By keeping connected while redirecting their homeland orientations, potential arises for migrants to realize their own aspirations as well—homeownership, retirement, vacationing, business, respectability, and sheer fun.

CHAPTER 4

Getting Around

Middle-Class Muslims in a Regional Town

From March 24 to June 2020, life in Anand came to an almost total standstill as a result of the nationwide lockdown that had been called for as a protective measure against the global COVID-19 pandemic. For three months, people sat in their houses, waiting. In the beginning, the lockdown reminded of the curfew of 2002, when they had been hiding in their homes for weeks. With time passing and news of coronavirus infections rising, the stillness acquired its own character. On WhatsApp, Zakiya Vahora (a young woman) wrote to me from Anand: "I miss everything! Friends, junk food, college, work!! Every single thing."

ACROSS THE WORLD, the COVID-19 lockdowns of 2020 exposed what had been habitual before: mobility. Zakiya's discomfort during the lockdown revealed that the residential segregation of Anand has not produced seclusion. Residents like Zakiya have actively nurtured connections with various other people, including those of other religious groups. They experience Anand's Muslim area as a well-connected place from which it is easy to travel—as a hub of intersecting routes and transport modes. Transnational mobility has gained in importance, too, although in many families such overseas ventures remain no more than an aspiration.

Zakiya and her relatives represent a perspective of an aspirational Muslim middle class, for whom such linkages beyond the Muslim area are of great symbolic and practical importance. Other aspiring middle-class groups in India, too, cultivate lifestyles and practices through which they seek to participate in desirable professional and social networks and transcend imposed social boundaries (Baas 2020). When Muslims in Anand similarly demarcate themselves as part of an urban Indian middle class, their efforts to seek inclusion in relevant social networks obtain a distinctive spatial component due to their distinctive location in the town. For this aspiring urban middle class, then, the capacity to be geographically mobile becomes an important vehicle of social class mobility and social inclusion.

Middle-Class Muslims

My understanding of Anand's mobility is informed by my position in the Majestic Housing Society: a cluster of houses in Anand's Muslim area that is regarded by its residents as a middle-class space. Residents differentiate among each other in terms such as middle-class versus poor, educated versus uneducated, business families versus service families, Chaud versus Arsad, Vohras versus other Muslims, and Sunnis versus Tablighis.

The Majestic Housing Society is an extended neighborhood of spacious, detached two-to three-story houses, freshly painted and surrounded by low walls and terraces, interspersed occasionally with empty, yet-to-be-developed plots. Morning starts here with the sound of *azaan* (the call for prayer) from every direction. This is followed by the loud thumps of clothes being washed by hand behind the houses by homemakers and their servants. Next, are the sounds of two-wheelers, rickshaws, and an occasional car starting, as men and some women leave their houses to attend to business or work, and young people travel to school or college.

The label "middle-class," used by the residents of the Majestic Housing Society to describe themselves and their direct neighbors, holds a number of connotations: it implies that they are wealthier, more educated, more internationally connected than others, and, according to some, even more civilized than others. Almost all the residents describe themselves as followers of the Tablighi Jamaat, an Islamic reform movement. With these and other labels, they position themselves as different from the poorer parts of the Muslim area, where residents have less access to stable employment or business. These poorer residents are considered (by the middle classes) to be less educated, less in tune with modern religious norms, and less well connected.

Another important local mode of distinguishing between different groups of Muslims is by community identity, often discernable from the surname of a family. While most of my neighbors were Vohras, other recurrent surnames included Diwan, Pathan, Sheikh, and Malek: Gujarat-and Hindi-speaking Muslim communities. Vohras are the largest and most visible Muslim community in Anand, and they are dominant in the sense that they frequently take on leading roles in local schools, madrassas, hospitals, and other social organizations.

One way of discussing status differences between these Muslim groups is the Ashraf/non-Ashraf hierarchy—a common framework for discussing caste status among South Asian Muslims. Muslims in Anand are aware of this classification, although it seems to be less important here than in some other regions of India (e.g., in comparison with Bengal, as described by Anasua Chatterjee

[2017]). Ashraf communities claim to be the descendants of Arab traders and saints who emigrated to India. They are considered elite. Non-Ashraf groups are people with an acknowledged Indian origin, who have converted to Islam. They are seen as the common people (Dumont 1980, 207). The majority of Muslims in central Gujarat are non-Ashraf. Vohras are also positioned in the category of non-Ashraf groups.

Insofar as the residents recognize a group of Ashraf "nobles," this position is attributed to the Saiyeds, a group of saints. None of the families in the Majestic Housing Society was Saiyed; nevertheless, Saiyeds are well known and regularly discussed. Saiyeds are connected to some of Anand's households as religious experts, and the tombs of their ancestors are popular places of worship in the region. Their religious authority is continuously called into question, however, especially by those among the Vohras who themselves are active in the field of religious leadership as teachers and preachers. This situation is very similar to descriptions of status competitions between Muslim communities in other parts of Gujarat (Simpson 2006, 104; see also Jasani 2008, 453) and elsewhere in central Gujarat (Heitmeyer 2009a, 83).

In terms of their Islamic affiliations, residents identify two main religious categories—Sunnis and Tablighis—and they link these categories with understandings of education. In the Majestic Housing Society, where almost all families self-identified as Tablighi, the Sunnis were dismissed with the derogatory term "uneducated," and as less religiously modern and progressive than themselves. It must be noted that this usage of the term "Sunni" is different from its global meaning. In global discourses, Sunni Islam is an umbrella category defined as contrary to Shia Islam. Vohras, too, when they describe themselves as "Charotar Sunni Vohras," use this umbrella meaning to differentiate themselves from Shia groups. The Sunnis and Tablighis of Anand, however, both fall under this larger umbrella term of Sunni Islam. While Shia communities exist in Anand (Momins from north Gujarat, Khojas, and Daudi Bohras), the Shia-Sunni divide hardly seems important. Instead, the internal differences among Sunni Muslims are a recurrent topic of conversation.

The local discussions about the Tablighi-Sunni divide within Sunni Islam may have been spurred by a pronounced growth in the number of mosques of both orientations in the town. In a survey[1] in 2012, the number of mosques in Anand was fifty-one, of which thirty-four were associated with the Tablighi Jamaat and sixteen were described as Sunni (one mosque did not fit either of these categories). Of these fifty-one mosques, twenty-six had been constructed after 2002, with the number of mosques of the Tablighi Jamaat rising from eighteen to thirty-four and the number of Sunni mosques from 6 to sixteen. This spur in construction after 2002 seems to reflect a competition between religious leaders on both sides to find followers among the newly arrived Muslims.

The Tablighi Jamaat is a religious reform movement that has a presence throughout India and has a large following in Anand. An educational institute for religious reform was founded in Anand around 1920, and has grown into a large madrassa with dense regional networks, offering a complete religious education from kindergarten to postgraduate studies, a government-supported school with a mainstream secular curriculum, and more than a hundred small madrassas that offer primary religious education to the rural youth in the surrounding villages. While the residents discuss Anand as a center of Islamic reform in the Charotar region, the presence of other mosques shows that the Tablighi Jamaat is not hegemonic, and religious practices are as contested here as they are among Muslims elsewhere in India.

Existing literature on Islamic reform movements in South Asia indicates that in broad terms, Muslims distinguish between two versions of Islam: on the one hand, a mystical form of Islam, in which saints act as intermediaries between people and God; and, on the other hand, a "reformist" Islam, in which people develop a more direct relation with God through the study of the Islamic texts, prayer and reflection, and ritual sobriety (F. Osella and C. Osella 2008a; Simpson 2006, 14). The two categories should be seen not as two separate sects, but as potential courses of action that an individual can decide to follow (see Simpson 2006, 108–9; 2008). Reform has been described as a device for the rich to reinforce their economically dominant position by claiming religious superiority (Gardner 2001, 236–37), and also as a means by which individuals in low-and middle-ranked caste groups seek to improve their status (Jasani 2008, 453). In Gujarat, too, articulations of religious difference become a platform on which Muslims can compete for status and superiority with other Muslims (Simpson 2006).

In Anand, the appeal of reform to residents who self-identify as middle-class is its emphasis on learning. Shahinben—one of the more highly educated women in the neighborhood, with a bachelor's degree in English and another degree in education, who worked as an English teacher in a local school—thought that the advantage of the Tablighi Jamaat is that "you don't need a religious teacher to tell you what to do," how to pray, how to celebrate festivals, or how to behave. Instead of consulting a *bapu* (Saiyed saint) about religious matters, she felt that as a Tablighi, she can read and think on their own. Her feelings are congruent with those of middle-class groups elsewhere in India, who "associate religious reformism with a self-consciously 'modern' outlook;

the promotion of education; rallying of support from the middle classes" (F. Osella and C. Osella 2008b, 317).

These ideas about religious reform are entwined with ideas about the rural-urban divide. My neighbors in Anand observed that new arrivals who had lived in a village before settling in town tend to fall "under the influence" of the religious atmosphere in town after some time, and then gradually reform their religious practices. In a neighboring household, for example, a man had started to pray five times a day after coming to live in Anand. While this surprised his wife, because he had never done so previously, she was told that this is a normal part of the process of adaption from a rural to a more urban and modern lifestyle. On the other hand, Vohra residents of the small town of Sultanpur suggest that they themselves observe Islamic tenets, such as the five daily prayers, less strictly than their urban relatives in Anand (Heitmeyer 2009a, 174), and see Anand as a space where manifestations of piety and an Islamized middle-class urban lifestyle are more important than in Sultanpur. These categories, however, are not as stable as the narratives suggest. In practice, the rural-urban division is less a boundary and more a continuum (Tacoli 1998); moreover, religious practices are dynamic in both rural and urban households.

These descriptions bring out another key term of differentiation: education. "Education," indeed, was on everyone's lips throughout my stays in Anand. Among the first items of information exchanged when two new people meet each other here is the educational level of their children. Education is also among the first things mentioned in local gossip, in the sense that criticism directed at a common acquaintance is almost inevitably accompanied by the qualifier that they are "not educated." Education has become a symbol of community (Cohen 2000, 19)—more particularly, a symbol of an urban, middle-class community that derives its prosperity and social standing from the social and cultural capital acquired through education (Bourdieu 1986).

Education is linked with another important marker of difference in the neighborhood: the one between business families (self-employed) and those "in service" (indicating employment irrespective of the sector). Both types exist in the Majestic Housing Society, and both are considered middle-class, but they are conceived of as differently positioned. The business families are thought to have invested less in formal education, preferring to hand over the family business from father to son, as a result of their traditionally privileged position, having land, shops, or other economic assets in their villages of origin. Other families derive their income and status not from trade but from employment in white-collar work, preferably in government offices, and thus are said to focus more strongly on education as a way of seeking access to secure employment. Again, these categories are not fixed—even business families often send their children to institutions of higher education in Anand. Some develop mixed economic strategies, with one son maintaining the family business while other sons and daughters are sent to college to enhance the chances of employment or migration overseas, and to increase their chances on the marriage market.

Vohras report a growing importance of education, which heightens long-term negotiations around status and hierarchy. In the Vohras' internal community hierarchy, there is a class division between a group of traditionally wealthy business families and a less privileged group without traditional capital, who have achieved wealth and status in the town through education and employment ("service"). The first group is associated with the Chaud marriage circle of the Vohra community, and the second is associated with the Arsad and Makeriya marriage circles. In Anand, there is growing competition between these groups, residents have said, because the families of the Arsad and Makeriya group are catching up so fast that they are now surpassing the Chaud families in status and wealth—and this would be a major impetus for Chaud families to send their children to be educated as well. Some claimed that the status difference between the groups has completely fallen apart. Others contest this, pointing to the ways in which business families are able to maintain family-owned property, land, and profitable relations in the villages of origin, even after having moved to the town.

These various social boundaries through which Muslims in Anand understand difference and commonality illustrate the complexity of status differentiations and negotiations in the neighborhood. The terms "middle-class" and "poor," "service" and "business," in particular, are relevant to the everyday mobility practices of the residents, which are shaped by their occupational practices and educational aspirations. Within these multilayered patterns of differentiation, the capacity to be mobile can be regarded as an additional modality of social differentiation.

Rural-Urban Linkages

Vohras' narratives of their regional community point to a long-term economic engagement with the rural economy through agriculture-related occupations and alliances with Hindus in a shared regional economy. These regional narratives are expressed from a position of rupture, following trends of urbanization, displacement, and segregation. But urbanization has not completely erased the Vohras' relations to the Charotar lands. On the contrary, in Anand they remain embedded in aspects of the rural and peri-urban economy, along with their urban-based residency and occupations. Their experiences of rural-urban mobility are aligned with descriptions of Anand as an example of a town with a well-developed rural-urban road and railway infrastructure, intimately connected to the rural hinterland through dense economic and social networks (S. Patel 2006, 26).

While these networks have changed in response to the recent history of segregation, they are still significant. This is not only the case for elderly people, but is also the lived experience of a younger generation, for whom the present situation of urban life is already taken for granted, but who still maintain various ties to people and places beyond the town. Their parents maintain such ties themselves and also actively pass on this knowledge to the next generation.

For business families in particular, especially the traditionally wealthy families who hold family-owned property and businesses in the villages, the cultivation of relationships in places besides Anand is a crucial economic strategy. If they own land, this can be retained and rented out to acquaintances or dependents, they can farm it and generate profits, or the land can be sold and reinvested. Such activities are dependent on sustained relations with relatives, friends, and business partners in the villages, including with people from other communities and castes. Their wide networks came to the surface when interlocutors took me along to visit nearby villages, where they mingled with obvious familiarity despite, in some cases, some performative disdain for the rurality of the place. Here, the village was devalued as a remnant of a rural past but obviously also reinvigorated with meaning as a source of relationships and resources, from which a privileged group of landowners in the town also derives its wealth and power.

The London-based businessman, Idris, is an example of this business perspective (see chapter 3). Another business family, who were among my neighbors in Anand's Majestic Housing Society, also illustrate how residence in a segregated town has not stopped entrepreneurs from remaining active in the wider region of Charotar. The dispersal of their trade depends on their widely spread social relationships in the region and their social labor and skill in maintaining them. They were active in the potato trade before, but currently they are almost exclusively involved in real estate. In 2012, they were constructing a shopping complex in a nearby town in Umreth. Vasim is the oldest son of this wealthy Chaud Vohra family in Anand.[2] Vasim's father had instructed him to manage the day-to-day operations at the shopping mall under construction, and he spent five days a week there, waiting for potential investors who visited sporadically to enquire about buying a shop.

One day, Vasim invited me to come along. That day, he wiped the dust from the seat of his white two-wheeler with an old cloth, put a scarf over his nose and mouth as protection against the dust, and instructed me to do the same. We hit the road. The heat was soaring. "Normally I go on scooty [two-wheeler]," he remarked, "but from tomorrow onwards I'll take the bus. Now that summer is coming, the heat is getting too much. My father has a car but I still haven't learned how to drive it." While passing the Ekta and Tip Top restaurants, Vasim pointed to the latter and said, "This is a new restaurant. I want to open a restaurant myself around here, maybe next year." The road then led away from Anand and through agricultural fields.

Finally, we stopped in a largely uninhabited area with a noisy road, fences, and a few half-constructed buildings—the outskirts of Umreth. Other than the construction workers and traffic, there were few people around. It was a patchy landscape, dry, and seemingly empty, lined by low concrete walls marking the boundaries of private properties from each other, and dotted with widely dispersed and mostly unfinished buildings. Vasim remarked, "Now, this area is nothing. But in ten years it will be fully developed. Value will rise. We are building a shopping center with two floors. If all goes well, we want to build a multiplex cinema on the third floor. At this point we are building and selling at the same time." He said that Umreth is

> a good place for investment. Before, my father constructed several buildings in Anand. He planned to buy a new plot in Anand as well, but the price was so high he decided not to do it. Anand is already totally developed. The prices are so high that they can hardly rise further. We prefer investing in small places, villages that are growing, where you can still buy land at a reasonable price and then make profit at a lower risk. Umreth is cheaper than Anand, because it is still small. But it is growing. Many people from the surrounding villages come here to shop.

For Vasim, the Charotar tract is configured into zones of opportunity, profit, and loss. It is in the peri-urban zone of a growing town, on the edge of "development," where his family expects to make a profit. Like many in India today, this family has turned to land brokering: the speculative business of converting agricultural land into real estate.

In the absence of customers in the office, we relax and talk. Vasim asks questions about Amsterdam. Then he talks about the violence of 2002. He is very interested in talking about this: "Nowadays people forget, but the people who have lost their children, their houses, their business, how can they forget?" In the middle of the conversation, he suddenly warns me, "Now stop talking about this, a Hindu is coming." A man walks in, sits down, and starts chatting to us comfortably. When Vasim goes to the other room to pray, without me having asked any questions, the man starts talking to me. His message: "There is no Hindu-Muslim tension here." Vasim later explains that this person arranges government permits for the construction business. "He knows very well how to get things done around here. He used to be a bureaucrat with the municipality, until he got fired because of corruption. We pay him a lot for his service of dealing with government officials, but he does his work well." Vasim further explains that collaborating with Hindus is vital in the real estate business, because of the need to get permissions from government officials as well as the strict residential segregation in the region. The shopping mall under construction is located next to a temple.

> This area we are building in is a Hindu area. On that side there is a *mandir* [Hindu temple]; on the other side, Hindus are building an apartment complex. The customers who come to inquire about buying a shop with us are also mainly Hindus. We are the only Muslims here. I can tell you, if we had been Hindus, all the shops would have been sold by now, not just seventy out of 110. People are a bit hesitant about buying from a Muslim. They don't say so, but I can feel I have to deal with a trust issue. That is why we collaborate with Hindu partners. We put the names of the two Hindu partners on the sign board that advertises our shopping mall. They are not financially involved, but they are giving their name. In the same way, we help them if they want to do business in a Muslim area. My father has a lot of experience in this business; he knows how to do all these things.

Vasim, a resident of Anand since childhood, and having lived in London as a student for some time as well, is planning to get married and build his future here in Gujarat. As an apprentice in the family business, he is keen on learning the tricks of the trade from his father while developing a business mind of his own. As he makes clear, this includes learning how to conduct himself successfully in a Hindu-dominated environment. One way in which Vasim maintains a low profile is in the way he dresses. When he is at home in Anand, Vasim normally wears the white cotton attire that is popular among men who follow the Tablighi Jamaat. Vasim is active in the Tablighi Jamaat and would prefer to wear his religious dress every day, but he believes that "if I wear my white clothes . . . people look at me as if I am an animal. They fear. They look at me . . . *don* or mafia, they think." At the office, he experiments with different clothes, sometimes coming in trousers, sometimes in religious dress.

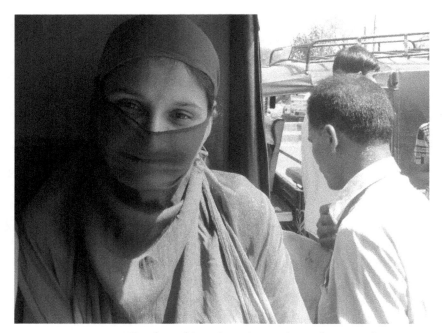

FIGURE 4.1. Resident of Anand traveling to the nearby town of Petlad in a shared autorickshaw, face covered with a dupatta to protect against dust on the road. (Photo by the author, 2012.)

THESE SCENES FROM a day of travel-along research demonstrate that urbanization and residential segregation have not erased the possibilities of maintaining economic and social links with people and places in the wider region of Charotar. For landed business families like these, members of an urbanized Muslim community in Anand, their occupations remain closely tied up with the surrounding region, and with various social networks. Their investments also symbolically reaffirm a link to the land itself, so that the everyday rural-urban exchanges of the landed business families can also be regarded as a concrete substantiation of Vohras belonging to the Charotar region.

For the service families, focused on education and white-collar employment, the relation with the village is not necessarily as important as it is for these business families. The social life of the service families I knew seemed to be focused on the town. Nevertheless, rural-urban connections exist in this group as well. When service families have relatives living in nearby villages, in some cases the town-based families offer a rural niece a foster home in their own house in Anand, so that relatives can participate in higher education despite their rural residency. These interactions generate a view of the town as a privileged space, and of the village as bereft of access to such privilege. This is different from the views in Vasim's family, where the rural arena is looked upon as a resource for potential profits. Thus, the views of the townspeople on their rural surroundings are affected by dynamics of occupation, property, and class, and there are differences between those with and without capital beyond the town.[3]

Getting Around Town

For middle-class Muslims who have established themselves as entrepreneurs and educated professionals in Anand, the town promises opportunity, self-realization, and a respectable social status. In a town that has become segregated along religious lines, however, the realization of these class aspirations is dependent on being mobile and getting around the town. The ability to be mobile, therefore, becomes an important line of differentiation alongside other markers of differentiation in the neighborhood. This is demonstrated by the case study of a middle-class Muslim family in Anand, whose lives are shaped by aspirations of class bonding (with the predominantly Hindu middle classes), as well as experiences of class distinction (within the Muslim-majority neighborhood). This is Zakiya's family, mentioned in the beginning of this chapter and in chapter 2 (during the festival of Uttarayan).

Siraj, Rakeem, and their four children moved to Anand in 2004 from the nearby town of Tarapur (an hour's drive from Anand). They are an example of a landowning Muslim family going through a process of urbanization, who have moved to Anand for education and to be closer to government offices (in this case, Anand's district court), while still holding onto assets in their village of origin. Their everyday practices straddle the rural-urban divide. Siraj is a notary lawyer with an office in Tarapur, where he also owns a house, and where one of his brothers is managing the family-owned agricultural lands. Since his arrival, Siraj had started up a second office in Anand. The office was turned over to his eldest son, Adam, after he graduated with a law degree. In 2017, Siraj returned to working full time in the village; his wife, Rakeem, joined him there a few days a week to manage their household while their son and daughter-in-law (who is also a lawyer) managed the office and household in Anand. On weekends, they were all together in Anand.

They are an example of a middle-class Muslim family who strongly emphasizes education. Education is important for anyone, Siraj says, but particularly for Muslims: "If you are good, people don't care about your religion." Many of his clients are Hindu, and they entrust him with handling their legal conflicts—he wants the same for his children. These considerations resemble those of Muslims elsewhere in India, who have invested in education to obtain not only employment but also respect (Jeffrey, Jeffery, and Jeffery 2008, 201), to highlight an achieved social status as "educated" over an ascribed social status as "Muslim" (Jeffrey, Jeffery, and Jeffery 2004).

The family also exemplifies a strong orientation toward middle-class Hindus. When the family showed me the wedding photo album of their son Adam and his wife, for example, they made sure I took note of the diversity of guests in my notebook, and especially that some of the guests were Hindus—a judge and several lawyers had come to congratulate the family and had joined in for a vegetarian dinner on the wedding grounds behind their house. Adam found this noteworthy, because normally "they [Hindus] don't feel comfortable coming to our area." Despite living in a segregated residential area, the members of this family actively maintain relationships with middle-class Hindus; moreover, they encourage the younger members of the family to develop such relations of their own. Education is one of the avenues through which such relations can be cultivated.

Getting Around for Education

To learn more about the mobility of middle-class Muslim life in a Hindu-majority town centered on education, I talked to teachers, and parents of students going to Anand's colleges and schools, as well as to the students themselves. What I learned was that higher education creates a link between the Muslim and Hindu parts of town. While public and political discussions about the education of Muslims in India tend to focus on madrassa education in Muslim-only environments,[4] I found that such Islamic schooling does not particularly appeal to middle-class Muslim families in Anand (see also Chatterjee 2017, 131).[5] This is partly because Islamic doctrine is so contested (as discussed above)—many prefer it be conducted after school hours, with selected private teachers. But it is also because education is considered a way of connecting to wider society, and of becoming familiar with the practices and spaces of the dominant groups in society. Going to a school with only other Muslims would defeat the purpose of obtaining crucial social and cultural capital through education. It is, however, hard to say anything general about the impact of these education experiences on Hindu-Muslim relations, as the students I have spoken to report experiencing both inclusion and exclusion.

From the perspective of the Muslim area, the educational map of the town can be divided into four zones. For higher education, the main site is Vallabh

Vidyanagar, with its many colleges and institutes—a Hindu-majority area. This space is dominated by the public Sardar Patel University, with many colleges and campus buildings, but it also contains many private colleges, which are mostly Hindu-dominated, and some Christian institutions.[6] Second, there are also schools and colleges in the urban center of Anand—closer to the Muslim area. Most of these are Hindu-majority spaces. While some of these are openly discriminatory toward Muslims, others accept diverse student populations. Third, most of the primary and secondary Christian schools are located in Gamdi. While they give preference to Christian students, the teachers indicate that nowadays the majority of their students are Muslims. Finally, a few schools started by Muslims are found within the Muslim area itself. Siraj is a trustee of one such school, but he would never have sent his own children there. It was started as an initiative to educate the children of the refugees who settled in Anand in 2002 and caters primarily to poor children without other options.

Siraj sent his own children to be educated in private English-medium schools and colleges of higher education, and thus all his children have commuted, for at least part of their lives, to Hindu-majority spaces. When I joined Siraj's youngest daughter, Zakiya, at college (in 2017), she talked about her college friends, who are predominantly Hindu, and she emphasized how she enjoyed spending time with these friends, in small eateries, parks, and ice-cream shops, where they hang out during study breaks—all located in "Hindu" spaces in and around Vallabh Vidyanagar. On the other hand, she mentioned that fellow students had said "bad things about us," that "Muslims are not good." She tried to ignore this: "I don't want to think about it too much."

In other families, student mobility sometimes causes anxiety over safety, as was explained by a grandfather who said he felt relieved every time his granddaughters returned from their classes in Vallabh Vidyanagar: "You never know when a riot will break out." When I asked Zakiya if she felt safe, she simply shrugged and said, "Sure, I feel safe in Vidyanagar; I go there all the time." Her mother Rakeem, not scared either, did take some precautions. After their Haj visit in 2012, Rakeem wore a *burqa* for a few months, in an effort to be a pious Muslim. At that time, however, she was also taking a course in English at the Sardar Patel University in Vidyanagar. During her trips to the university, she felt that everybody was looking at her *burqa* and became extremely self-conscious about standing out as a Muslim in a Hindu environment. As a consequence, she quickly abandoned the practice. Zakiya is also not recognizable as a Muslim from her dress. She goes to college in a *salwar kameez*, a common dress for women in her age group (irrespective of religion).

When Rakeem talked about abandoning the *burqa*, she did not seem annoyed or upset. She described it in a practical, matter-of-fact way, just as Shahinben had instructed me, matter-of-factly, never to bring meat into the university library of Vidyanagar. Another woman had told me that while I was in Vidyanagar, I should always introduce my research topic as "Charotar" (without immediately mentioning Muslims—such information could be shared later, once they had gotten to know me). With these instructions, they were, in effect, teaching me what they also teach their children: how to behave in Hindu-dominated spaces so that nobody would take offense. Potential obstacles can be prevented or overcome by prioritizing social roles—as classmates, colleagues, clients, or friends—rather than religious characteristics.

Anand's educational field is one of multiple sites in which Muslims are able to forge and sustain relations with Hindus. While I cannot give an exact answer about how interreligious relations have evolved in Anand,[7] my data suggest that relationships across religious boundaries are deemed important, and, moreover, that these middle-class Muslim families considered them to be a normal element of everyday life. Their everyday travels in the campus area of Vidyanagar indicate they habitually participate in the public life of the town beyond the Muslim area. The resulting Hindu-Muslim relations do not only produce potential social capital (e.g., in Siraj's work as a lawyer), but also hold great symbolic importance, in that they substantiate the perception of being part of an urbanized and educated Indian middle class shared by Muslims, Hindus, and Christians.

While moving into the Muslim area may in one way separate Muslims from Hindus, in another it enables them to access and make use of facilities in nearby Hindu spaces within the town, as students, consumers, and potentially as workers or businesspeople. The move contributes to making a Hindu-Muslim binary, but, when coupled with everyday mobility practices, still potentially enables the reworking of such prevalent categorizations along the lines of class.

Getting Around to Do Good

The literature about urban space in India has highlighted the efforts of middle-class groups to maintain their geographic and symbolic distance from the poor by withdrawing into gated communities and organizing the removal of the informal settlements of poorer residents ("slums") from their neighborhoods. In Indian city spaces, where different classes have often lived in close proximity to each other, this proximity now causes discomfort and anxiety among the urban middle classes, and they are closing their ranks vis-à-vis "slum dwellers" and "uneducated" members of society (Fernandes 2004), who are considered a nuisance

(Ghertner 2015) or negative role models (Nandy 1998). In India's Muslim areas, however, poorer and wealthier households live within close proximity to each other, grouped together only because of their imposed categorization as Muslim.

This proximity has been described in two contrasting ways. One description suggests that the proximity of poor people leads to considerable class anxiety for middle-class Muslim families. Middle-class Muslims in Kolkata, who live in exclusive enclaves with very little contact with the rest of the neighborhood, symbolically distance themselves from the less fortunate Muslims by expressing disdain (Chatterjee 2017, chap. 2). Such attitudes are quite similar to those of middle-classes Hindu families, who similarly feel pressure to constantly prove their class status (Dickey 2012; Säävälä 2001). Other observations point to an emerging cross-class solidarity between Muslims. In Ahmedabad, where wealthy and poor Muslims have settled in Muslim areas such as Juhapura after 2002, their proximity has prompted wealthy Muslims to organize and collect funds to build schools, hospitals, and other kinds of infrastructure in the neighborhood (Jaffrelot and Thomas 2012; also Turèl 2007). This has been described as a form of cross-class solidarity with the poorer residents of the neighborhood, through philanthropy and "upliftment."

In Anand, both mechanisms seem to operate simultaneously. While at times interlocutors would make it very clear that they would not, for example, visit the places I had been to the previous day, implicitly suggesting this would be below their standing, they were themselves involved in a variety of hierarchical networks with poorer as well as richer acquaintances. In Siraj and Rakeem's family, I had the chance to observe how such relationships between people of different social standing operate.

Siraj was a trustee of a small primary school.[8] The trust had been started shortly after the 2002 violence with the aim of providing education to Muslims, and the school had been built next to a refugee colony. The trustees were all Muslim men, mostly Vohra, and included two businessmen, two teachers, an office worker, a press reporter, and a politician. The trustees of the school would occasionally drive over to interact with the teachers, parents, and students. The teachers among them were the most active, but the others also showed up during special events such as school ceremonies, which the trustees were invited to attend as special guests. During these events, the trustees would sit on an elevated part of the grounds, visible to all students and parents, and make short speeches. They ceremoniously presented awards to students who had scored top marks, symbolically enacting their generosity and patronage. The principal of the school (a young woman) said that "our trustees have a plan," "they know what they are doing," and that they are good people who "take care of us." These ceremonial interactions espouse a moral idiom in which transactions between unequal actors are sanctioned, and provide a framework for well-to-do men such as Siraj to display their success while making a contribution to public life (see Piliavsky 2014, 13).

This is a small school, with classes up till the eighth standard. The school fees are low (₹300, in 2012), and the poorest pupils qualify for free education through a charity scheme funded by the trustees and other local donors. According to the books of the school, to which I was given access, 249 pupils (excluding the kindergarten class) were enrolled in the school in July 2011. Of the 249 pupils, 92 received free school tuition. In 2012, the school had grown considerably bigger, having 370 children, of which 150 received free admission. About the pupils who received charity, the principal explained: "They are so poor that they cannot afford a full school uniform. You see, their parents live over there . . . [pointing to a set of huts]. We give them a chance to study here."

On Independence Day in 2017, as Siraj was busy, his wife, Rakeem, took his place during the school's celebrations and sat on the stage as a trustee. I took some pictures of the ceremony and the school's surroundings. When she saw them that afternoon, her attention lingered on an image of the only road leading up to the school. In this part of town, the road was unpaved, muddy, and full of potholes—a striking contrast with the freshly painted school building. According to the residents there, rickshaw drivers rarely entered these bumpy streets unless they resided in the area themselves, or charged higher prices than normal. This impinged on the residents' ability to get to work, hospitals, and markets. Seeing pictures of the road goaded Rakeem to action. Her own housing society has a fine interior road, yet she used the term "we" when she exclaimed, on behalf of the residents nearby the school, "We are also taxpayers!" In a flash, she decided: "Let's go to Chinakaka." Chinakaka is the nickname of a local politician.

RAKEEM HAS HER own scooty. With me on the back, she drove it to Chinakaka's house. The street was paved in this part of the Muslim area. The house was big. Chinakaka is a BJP party worker. Being Muslim, he had run several times for elections as the BJP representative from the Muslim area, although he kept losing to Congress (the preferred party for most Muslims of Anand). When we entered the house, his wife offered us ice cream, and he showed us the promotional materials from his last election campaign, in which he had promised infrastructural improvements. Rakeem told me to show him my pictures of the road leading to the school, in support of her argument that a new road was required. Chinakaka responded, "It will take time. There are town planning schemes. At this moment, they are working on T.P. scheme eight or nine, and this area is planned for in T.P. scheme twelve. It will take years before town planning will arrive there." He further clarified why his hands were tied: "BJP is in power in Anand and everywhere in Gujarat. But in this neighborhood, everyone is voting Congress, so the BJP is not taking any effort to develop it."

Despite Chinakaka's lack of power and his inability to make any promises, Rakeem looked very content thereafter. On the way back home, she said, "I want to do good work for my community. I want to be an example in my community. This is why I started studying." When we arrived at her house, she told a neighboring family enthusiastically what we had done. In the future, she wants to "sit in a chair" in this school, or, in other words, to be a leader. This was precisely what she had done that day, by positioning herself as a mediator, a "broker" (Berenschot and Bagchi 2020), between the roadless housing societies surrounding the school and the politician.

Theories about middle-class India highlight the desire of middle-class groups to separate themselves symbolically and spatially from the poor. Indian Muslims tend to live in neighborhoods where people of different classes live close together. This residential proximity of wealthier and poorer Muslims can generate class anxiety, but also invites distinctive forms of cross-class solidarity through charitable endeavors. The situation in Anand shows how these two strategies are not diametrically opposed, as charitable work can itself also become a way of enacting and expressing class distinctions. The case of this school shows how such interactions with the local poor can be expressions of the moral value that "differences of rank do not prevent relations but promote intimacy between parties in distinct and complementary roles" (Piliavsky 2014, 30).

Fragile Futures and Transnational Aspirations

In 2020, Zakiya completed her Bachelor degree in electrical engineering. She was preparing to continue her studies abroad. She was taking English classes, obtained a driver's license, and asked around for advice about the best destination: the United Kingdom, Germany, Canada? Hearing about the difficulties of Indian students in the United Kingdom, aggravated as a result of the COVID-19 lockdown, by the end of the year she had made up her mind and was arranging fingerprints for a Canadian visa application. In 2021, her Canadian visa application was approved; her older brother Adam obtained a visa for the United Kingdom. The family was among the majority of Muslim families in the neighborhood, who had no previous personal connections with Indian diaspora networks, and who are now investing considerable resources in international migration.

Anand is a global town. On the Anand-Vidyanagar road and all around the Vidyanagar campus area, billboards advertise the services of visa agents to help students gain admission to foreign colleges. In 2015, we counted thirty-three visa consultancy agents, most of them in easily accessible locations such as shopping areas (Verstappen and Rutten 2015). The proliferation of such commercial services, catering to the masses, demonstrates there has been a shift in transnational migration patterns. While earlier migrants from central Gujarat migrated using family, caste, and village networks (as explained in chapter 3), at present, agents offer temporary work and student visas that make it easier for those without privileged migration networks to migrate as well.

Broader opportunities to migrate offer Anand's middle-class Muslim youth new hopes. Migration has been relatively limited among the Vohras of central Gujarat in comparison with, for example, the Patels of central Gujarat, or the Muslims of Gujarat's coastal regions. But in Anand, approximately a third of the families who participated in my household survey had transnational links, and many other families hoped to send their children overseas in the future. The migration aspirations of these middle-class Vohra families reveal some of their expectations for India's future.

Given the focus of my research on mobility, I have spent a considerable amount of time talking to local youth and their parents about their migration aspirations. By far the most recurrent narrative came down to anxiety about job scarcity: "there are no jobs." The lack of employment opportunities for educated youth is a nationwide problem, and has been widely discussed by economists of India, and also in Gujarat. While the neoliberal economic policies of the Gujarat government resulted in economic growth, this growth did not translate to economic welfare for the majority in Gujarat (Hirway, Shah, and Shah 2014; based on data over the period 2002–2012). The tax breaks and subsidies granted to the corporate business class attracted investors, but they did not produce what economists refer to as "decent jobs" (Unni and Naik 2012). Employment in the public sector declined, as did employment in industry and agriculture, and the remaining jobs in the service sector did not provide regular wages or social security.

This has caused significant tension in Anand. Many Muslim families in Anand live in good houses, own a scooty or motorbike, invest in education, and have middle-class aspirations and urban lifestyles. They, however, are also confronted with rising land, housing, and food prices, and worry about the next generation's capacity to be financially stable enough to find a job, marry, buy a house of their own, and provide for a future family. Discrepancies between current living standards and future prospects are widely discussed, even among relatively privileged self-employed families like Siraj's. Concerns over absent jobs are felt most acutely by the service families who have gained status and prosperity through education and secure employment, and who now see their children struggling to find even a low-paid temporary job. Within this group, given the increasing scarcity of secure jobs in a neoliberal economy, their currently comfortable middle-class status seems very fragile in light of the limited economic prospects for the next generation. One question these employed parents ask themselves is, "Will our children be able to keep up our lifestyle in the future?"

This lack of secure employment is one of the reasons why these middle-class families take out loans to send their children abroad. Shahinben's family is an example of a service family who is also one of the more transnationally connected families in the neighborhood, with two sons in Australia. Shahinben, a teacher in a government-aided Catholic school in Gamdi,[9] earned a salary of ₹40,000 ($812)[10] per month in 2011–2012. This was a very good salary by local standards (in comparison, a teacher in a privately funded primary school earned between ₹3,000 and ₹4,000). Therefore, even if her husband was selling samosas on the market, Shahinben was the main breadwinner of the household. Her government-funded employment, moreover, came with several social security benefits, such as a profitable pension to look forward to. Her retired father, who had worked for the government, received a pension of ₹70,000 ($1,422) per month—this meant, Shahinben said with a smile, that "he is very happy."

Shahinben was not so optimistic about the next generation, however. This is why she had taken loans to send her sons to Australia. She reasoned:

> We have two sons. Both are in Melbourne. When we sent my second son to Melbourne, people told us, "Why, you will be all alone! Don't do it!" But we did it anyway. My husband and I wanted him to stand on his own feet. He was not earning anything here. He and his wife both have a B.Ed. [Bachelor of Education degree] and a B.A. [Bachelor of Arts], but could not find a stable position in a government school. Both were working [as teachers] in private schools. Their salary was very low. Our youngest son was earning ₹1,500 [$30] per month as a teacher, and it was not even a secure job. His wife became a principal and received ₹3,500 [$71] per month. Financially, they were totally relying on me and my husband. We wanted him to be independent of us and make his own money. We paid a donation of three lakh [₹3,00,000/$6,093] to get him a job in a government school,

but even then, they only gave him a temporary contract. So, we thought it was better to take another loan and send him abroad.

We have taken soooo many loans in our life. When we sent my eldest son to Melbourne, for two to three months I lay awake at night; we had taken a loan for his visa, and at first, he couldn't find a job. But now they are OK over there, earning their own money. My eldest son has PR [permanent residence], so the younger one will surely get it also. We are paying off our last loan now and will never borrow money again.

Parents like Shahinben, who themselves have stable jobs and have invested a considerable part of their income in the education of their children, feel that the return on this investment is poor in India now that their educated children remain unemployed. Sending a child abroad is not easy either, because, besides the initial loan, several other costs had to be incurred, such as living expenses overseas in the first months, and the unexpected costs charged by local visa agents to extend the visa.

An additional hurdle that applies to Muslims is the risk of discrimination on the labor market. While the Gujarati job market is challenging for everybody, being Muslim does not improve one's chances. One father said that his sons went overseas "because of Modi." When I asked him what he meant by this, he replied that after the 2002 violence, many companies stopped hiring Muslims, and in some of them Muslims were fired. He himself had worked for twenty-one years as a clerk in a government office, earning approximately ₹20,000 per month ($406). His two eldest sons, however, both of whom held degrees, had been unable to find jobs. One left for South Africa, and the other moved to London. The youngest son, who does not have a degree and remained in Anand, is working in a local shop and earns around ₹3,000 ($61) per month, plus a variable commission of ₹2,000 ($41) on average per month (totaling ₹5,000, or $102). According to local standards, this is not enough to sustain a family.

A counterexample of a young Muslim man, who did obtain secure employment as a professor in a local college, did not generate more hope either. He said:

> When I applied for my job as a professor, none of the other applicants had higher marks than me. Otherwise I would never have got the position. Muslims can only get jobs on the basis of merit. If you have average marks, there are no chances. I didn't know anybody in the college, my family has no political contacts and not enough money to pay donations. Now that I am hired, I have not been paid the full salary according to government regulations. This is illegal but what can I do?

The story of mobility—and of mobility as a trademark of an urban middle-class lifestyle—is thus fraught with ambivalence and inequality. With mobility emerging as such a central value of middle-class life, the risk of stagnation has become a source of concern. Future research will need to pay special attention to these entwined experiences of mobility and stagnation, and how they are felt in different sections of segregated towns.

Conclusion

The everyday practices of Muslim middle-class families in the town show that Anand's segregation has been accompanied by the retention of connections, and in some cases even a subjective experience of enhanced mobility. This has implications for the study of residential segregation in India. It raises questions about how our understanding of segregation might change if we revisit it through a mobility lens. At the moment, various researchers are working to refine our understandings of segregation in India (e.g., Susewind 2017). Some of them have started to specifically challenge the hypothesis of "estrangement" that has been a central element in the ghettoization thesis (Gayer and Jaffrelot 2012), alongside perceptions of segregated Muslim neighborhoods as "open air prisons" (Shaban 2012b, 223). In the town of Bhuj in Kutch, for example, it is argued that the segregation of a Muslim neighborhood has been accompanied by the persistence of various heterogeneous networks (Ibrahim 2018, 123). Similarly, in the Muslim *mohalla* (neighborhood) of Zakir Nagar in Delhi, borders are permeable so that people come in and out "anywhere from several times a day to once a week to only a few a times a year, depending on the individual" (Kirmani 2013, 112). The case study of Anand adds a regional and transnational dimension to these demonstrations. It invites us to explore how segregated cities and towns are shaped by rural-urban and local-global linkages alongside intra-urban ones. And it invites further research into how residential segregation can be differentially experienced and navigated by people with different capacities to be mobile—for example, when the availability of roads, two-wheelers, or visa becomes a way of indexing the relative privilege and marginality of residents.

Conclusion

New Lives, New Concepts

How do people move on with their lives after an episode of violence? How, in the process, are spaces and societies remade? The concepts of center-making and reorientation can be used to answer this question. The sociological concepts of "ghetto" (applied to marginalized Muslim areas) and "suburb" (applied to middle-class residential areas), which are more commonly used in the literature on urban landscapes in India, resonate only partially with life in Anand's Muslim area. Instead, the Muslim area can be conceptualized as a center or a "hub". Of the concepts used in discussing the social-spatial consequences of violence, "reorientation" can be added to broaden the conversation about "displacement." In this way, the space for conversation about the position of Muslims in India and about comparable situations elsewhere in the world can be expanded.

Ghetto and Suburb

Two possible ways of characterizing a neighborhood that exists on the outskirts of a growing city, and to study the relation of this neighborhood with the rest of the city, are the lenses of the ghetto and the suburb. Both terms have had a rich history in discussions on urban transformation in India. In India, the term "ghettoization" (Gayer and Jaffrelot 2012) is used mainly to describe the displacement of Muslims to marginal spaces; "suburb" (Rao 2013), in contrast, describes distinctly middle-class residential areas on the outskirts of the town. Both terms have some application to explain and describe the formation of a Muslim area in Anand town. Over time, however, I came to recognize not only the value but also the limitations of using these terms. Both terms can be considered as viewpoints, or lenses, that offer relevant insights into the formation and consolidation of Anand's Muslim area. Neither of them, however, is sufficient in isolation.

Walls and *chowkidars* (guards) have been a part of South Asian cities long before the term "ghetto" entered the Indian vocabulary. South Asian cities have historically been organized in clusters to establish and consolidate social distinctions. The morphologies of this residential clustering are complex, involving aspects of race, caste, class, and religious identity, as well as regional and language

Conclusion 117

distinctions. Under colonial rule, for example, "white towns" were created (Marshall 2000) along with "hill stations," in which the colonial elites could enjoy the cool air of the mountains (Kenny 1995). In postcolonial India, strategies to create exclusive spaces for the privileged sections of society still shape residential spaces, but in different ways. For example, municipal governments now build gated communities with world-class amenities for a global corporate class, while demolishing slums and resettling slum dwellers to the outermost peripheries of the city (Goldman and Longhofer 2009). The urban middle class distances itself from the urban poor through gated communities (Falzon 2004), "nuisance talk" (Ghertner 2015) and, on social media, activism around cleaning the city (Doron 2016). The dynamics of caste exclusion, too, continue to shape these urban landscapes, with marginalized Hindu caste groups relegated to specific residential neighborhoods, because they face discrimination in other parts of the city (Banerjee and Mehta 2017).

In Indian newspapers and academic discussions, the term "ghettoization" is used to describe one particular mode of residential segregation, where Muslims are relegated either to the outskirts of the city or to the old inner city. Instances of ghettoization have been recorded in many parts of India, but the state of Gujarat has been discussed as a paradigmatic case due to the unprecedented spatial marginalization of Muslims in Ahmedabad (Gayer and Jaffrelot 2012; Jaffrelot and Thomas 2012). Scholars of India have found the framework of ghettoization useful in drawing attention to the spatial marginalization of Muslims as a consequence of the rise of anti-Muslim violence in India, and have proceeded to test its premises.

The Muslims of Anand show that seeking safety in numbers after violence occurs not only in Indian cities, but also in towns and villages. The anti-Muslim pogroms of 2002 in Gujarat were not confined to cities—mobs swept the countryside, attacking Muslim homes in village after village. In the Charotar region, Ode was the worst-affected village, while the town of Anand became a safety zone. The pogroms reached only some parts of Anand town, such as Vidyanagar, where Hindus were the majority. The mobs bypassed the area around the railway tracks, where some Muslim-majority housing societies already existed at the time. It was this safety zone, on the eastern outskirts of Anand, that refugees sought when their homes in the villages had been set aflame or when they feared they would be attacked. In the years thereafter, many more Muslims arrived in Anand from the nearby villages. The eastern outskirts of Anand, which consisted of agricultural and communal lands before, were developed into residential areas. In areas where Muslims moved in, Hindus and Christians moved out. Most residents moved only a few kilometers away; still, they remember this episode as a turning point in the town's history. Some call it a partition.

In this rural region, urbanization has been accompanied by the emergence of new spatial imaginaries, with "Hindu villages" and "Muslim villages" in the countryside, "Hindu areas" in the main urban centers of government and education, and a growing "Muslim area" in the urban and peri-urban outskirts of Anand town. Anand's municipal government is locally famous for its meticulous town-planning schemes, but town planning had not yet arrived in most parts of the Muslim areas ten years after the violence. In the period 2011–2012, I walked around a patchy landscape with new, freshly painted houses amid green patches, on (mostly) unpaved roads. When I returned in 2014 and 2017, new street lights had been added and more streets had been paved, yet others remained dirt roads. Residents understood the unevenness of infrastructural development as a result of the political constellation in the town: the municipal state authorities have been dominated by the BJP in this period, but most Muslims in Anand voted for the Indian National Congress party.

The development of these urban spaces was an outcome of political and social developments that involved the regrouping of people on the basis of their ascribed (religious) identities in response to violence. These are characteristics that define a "Muslim ghetto" (according to the analysis in Gayer and Jaffrelot 2012, 21–22). But the concept of the ghetto does not fully capture the themes and concerns that emerge in this site, for three reasons. First, the residents themselves do not use the term. Second, the negative connotations of the term do not resonate well with the residents' experiences. Both public and state narratives present the Muslim ghetto as a problematic space, either because it is perceived to be criminal and deviant (in Hindu majoritarian narratives), or because it is neglected, isolated, and deprived (in the critical narratives of activists and journalists). Scholars who use the term "Muslim ghetto" as an analytical tool also present it primarily in negative terms—as a symbol of marginalization. Third, and most important in my analysis, two key aspects of the definition of a Muslim ghetto do not describe Anand: the "estrangement" and the subjective "sense of closure" of these Muslim residents from the rest of the city.[1]

Rather than experiencing estrangement and closure, the Muslim residents of Anand consider their homes to be well connected to the rest of the town and the wider region. They feel that their residences in the town are better connected geographically than their former homes in the villages, because they have better access to road networks and public transport facilities. Anand has a railway station that connects them to nearby cities, and a vibrant bus station and shared rickshaw system that connects them to the surrounding region and other parts of the town. The area is close to institutes of higher education, various marketplaces, and government institutes and private offices that offer coveted white-collar jobs. These are some of the reasons why they consider their new residential area a privileged space, a "lucky space" that is better connected, more convenient, and more desirable than the village.

While moving to the Muslim area of Anand may, in one sense, separate them from the majority society of Hindus, in another sense, it enables Muslims to access the facilities in the Hindu-majority areas of the urban conglomerate as students, consumers, and potential workers or businesspeople. The setup of Anand enables them to move between these different spaces and social realms, thereby maintaining long-standing relations while also exploring new kinds of relations within and beyond their own neighborhoods. Thus, their residence in Anand has become a way of broadening their scope and seeking new ways to connect with the wider society dominated by Hindus. Paradoxically, it is by moving into a Muslim area that some Muslims seem to be able to reconfigure themselves as part of an urbanized and educated Indian middle class.

The Hindu areas of the town and the surrounding region are not no-go areas for Muslims; rather, these are important spaces of education, work and business, and consumption. Ventures into Hindu areas require some skills and knowledge, as shown in the cases of students or businessmen who skillfully adjust their attire and demeanor when they operate in such spaces. The businessman Vasim (in chapter 4), for example, carefully controls his self-presentation to be perceived as socially acceptable by his non-Muslim customers and partners. As Vasim explains, he learns these skills of building and maintaining relations from his more experienced father. These relations have long histories, and they remain important to economic and social life even in the present context of residential segregation.

Altogether, Anand's Muslim area does not fit in the existing classifications of estrangement and closure. The absence of language with which to capture my observations has led me to consider whether another notion (instead of the ghetto) is more suitable. The residents' feelings of being well connected and privileged in Anand suggest another label: the Indian suburb. This notion draws on Nikhil Rao's historical account of colonial Bombay (1898–1964). Rao describes the "suburb" in contrast to the "old city," which the colonial state authorities regarded as cramped, chaotic, and unruly. They constructed new residential spaces on the outskirts of the city, where traffic, people, and air could be better controlled (Rao 2013, 21–58). These spaces were intended to attract middle-class residents, but it was not the established urban middle classes of the inner city who relocated there. The people who moved into the suburb (from the 1920s onward) were aspiring middle classes from the rural south of India, attracted to the white-collar office jobs that were available in the city for educated individuals at that time. Over time, this new middle-class suburb also turned into a neighborhood with a distinctly South Indian identity (Rao 2013, 96).

There are obvious differences between colonial Bombay and contemporary Anand—for example, Bombay's suburbs consisted of apartments while most of Anand's middle-class families live in houses. Still, in several ways Rao's characterizations of a suburb do apply in Anand. Like other Indian suburbs, Anand's housing societies house middle-class residents with a history of rural-urban relocation and share the characteristic rhythm of life in a suburb—especially the daily commute to places of work, business, and studies in the commercial and office centers of the city. They also display an evolving social identity as spatial, ethnic (religious), and social-political communities. The middle-class Muslims of Anand see their neighborhood as one in which they can find safety as well as certain forms of modernity, enhanced social status, and improved religious propriety. In these ways, defining it as a suburb fits Anand's Muslim area very well. The spacious houses, the two-wheelers and cars parked around these houses, and the astronomic land prices—in comparison to the rest of the region—shape the experience of Anand's Muslim area as a relatively privileged space; the constant in-and outflow of visitors from America, England, and Australia further reinforce this idea of a Royal Plaza (the name of a local landmark building).

When one spends enough time on the rooftops and in the living rooms of this neighborhood, however, another story emerges. Worried parents start to talk about their troubled sons, who are frustrated that they cannot find a job, or about their daughters, who are educated but cannot find a spouse with a reliable income. It is the absence of decent employment that troubles the residents the most. Those with considerable economic and social capital run their own businesses, while those who are less privileged strategize to land government jobs or migrate overseas. This is what life looks like, not just for Muslims, but for many middle-class people in small-town India.

If the term "suburb" captures some aspects of life in Anand's Muslim area better than the term "ghetto," it is also, ultimately, not a satisfactory description. This is because the proliferation of separate residential areas is the product of a specific history of marginalization and exclusion of Muslims in India. This needs to be recognized and factored into the discussion. Thus, the middle-class

Muslim area of Anand does not neatly fit in with either of these categories, the ghetto or the suburb. In what terms, then, can we aptly describe it?

Hub

Anand's Muslim area has been described here as the headquarters of the regional Vohra community, as a new hometown for overseas Vohras, and also, jokingly, as a "Mecca" for Vohras. Its residents have described it as a new space that signifies upward socioeconomic mobility as well as enhanced geographic mobility and connectivity. Muslims in nearby villages and towns have described Anand's Muslim area as a place that they aspire to move to in the future. The fact that overseas Muslims have also bought property in the town has further reinforced this idea of Anand as a well-connected space onto which aspirations for better futures can be projected. For members of the Charotar Sunni Vohra community, Anand has also become one of few places in the world in which Vohras are a large, dominant community among Muslims.

When overseas Vohras in the United Kingdom and United States visit their home region, they see that their relatives have moved—some of their houses in the villages having been ransacked and abandoned, others having been sold or rented to others. The overseas Vohras have responded by following their relatives, or even actively encouraging them to move to Anand, playing a proactive role in helping refugees resettle in the town. Some have bought new houses in Anand themselves. Through their investments, business endeavors, and charitable projects, they provide local Muslims with support and simultaneously carve out a space of their own. In this way, a town in which they previously had little interest has become their new home in their region of origin. When they come to visit, they do not limit themselves to their houses in the Muslim area of Anand; on the contrary, they see their house as a convenient central location from which to maintain relations within the wider region. For those among them who continue to be involved in business affairs in Gujarat, their relationships with powerful Hindu friends remain a form of social capital that safeguards their access to various resources, including the ability to participate in the region's omnipresent land brokerage business.

The notion of the hub implies that residential segregation does not need to be accompanied by estrangement or a subjective sense of closure. It invites us, instead, to look at a space as being embedded in multiple networks. Both ghettoization and suburbanization analyses are usually contextualized within an urban studies framework; the geographic focus is the city, and the analysis itself is focused on the neighborhood. Broader networks, however, shape urban life in India to a great extent. The alternative notion of the hub makes it possible to understand an urban neighborhood as outward-looking and shaped by diverse, intersecting mobilities, connected with the rest of the city and its broader surroundings. It invites us to reconsider the false binary distinction between segregation and connection that is often implicit in discussions about residential segregation.

My observations in Anand's Muslim area align with other descriptions of small-town India as regional centers—as market towns, transport nodes, and as centers of networks of rural-urban exchange.[2] In Gujarat, historical and sociological descriptions of small towns have repeatedly evoked this imaginary of small-town connectivity, and towns have been described as being tightly interwoven with rural hinterlands through roadways and rivers, containing dynamic histories of economic and sociocultural exchange (Sheikh 2010; Spodek 1976; Tambs-Lyche 1997). These multiple, intersecting mobility patterns may thus be specific to small towns. Further research is required to compare these observations with other towns and metropolitan cities in India. Now that communal violence has shifted from attacks on Muslim homes to Muslims traveling in cars, and on buses and trains, it is even more necessary for scholars of Muslims in India to incorporate mobility as an analytical category and methodological challenge.

This requires an analytical shift in the scale of the research, to look at the spaces where Muslims live not only as a neighborhood-in-a-city, but also as a neighborhood-in-a-region and a neighborhood-in-a-transnational-network. The scales discussed in this book—the city, the region, the nation, and the transnational social field —have been conceptualized as different yet interconnected social networks of the residents. This multiscalar perspective has been developed through a multisited ethnographic research methodology, mobile yet still grounded in a locality, which entailed the mapping of the relations and the following of the flows that emanate from their neighborhood.

With regard to the power structures that affect people's opportunities, aspirations, and social relations, Anand's Muslim area is complex. Anand has been a prime location for growth, investment, district government offices, and education, and can be considered a central market and service town to its surrounding region; however, its Muslim area has been marginalized in the municipality's development schemes. My findings show that this marginalization is discussed but still most of the time ignored by the residents. It is also by and large ignored in the narratives of Vohras residing in the surrounding villages, when they speak of Anand as a site of aspiration, and by the overseas Vohras who speak of Anand as a new home or holiday destination. Their narratives do not exclude marginalization but invite us to also consider other possible interpretations.

While writing this book, I have grappled with the terminologies used in the existing debates about Muslims in Indian cities. Over the years, I have become increasingly concerned that the prevalent terms of the debate prohibit an understanding of on-the-ground realities; in fact, they might even be hindering us. By using the term "hub," I aim to make a fresh start, but this is not meant to be the end of the discussion; it is, rather, an entry point for further reconsideration of what the terms of the debate could be. This notion of a hub, like the ghetto and the suburb, can ultimately capture only certain aspects of life in Anand town. It generates a risk of its own: it bypasses—and thus, risks erasing—the memory of violence and displacement. This suits the self-perception of those who attempt every day to create a life on their own terms, and who do not wish to be defined by or reduced to the incidents of 2002. Documenting their perspective has been at the core of my effort in this research—to look at a Muslim area from the inside, based on the perspectives of those who participate in its making.[3]

Regional Orientations and Reorientations

The importance of regional identities is mentioned in existing research on Indian Muslims (e.g., Kirmani 2013), and especially in Gujarat, where Muslims have been represented as threats to the territorial integrity of the nation and the state, so that they are challenged to formulate alternative views of space and belonging (Ibrahim 2011). Vohras, too, present themselves as a Gujarati community—more specifically, a central Gujarati community—who also happen to be Muslim. Their story presents a challenge to prevalent interpretations of the Gujarati regional identity as one that excludes Muslims. It offers insights into the ways Muslims represent themselves beyond the Hindu-Muslim binary (Gottschalk 2000), and conceive of religious boundaries as only one aspect of a complex and multilayered constellation of identities, including location, class and occupation, *samaj* and marriage circle, gender, age, and regional identity (Kirmani 2008). It presents, moreover, new insights into how transnational identities in South Asia are regionally produced (Gardner 2001; Ballard 1990), and how pathways of rural-urban and transnational mobility become entwined in response to regional-level politics in migrant-sending regions (King and Skeldon 2010; Sheller and Urry 2016).

The notion of reorientation has been used here to capture the dynamism of the Vohras' regional orientations. The Vohra community identity is produced through narratives, practices, and networks that are passed onto a new generation of young Vohras by their parents and other elders of the community. These practices and relations have been spatially redirected as a result of the post-violence displacements and other developments described in this book, and a shift has occurred in the conceptualization of the regional community. A regional concept of dispersed yet entangled village groups—with a varied set of leaders and family homes in hundreds of villages in the Charotar tract—has been maintained, yet converges with a new regional concept, in which Anand becomes the center of this region and of the regional Vohra network. This reconceptualization of the region is shaped by spatial shifts in the post-violence landscape but also by new social and economic practices that are associated with the shift to the town.

The regional community of Charotar Sunni Vohras was first organized in the 1920s, and, during conferences organized between 1926 and 1940, issues of community unity, education, and marriage were discussed. The community organization lost traction after Partition, when the Vohras reorganized themselves independently on both sides of the India-Pakistan border, but meetings were again organized in Gujarat in the 1950s. One point of internal discussion and regulation was the ideal of endogamous marriage (to preserve unity within the community) and the system of marriage circles that existed informally and was formalized in the 1950s (Heitmeyer 2009a, 170). The Vohra marriage system categorizes the wealthier and less wealthy sections of the community in two related yet broadly endogamous marriage circles (Chaud and Arsad). Membership in a circle is defined by a family's village of origin, as each village is attributed a distinctive place within the marriage system.

This development of the Charotar Sunni Vohras as a regional community, with its marriage system linked to a specific subset of villages in the region, is in many ways analogous to the history of the Patidar caste (described by Pocock 1972, 1973). Patidars, too, have delineated hierarchically related marriage circles, in which every family is assigned a status on the basis of its home village. These marriage circles feature in descriptions of the Patidar caste as a central aspect of internal caste politics, as the boundaries and meanings of these circles are constantly being renegotiated (e.g., Rutten 1995; Tilche 2016). These analogies between Patidars and Vohras have been described in various resources (e.g., Heitmeyer 2009a; Mahammad 1954). They are also known to the Vohras themselves, who consider themselves as similar in practices and outlook to the Patidars, although they also observe differences—for example, in terms of the different treatment of hierarchy within the community. Vohras in Anand describe their regional community as one that is very similar to the locally dominant Hindu caste, yet distinctive: e.g., in promoting (Islamic) values such as equality in a caste-based society.

Despite the shared claims to local ancestry and rootedness in local villages, the relations Vohras and Patidars maintain with the designated villages have evolved differently: while Patels can claim dominance in most of "their" villages, Vohras were always a minority in most villages and, following their expulsion in 2002, have lost the claim to village space even further. In Anand, their regional orientation stands out as a recurrent theme in the Vohras' narratives, but becomes something that has to be actively cultivated after the post-violence ruptures of displacement, urbanization, and residential segregation. Among Vohras in Anand, regional orientation is marked through a shared lexicon of words (village names, and the recurrent use of the unifying term "Charotar," for example) and everyday practices that substantiate the sense of regional belonging as a lived experience. Businessmen maintain partnerships and friendly relations with a variety of their collaborators within and beyond the Vohra community. Vohras' patrilocal marriage practices reveal the active role women play as keepers of dispersed kinship networks, when they marry and move to the household of their husband while maintaining relations with their maternal kin, thus connecting dispersed families across the region.

When overseas Vohras visit their region of origin on vacation or during retirement, they participate in these dispersed networks as well. In this inland region of central Gujarat, with its long history of transnational mobility, migration has been caste-specific, and for a long time it has been mostly limited to the caste networks of the Patidars. As a result, Vohras migrated later than others and in fewer numbers, but those who did settle overseas are now well equipped to travel back and forth. They have the financial capacity to make investments and conduct business in their region of origin, and as these endeavors remain largely dependent on the networks and wayfinding capacities of their local relations, local and transnational pathways have become intricately entangled.

The local and overseas reproduction of these regional orientations is significant, given the prevalence of interpretations of regional identity that exclude Muslims from the Gujarati imagination. The story of a regional community, as it was told to me and is passed on to a next generation of Vohras, is told from a situation of rupture. The stories recognize this rupture by describing the Vohras as an urbanizing community with rural roots, which operates from a Muslim area and maintains social and economic relations beyond it. Mobility becomes a crucial aspect of this regional conceptualization, because it is in the constant mobility across the rural-urban continuum that people are able to reproduce, as well as reshape, their regional orientations.

The process of reorientation described here occurs both in India and transnationally, involving not only the local residents but also their overseas relatives who have migrated away from their region of origin, yet maintain connections with it. In India, there is a shift from being a rural to an urban community, with Anand emerging as a focal point for the regional community. Transnationally, there is a similar shift in the homeland anchoring of overseas Vohras toward the urban space of Anand, even as relations with other villages are maintained as well.

What, then, does this lens of reorientation offer? How may it enable us to look from the housing societies of Anand toward the wider world, where comparable processes occur? An anthropology of reorientation offers a people-oriented perspective of post-displacement transformation, and it invites us to think in the broadest possible sense about the social-spatial consequences of violence-induced, forced migration.[4] It allows us to examine how people find their way anew through shifting terrains, and how, through their adjustments, they themselves become part of producing a changing landscape. It enables us to study how people engage with a changing landscape, which they assist in coproducing, and, especially, how their carving out new pathways is paired with the reconceptualization of sociality—in this case, of a regional community. An anthropology of reorientation is an empirical and exploratory approach, in that it foregrounds the places, practices, and narratives that emerge as significant to the people being researched. It is also a translocal approach, since the "local" knowledge under study is common to the residents and their overseas acquaintances.

In Anand, reorientation has been an experience shared by differently positioned people—young and old; rural and urban; resident and nonresident; Muslim, Hindu, and Christian. It started with the displacement of some and the disorientation of many; this temporary but dramatic moment then turned into a gradual, long-term process of adjusting to a new situation. People's places of residence changed, their sense of direction changed, and a new locality emerged as a shared space of community-making and home-making. This reorientation process was influenced by complex constellations of power, including religious politics, class/caste dynamics, and rural-urban inequalities, as well as regional patterns of socioeconomic exchange that continue to influence the lives of Gujarati Muslims at home and abroad.

The second underlying aim of this book has been to explore how the violence and its aftermath of urbanization and residential segregation affected a range of people—both within the region and overseas—far wider than that of the direct perpetrators and victims. Other ethnographic work that has described the consequences of communal violence in Gujarat have focused on displacement (Lokhande 2015), reconstruction (Jasani 2008), community making (Ibrahim 2018), religious dynamism (Simpson 2006), politics (Simpson 2013), and the impacts on Muslims' relations with the state (Ibrahim 2008; Jasani 2011). My ethnography has described a range of social, spatial, and economic practices that I observed and have conceptualized jointly as a process of reorientation. I have incorporated but also looked beyond the vocabulary of violence, displacement, reconstruction, and the figure of the refugee. These terms remain important anchors in discussions on citizenship and rights, but can be complemented with explorations of a wider range of practices and narratives that reveal the long-term consequences of the pogroms as they unfold slowly, sometimes almost imperceptibly, and in combination with other factors.

It has taken me a long time to write this down. Finding the words has not been easy in a climate of polarized public debate. If the protests against the Citizenship (Amendment) Act in Delhi in 2019–2020 opened new opportunities for Indian Muslims to express themselves in terms different than the ones imposed on them, they also revealed that those doing so were regarded as dissenters and vulnerable for attacks. Books can make a contribution to extending the conversation, by revealing the diversity of perspectives that exists in India's cities, towns, and villages, and by broadening the language and frameworks through which we discuss them. I hope this book will be a source of information and encouragement for those who are concerned about the unfolding developments, and who wish to imagine a society in different terms.

APPENDIX: TABLES

TABLE A.1. Rural and urban population by religious community, Anand district, 2001–2011

	Hindus: total district population	Hindus: rural	Hindus: urban	Muslims: total district population	Muslims: rural	Muslim: urban
2001	1,616,127	1,228,924	387,203	199,263	102,688	96,575
2011	1,798,794	1,328,863	469,931	250,919	111,199	139,720

SOURCE: Census 2001 and 2011, Table C-01, State 24 (Gujarat).

TABLE A.2. Population by religious community, Anand town and urban outgrowth, 2001–2011

Anand (M+OG)*	Hindus	Muslims	Christians	Jains	Total persons
2001	118,355	25,099	9,963	1,972	156,050
2011	151,400	45,932	8,487	2,161	209,410

SOURCE: Census of India 2001 and 2011, table C-01. Buddhists, Sikhs, "other religions," and "religion not stated" each represent less than 1% of the total population.
* Town and outgrowth

TABLE A.3. Population by religious community, Gujarat and Anand, 2001

Place	Total population	Hindu	Muslim	Christian	Sikh	Buddhist	Jain	Other religions and persuasions	Religion not stated
Gujarat	50,671,017	45,143,074	4,592,854	284,092	45,587	17,829	525,305	28,698	33,578
Anand (district, total)	1,856,872	1,616,127	199,263	29,461	1,004	81	10,151	60	725
Anand (district, rural)	1,348,901	1,228,924	102,688	14,311	175	3	2,208	18	574
Anand (district, urban)	507,971	387,203	96,575	15,150	829	78	7,943	42	151
Anand (town and outgrowths M+OG)	156,050	118,355	25,099	9,963	579	18	1,972	15	49
Vallabh Vidyanagar (M)	29,378	28,026	628	346	86	6	261	8	17

SOURCE: Census 2001, Table C-0101, State 24 (Gujarat).

TABLE A.4. Population by religious community, Gujarat and Anand, 2011

Place	Total population	Hindu	Muslim	Christian	Sikh	Buddhist	Jain	Other religions and persuasions	Religion not stated
Gujarat	60,439,692	53,533,988	5,846,761	316,178	58,246	30,483	579,654	16,480	57,902
Anand (district, total)	2,092,745	1,798,794	250,919	29,789	1,524	267	8,591	142	2,719
Anand (district, rural)	1,457,758	1,328,863	111,199	14,197	291	116	1,453	72	1,567
Anand (district, urban)	634,987	469,931	139,720	15,592	1,233	151	7,138	70	1,152
Anand (town and out-growths, M+OG)	209,410	151,400	45,932	8,487	866	39	2,161	22	503
Vallabh Vidyanagar (M)	23,783	22,786	331	287	61	21	202	5	90
Gamdi (CT)	14,582	10,797	1,222	2,447	29	4	19	0	64

SOURCE: Census 2001, Table C-0101, State 24 (Gujarat).

TABLE A.5. Incidents of the 2002 riots reported in the *Times of India* for Anand district

Subdistrict	Town/village	Date of incident	Killed	Cause of incident, as reported in newspaper	Clash between police and attackers?	Clash between Hindus and Muslims?
Anand	Ode	March 1	27	Prev violence (communal)		Yes
	Anand/Vasad	March 2	3	Prev violence (communal)		Yes
	Anand	March 3		Prev violence (communal)		Yes
	Anand	March 27	1	Prev violence (communal)		Yes
	Adas	March 29		Protest against police action	Yes	Yes
Anklav	Umeta	March 30		Prev violence (communal)		Yes
Borsad	Borsad	March 24		Prev violence (communal)		Yes
	Borsad	April 3		Prev violence (communal)		Yes
	Borsad	April 8		Prev violence (communal)		Yes
	Borsad	September 16	2	Other (accident)		Yes
Khambhat	Khambhat	March 30		Prev violence (communal)	Yes	No
	Khambhat	March 30	1	Prev violence (communal)		Yes

Petlad	Petlad	March 2	1	Prev violence (communal)		Yes
	Petlad	March 30	3	Prev violence (communal)		Yes
	Petlad	July 12		Public ritual		Yes
	Petlad	December 15		Political elections		Yes
Sojitra	Sojitra	March 2	1	Prev violence (communal)		Yes
Umreth	Umreth	April 2	1	Prev violence (communal)		Yes
	Bhadran	March 24		Prev violence (communal)	Yes	No

SOURCE: *Times of India*. Courtesy Raheel Dhattiwala, who acquired a dataset of violent events mentioned in news reports in the *Times of India* (Dhattiwala 2013; 2019). Notes recorded in the dataset: March 1, Ode: "Using figures as on May 15, 2008, in TOI Ahmedabad"; March 2, Anand/Vasad: The incident is recorded as having occurred "near Vasad." Vasad is located 20 kilometers from Anand town; March 3, Anand: The incident is recorded as "mob violence in Akhbarpura"; March 27, Anand: The incident was recorded: "Two stabbed nr Gujarati chowk, dies on Mar 28 (rept mar 29)"; March 29, Adas: The incident was recorded: "Police attacked by mobs being prevented from attacking Adas."

TABLE A.6. Growth of Anand's total population since 1991

	Anand town*	Anand (town and outgrowths)**	Anand (urban agglomerate)***
1991	110,266	131,104	174,480
2001	130,685	156,050	218,486
2011	198,282	209,410	288,095

SOURCE: Census of India 1991, 2001, 2011.
*Anand town (M).
** Anand and outgrowths (M & OG), including Mogri and a part of Jitodiya (Census 2011).
*** Urban Agglomerate (UA). Included in Anand's urban conglomerate are Gamdi, part of Jitodiya, Karamsad, Mogri, Vallabh Vidyanagar, and Vithal Udyognagar (Census 2011).

TABLE A.7. Shop owners in Anand's central market area ("supermarket"), 2012

Classification of shop owners	Total	Subtotal
Muslim	65	
Vohra		48
Nadiadi Vohra		14
Other Muslims		3
Hindu	35	
Sindhi		22
Punjabi		13
Total respondents	100	100

SOURCE: This record was established by research assistant Sajid Vahora, in 2012, who did a survey of 100 shops on the ground floor of "supermarket," the central marketplace in Anand town.

TABLE A.8. Occupation of heads of household in "Majestic Housing Society," Anand, 2011–2012

Occupation	Heads of household
White collar *	6
Business **	6
Transport/driver	2
Engineer	2
Mechanic/electrician	2
Housewife	1
Unclear ***	2
Farmer	1
Total	22

SOURCE: Household survey Anand, 2011–2012. The table is based one of the housing societies included in Survey A, with the pseudonym "Majestic Housing Society." There were two "closed houses," where the residents were absent at the time of the survey, bringing the total number of houses in the society to 24.
* In the category "white collar" are included a tax officer, clerk, advocate, bank employee, teacher and professor.
** The category "business" is a common umbrella term, which was not further explained by most of the respondents. It includes owners of large corporations and small-scale entrepreneurs.
*** One stated only "retired"; the other, "working."

TABLE A.9. International migration in six housing societies in Anand

	Six housing societies	One selected housing society ("Majestic")
Total houses	147	24
Houses with a link to abroad:	42	10
Total residing families with a member abroad	36	8
Families with one or more children abroad	26	8
Closed houses; family (probably) abroad	4	2
Return migrant (temporary or permanent)	4	1

SOURCE: Survey A (conducted by the author and research assistants), in 147 houses in 6 housing societies in Anand town, 2011–2012.

TABLE A.10. Characteristics of survey participants in the United Kingdom and United States

	UK	USA
Total number of participants	**35**	**15**
Surname		
Vohra/Vahora/Vhora/Vora/Bora	34	15
Other	1	
Duration of stay		
5 years or fewer	9	1
6 to 10 years	2	4
11 years or more	21	9
Born in the UK/USA or arrived as a young child	3	1
Legal status		
Temporary visa	9	0
Citizenship or permanent residence ("indefinite leave to remain" in the UK)	24	12
Not discussed in the interview	2	3

SOURCE: In the UK: Survey B (conducted by the author), among Muslims from Charotar in the UK, 2012. In the USA: interviews recorded on video by the author during a social gathering, the Vohra Families Reunion, in 2015 and 2018.

LIST OF CHARACTERS

Some of the characters and place names in this book are pseudonyms, in order to preserve anonymity.

Vinod Bhatt (b. 1988). Resident of Anand. Student of rural management. Vinod's family lived in a residential quarter adjacent to Ismail Nagar. After 2002, they moved out of this quarter to a Hindu-majority housing society near Ganesh Chokdi in Anand.

Amrapali Merchant (1944–2014). Professor of Sociology at the Sardar Patel University in Anand.

Mr. Parmar (b. 1963). Teacher. Resident of a Christian housing society in Gamdi. After 2002, he and his nuclear family moved to the campus area of Vallabh Vidyanagar, while his elderly mother stayed in Gamdi.

Samir Vahora (b. 1975). Resident of Baltimore, previous resident of Nadiad, regular visitor of Anand. He migrated from Gujarat to the United States as a teenager, with his parents. In 2011, he started a transport company in Anand.

Shahinben Vahora (b. 1956). English teacher in a Catholic secondary school in Gamdi. Resident of Anand, who grew up and married in Anand. Her two sons moved to Australia, and she and her husband followed them there in 2012. They still live in Australia.

Siraj Vahora (b. 1966). From Tarapur; resident of Anand. Lawyer. Married to **Rakeem Vahora** (b. 1971), from Kheda: housewife and student of English. Their eldest son, **Adam** (b. 1992), is a lawyer, and their youngest daughter, **Zakiya** (b. 1999), is an engineering student.

Vasim Vahora (b. 1985). From Kanjari; resident of Anand. Lived as a student in London for two years; returned to Anand in 2011 to become a real estate broker, working beside his father in the family business.

Ahmad Vohra (b. 1966). From Boriavi, Gujarat; resident of London. Born in Gujarat, grew up in Mumbai, moved to the United Kingdom in 1973. Customs officer. Had been active in organizing social activities for Vohras in London. He was a regular visitor to both Mumbai and Anand, and bought a flat in Anand for these recurrent visits.

Faridaben Vohra (b. 1947). Lives with her joint family household, including **Farhan Vohra**, her twenty-two-year-old cousin, in a village in central Gujarat. They hope to move to Anand in the future, following the other Muslims of the village—when the time is ripe.

Ibrahim Vohra (b. 1975). A mechanical engineer who grew up in London. Married to **Salma Vohra** (b. 1976), who moved to the United Kingdom from a village in Gujarat after her marriage. Salma and Ibrahim reside in west London with their children.

Idris Vohra (b. 1974). From Anand. Resident of a town in west Sussex, United Kingdom. Grew up in Anand; moved to the UK in 1999. Taxi driver and factory worker in the United Kingdom; real estate broker and trader in Gujarat.

Yousuf Vohra (1946–2013). From Sunav; resident of London. Born in Gujarat; moved to the British colony of Tanganyika in 1951, and to the United Kingdom in 1965. Regular visitor of Anand.

GLOSSARY

Arsad marriage circle of sixty-eight villages in the Charotar Sunni Vohra *samaj*

Bajrang Dal Youth wing of the *VHP*, founded in 1984
bapu saint
BJP Bharata Janata Party (Indian People's Party); political party in India

closed house house in Anand with an absentee landowner
Charotar region in central Gujarat
Charotar Sunni Vohra *samaj* an endogamous community of Sunni Muslims in the Charotar region, not to be confused with the Baruchi Vohras (from the region of Baruch), Surti Vohras (from the Surat region), or Daudi Bohras (who are Shia)
Chaud marriage circle of fourteen villages in the Charotar Sunni Vohra *samaj*
Congress Party political party in India

dupatta shawl, commonly worn by women as part of a *salwar kameez* outfit

endogamy marriage within a group

ghetto term used in India to indicate marginalized residential areas inhabited by Muslims
ghettoization term used in India to indicate residential segregation along religious lines

haj pilgrimage to Mecca (pronounced *Makka*)
Hindutva term used to denote the ideology of Hindu nationalism, or Hindu majoritarianism
housing society common residential area in Anand, in which a group of house owners within a residential complex is legally registered as a cooperative
hypergamy marriage system in which a lower-status female is married to a higher-status male

land conversion legal procedure, during which the agricultural status of a plot of land is converted to a nonagricultural status

madrassa religious school or institute
majid mosque

majoritarianism a political ideology that asserts that a majority of the population is entitled to have primacy and power in society
maulana religious teacher

pir paternal home (of a married woman)

RSS an organization, founded in 1925, which organizes training to instill Hindutva values and discipline in participants

salwar kameez a clothing set of wide trousers and a long short
Sangh Parivar a group of organizations that promote the Hindutva ideology
samaj community
scooty light motorized two-wheeler
suburb term to denote an urban space with a distinctive middle-class identity
Sunni an umbrella category in Islam. In global discourse, "Sunni" is the opposite of "Shia" Islam, but in Anand more likely to be presented as part of a different opposition, between "Sunnis" (the followers of saints) and "Tablighis" (the followers of the Tablighi Jamaat)

Tablighi Jamaat Islamic reform movement
T.P. scheme Town Planning scheme

Vohra/Vahora/Vora/Bohra/Bora surname within the Charotar Sunni Vohra community
vatan home, place of origin, motherland (of a man)
VHP an organization, founded in 1964, with the aim of promoting Hinduism worldwide

ward locality that constitutes a voting unit during elections

NOTES

Preface

1. Professor Amrapali Merchant was a former vice chancellor of the Babasaheb Ambedkar Open University, honorary professor at the Gujarat National Law University (GNLU), and the president of the Gujarat Sociological Society. She unfortunately died on December 23, 2014.

2. Following an earlier research project (Rutten and Verstappen 2014) I had become acquainted with several young people in London, most of whom were Patels from villages or cities nearby Anand. When I conducted research in Anand in 2011–2012, some of them had returned to their parental home in Gujarat and we remained in contact.

3. Survey A (2011–2012) was conducted in six housing societies in Anand's Muslim area, within walking distance of each other. They were chosen because we had access to them through personal connections; we knew that at least one household in them had a relative abroad. Research assistant Minaz Pathan conducted most of the survey, with the help of Abedaben Vahora, Sajid Vahora, and Shifa Vahora. The response rate was high: in all except three houses a resident was available and willing to answer the survey questions. All six societies surveyed were occupied solely by Muslims and mainly by middle-class residents. I lived in one of these housing societies during 2011–2012. We conducted the survey in a seventh housing society, occupied mainly by Christians, but the findings of the seventh society are not addressed in this book.

4. During my initial visits to organizations, I was often accompanied by Asif Thakor, a social worker. He helped organize a stakeholders' event in 2012 to inform representatives of these organizations about the preliminary findings of my research.

5. I also organized a survey among Vohras in Australia, conducted by Abedaben Vahora in 2012. As I have not followed up on these links personally, however, the findings are not used here.

Introduction

1. These atrocities have been recorded in a range of reports; for example, "Compounding Injustice: The Government's Failure to Redress Massacres in Gujarat." *Human Rights Watch* 15 no. 3(C) (July 2003), http://www.hrw.org/reports/2003/india0703/Gujarat-07.htm.

2. Examples of scholarship on the segregation of Muslims in Ahmedabad include Bobbio 2015, chap. 6; Chaudhury 2007; Dhattiwala 2019; Ghassem-Fachandi 2008; Jasani 2008, 2010; Mahadevia 2007; and Rajagopal 2010. For related discussions based on studies of Indian Muslims at the national level or in other cities, see Ahmad 2009; Ahmed 2019; Basant and Sharif 2010; Mistry 1992; Punathil 2018; Shaban 2012a; and Susewind 2013.

3. According to Tommaso Bobbio (2015, chap. 6), the term "ghetto," like "slum," does have a place in the everyday language of citizens in Ahmedabad. I have not conducted research in Ahmedabad, but when I asked a Muslim resident of the so-called ghetto of Juhapura in Ahmedabad (who visited Anand in 2017) about the term, his response was confusion. He was a talkative man (in Gujarati), and very opinionated about the segregation of Muslims in Ahmedabad (considering it worse in Ahmedabad than in Anand), but he was unfamiliar with the word "ghetto." This chance observation raises an unanswered question as to which citizens use the term "ghetto" in Ahmedabad, and whose experiences its usage reflects.

4. In these interviews, residents also indicated that they deemed the word *mohalla* (used by Muslims of Zakir Nagar in Delhi; Kirmani 2013) inappropriate to describe Anand's Muslim area.

5. For research in towns and villages in the coastal region of Kutch—where the impact of the violence in 2002 coincided with the aftermath of the 2001 earthquake—see Farhana Ibrahim (2008) and Edward Simpson (2013). I build on these works, alongside Carolyn Heitmeyer's study of Vohras in a small town in central Gujarat (2009a), as comparative resources in this book.

6. For foundational discussions on transnationalism in migration studies, see Glick Schiller, Basch, and Blanc-Szanton 1992; Kivisto 2001; Levitt 2001; Portes 2001; and Vertovec 1999. For overview discussions on migration and development, see Bastia and Skeldon 2020; Faist, Fauser, and Kivisto 2011; and van Naerssen, Spaan, and Zoomers 2008. My approach of mapping practice and narratives of development from the perspective of overseas migrants and their acquaintances in the region of origin is inspired by ethnographically oriented work by Katy Gardner (2018) and David Mosse (2013), among others.

7. For discussions about the relations between migration and development specifically in South Asia, see Ballard 2003; Gardner 2001; Kapur 2010; Kurien 2002; Taylor, Singh, and Booth 2007; and Upadhya and Rutten 2012. These studies have explored how migration brings into being new axes of economic inequality in migrant-sending regions, or reinforces existing ones, and some have paired economic concerns with research into domains of cultural expression (e.g., Osella and Osella 2000, 2006) to reveal how migration is also paired with new dreams, styles, and social practices.

8. Part of the research for this book was conducted as a team member of the collaborative research project Provincial Globalisation, directed by Mario Rutten and Carol Upadhya. "ProGlo" was a five-year collaborative research programme of the Amsterdam Institute for Social Science Research (AISSR), University of Amsterdam, the Netherlands, and the National Institute of Advanced Studies (NIAS), Bangalore, India, funded by

the WOTRO Science for Global Development programme of the Netherlands Organisation for Scientific Research (NWO), the Netherlands, initiated in 2010. My direct colleagues were Sanam Roohi, Sulagna Mustafi, Leah Koskimaki, Puja Guha, and in Gujarat Amitah Shah and Amrapali Merchant.

9. The shifting meanings of "development" in India have been discussed by David Ludden (2005), Peter Sutoris (2016), and, in the context of "migration and development," by Caroline Osella and Filippo Osella (2006).

10. Claims of autochthony, which seek to establish the right to belong, have come to the fore in many parts of the world. The anthropologist Peter Geschiere (2009) calls this a flip side of globalization, which often results in fierce struggles over who may be included and who excluded.

11. My household survey among 147 middle-class Muslim households in Anand town (Survey A) indicated that 66 percent of the households were Vohra.

12. I describe the perspectives of Sunni Vohras only—Daudi Bohras in Anand were a very small group of an estimated twenty-five families in 2012, and I have not interviewed them. Daudi Bohras and Sunni Vohras have the same surname but constitute separate endogamous groups without interlinked kinship ties. From what I have seen in Anand, there is very little interaction between them.

13. For examples, see Hardiman 1981; Michaelson 1979; Pocock 1972; Rutten 1995; Rutten and Patel 2003; Tambs-Lyche 1980; Simpson and Kapadia 2010; and Tilche 2016.

14. See the film *Transnational Village Day* (2015), by Dakxin Bajrange, Mario Rutten, and Sanderien Verstappen, Noman Movies and University of Amsterdam.

15. See the *Profile of Internal Displacement: India* (2002) for a compilation of the information available in the Global IDP Database of the Norwegian Refugee Council, Geneva, page 44.

Chapter 1

1. To describe locally defined regions and distinguish them from officially defined ones, Willem van Schendel (1982) uses the term "microregions," which he borrowed from Peter Bertocci (1975, 351), who, in turn, was inspired by discussions among Bengal scholars. According to Bertocci, the term was first used in an unpublished paper by Ralph W. Nicholas.

2. The Gujarati script for the name of the community name is: ચરોતર સુન્ની વહોરા. There are different ways to transcribe the Gujarati word વહોરા into English. The spelling "Vahora" is more often used in Gujarat, the spelling "Vohra" is more often used overseas; "Vora" or "Vhora" are also found. The spelling "Bohra" seems to be the prevalent spelling in Karachi and is also used in some US families. The spelling is not considered a marker of distinction within the community, except that it can sometimes indicate one's residential base. The spelling "Vohra" is used in academic descriptions (Heitmeyer 2009b, 2011).

3. The association is also referred to as the "Sunni Vahora Young Men's Association," without the prefix "Charotar" (Vahora n.d., 78–100).

4. Although the year of publication is not stated, the date of the author's death is given: 22–10–1404 according to the Muslim calendar (July 22, 1984). The book was translated from Gujarati into English partly by Rashid Vohra in London and partly by Mayur Macwan and Monica Macwan in Anand for the purpose of this research.

5. The author explains that the name વહોરા ("Vohra," "Vahora," "Bohra") has been adopted in different contexts for different reasons. It is unclear whether these disparate groups are historically related to each other or merely share a name.

6. I collected seven copies of this pamphlet, which had been distributed by the association, dated between 2005 and 2011.

7. Charotar Sunni Vahora Makeriya Samaj, Gujarat, 1986, 1996, and 2006.

8. Dewataja Samajik Ane Shaikshanik Vikas Mandal, Gujarat, Anand, 2004.

9. Website of the Muslim Vohra Association of USA, accessed July 14, 2015. The website went offline afterward, while the association was working on a new website.

10. Among Patidars this system arose after the end of the nineteenth century and aimed to promote unity and equality in the caste. This was deemed an important way of diminishing the (hypergamous) practice of marrying a daughter into a higher-status family, which is often paired with colossal financial gifts (dowry) at the time of the marriage (Pocock 1972; Tilche and Simpson 2018).

11. Among Vohras in Anand, the interest in promoting equality within the Vohra community (as compared with the Patidars' strong focus on hierarchy) was attributed to ideals of equality in Islam. This interpretation is different from Carolyn Heitmeyer's argument that the Vohras' strong focus on equality is linked to their traditional occupation as traders, as different socioeconomic strata need to be kept together within the caste to secure property and cash flow in the community (2009a, 110).

12. There were very few Muslim families in the village; two of them were Vohra. Upon consideration of David Pocock's descriptions of the Vohras, Carolyn Heitmeyer (2009a, 75) notes that the Vohras he spoke about must have been Charotar Sunni Vohras, even though Pocock himself conflates the Vohras in the village with the urban-based Daudi Bohras. Pocock's brief description of the shopkeepers of the village does not include references to Muslims (1972, 53).

13. For an example of a website of an overseas Patidar community, see Charotaria Leuva Patidar Seva Samaj, http://www.clpss.org, or 14Gaam.com, https://www.14gaam.com/charotar-patel-patidar-samaj.htm.

14. See also our film *Transnational Village Day* (2015), by Dakxin Bajrange, Mario Rutten, and Sanderien Verstappen, Noman Movies and University of Amsterdam.

Chapter 2

1. A shortened version of this statement has been published in Verstappen and Rutten 2015, 243.

2. Census of India 2001, Population by Religious Community, C-0101-24-15-0004, Ode (M).

3. Basant Rawat. "23 Guilty in Gujarat Riot Case." *The Telegraph*, April 10, 2012.

4. For sections of the judgment on the Ode case, see Akanksha Jain, "Post Godhra Ode Massacre: Guj HC Upholds Conviction of 19 Accused, 14 Gets [sic] Life Term, 3 Acquitted [Read Judgment]," *Live Law*, May 13, 2018 (https://www.livelaw.in/post-godhra-ode-massacre-guj-hc-upholds-conviction-of-19-accused-14-gets-life-term-3-acquitted-read-judgment/). Insofar as I have been able to retrieve the names of the victims from available reports, they had the family name "Vohra."

5. Human Rights Watch 2002, 4. The Minister of State for Home Affairs, Sriprakash Jaiswal, estimated the post-Godhra fatalities at around one thousand: "790 Muslims, 254 Hindus Perished in Post-Godhra," *The Times of India*, May 11, 2005, https://timesofindia.indiatimes.com/india/790-Muslims-254-Hindus-perished-in-post-Godhra/articleshow/1106699.cms.

6. A research report on the long-term consequences for the displaced was published as part of a series of commemoration activities in Ahmedabad ten years after the 2002 violence (Janvikas 2012).

7. The director general of police, R. B. Sreekumar, stated before the Election Commission that 151 towns and 993 villages were affected, covering 154 out of 182 assembly constituencies in the state (Varadarajan 2002, 329).

8. "Gujarat 2002: The Truth in the Words of the Men Who Did It," *Tehelka*, November 3, 2007 (also see Laul 2018).

9. Sanjoy Majumder, "Narendra Modi 'allowed' Gujarat 2002 anti-Muslim riots," *BBC News*, April 22, 2011, https://www.bbc.com/news/world-south-asia-13170914. Modi has disputed that he would have given such orders: see Manas Dasgupta, "Never Asked Police to Allow Hindus to Vent Their Anger," *The Hindu*, February 24, 2012, https://www.thehindu.com/news/national/never-asked-police-to-allow-hindus-to-vent-their-anger/article2925341.ece.

10. For further analysis of the rise of Hindutva ideology in India and the organizations that are associated with its history, see Tarini Bedi (2016), Thomas Blom Hansen (1999), Paul Brass (2003), and Peter van der Veer (1994).

11. Speeches of Narendra Modi and other political leaders (recorded by documentary filmmaker Rakesh Sharma) indicate they denied the violence had occurred or trivialized it. See, for example, "Film-maker releases a dozen clips of controversial Modi speeches made just after Gujarat riots," *Scroll.in*, March 10, 2014, https://scroll.in/article/658119/film-maker-releases-a-dozen-clips-of-controversial-modi-speeches-made-just-after-gujarat-riots.

12. The meaning of the Zee TV interview statement has been contested, with some claiming that Modi was merely calling people to refrain from violence, as there should be "neither action nor reaction," and others focusing on his retaliatory tone, which was maintained in other speeches that also did not explicitly condemn retaliatory violence.

13. According to a (disputed) court ruling in 2011, the fire was started by Muslims. This event is said to have sparked the anger of Hindus, which escalated into three months of attacks on Muslims as "revenge." The image of the train appears in almost all newspaper articles, books, and reports on the subject as marking the beginning of the violence, and the word "Godhra" is often used to describe the entirety of the 2002 violence.

14. Quoted in Rowena Robinson (2005, 26) and Christophe Jaffrelot (2012, 82). (For further examples of statements by government actors, including prosecutors and police investigators, see Jaffrelot 2012, 81). Jaffrelot's analysis is based on primary reports from government institutions, NGOs, and newspaper articles, including Janyala Sreenivas (2003), "Justice? When P in VHP Stands for Prosecution," *Indian Express*, September 19.

15. This was a partial reduction, as many SIT members were drawn from local cadres. This decision was hailed by some as a victory for justice but criticized by others as a move toward acquittal, because the SIT concentrated on reaching verdicts in eight cases only.

16. Among the many newspaper articles that reported on the court proceedings was that of Basant Rawat (2012).

17. Some of the convicted people were residents of Ode. They belonged to the Patidar community. Some convicts escaped imprisonment by fleeing abroad. Natu and Rakesh Patel fled to the United States; Samir Patel was arrested in Gujarat but fled to the United Kingdom in 2009, while out on bail, and was again arrested in west London in 2016 to be sent to jail in Anand. Articles that give details about the convicts include "18 Get Life for Ode Killings," *The Indian Express*, April 13, 2012; and "Gujarat Riots Accused Nabbed in London," *Ahmedabad Mirror*, October 12, 2016.

18. The SIT stated that it could not find prosecutable evidence of his role in the 2002 violence. After an initial hearing, the courts did not press charges against Modi and sixty-three others due to the absence of prosecutable evidence. The BJP interpreted this as a "clean chit" for Modi, which freed him to run for national elections in 2014. In an interview with Reuters, Modi stated that he owes no explanation and is not accountable for the violence that occurred under his reign (Sruthi Gottipati and Annie Banerji, "Modi's 'Puppy' Remark Triggers New Controversy Over 2002 Riots," *Reuters*, July 12, 2013). For a critical comment, see Samat and Citizens for Justice and Peace (2013), "No Clean Chit for Mr. Modi." *Outlook*, July 15.

19. See Raheel Dhattiwala (2018), "'Blame It on the Mob': How Governments Shun the Responsibility of Judicial Redress.' *The Wire*, August 17.

20. For discussions on Hindu nationalism and communal violence in Gujarat, see Ward Berenschot (2011), Farhana Ibrahim (2008), Ornit Shani (2007), Edward Simpson (2013), Howard Spodek (2010), and Nikita Sud and Harald Tambs-Lyche (2011).

21. See, in particular, Ward Berenschot 2011; Jan Breman 2002, 2004; Raheel Dhattiwala 2019; Ornit Shani 2007; and Ashutosh Varshney 2002.

22. This number is derived from an interview with a resident of Anand who had been actively involved in organizing relief at the time.

23. In the village of Ode, according to one of the organizers, sixty-three houses were built through this initiative—sixty-two for Muslim families and one for a Hindu family whose house was damaged.

24. The housing societies were not built by the state, but by NGOs, community associations, and religious organizations. The Islamic Relief committee, which was one of the supporting NGOs in Anand, is said to have built 1,321 new homes and repaired an additional 4,946 damaged homes across Gujarat. See Habitat International Coalition (2014, 24).

25. Janvikas provided me with the specific data on Anand town, in addition to their published compiled report (2012). The local data show that 1,049 people resided in 205 houses in Anand's relief societies in 2012. Other relief societies for refugees in Anand district that were surveyed in the report are in Anklav, Sojitra, Tarapur, Borsad, Khanpur, Khambhat, and Hardgud.

26. I learned about these signs from residents of Anand, although when I looked for them in 2012, nobody could tell me their whereabouts. In the same village, a journalist reports, statues of "martyrs" were erected. These were statues of men who died while looting a Muslim house because other arsonists set fire to the house (Mander 2010, 64).

27. Nutan Nagar was constructed on the former premises of the Polson dairy. The Polson Diary was established in Anand in 1930 but, in 1946, in connection with the Independence movement, farmers set up the Amul Dairy Co-Operative, a milk producers' cooperative, to counter the low prices offered for their milk (https://en.wikipedia.org/wiki/Polson_%28brand%29).

28. For further details about the development of Anand as an educational hub, see Sanderien Verstappen and Mario Rutten (2015). We established the number of colleges in 2014 through internal documents provided by the Sardar Patel University, and online searches of educational institutes and their websites.

29. Sanjeevini Lokhande's analysis is based on interviews with BJP spokespersons and NGO workers, and on reports published by both government institutions and NGOs. An example of the "resettlement" (rather than refugee) framing is the Government of Gujarat's report "Status Report of the Displaced Families in Gujarat with Reference to NCM Delegation Visit on 15/10/2006," File RTI-102008-Information-18-A1, Social Justice and Empowerment Division, Sachivalay, Gandhinagar, August 2008 (in Lokhande 2015, 90).

30. For an online version of this history, see the "About" page of the website of St. Xavier's Catholic Church, Gamdi-Anand, https://www.xavierchurchanand.com/about.

31. The Census of India (2011) indicates the majority of the population of Gamdi is Hindu, with a sizeable Christian population of 17% (table A.04).

32. Historical conversion rate as at February 1, 2001, https://www.xe.com/currencytables/?from=INR&date=2010-02-01.

33. The name Vinod Bhatt is a pseudonym. After I had introduced my research at a meeting in Anand in 2017, Vinod (a B.A. student) came up to me and volunteered to share his experiences in an interview. He thought that it was important to also discuss the movement of Hindus within the town, not just that of Muslims.

34. Tommaso Bobbio 2015, chap. 6; Christophe Jaffrelot and Charlotte Thomas 2012; Rubina Jasani 2008; and Arvind Rajagopal 2010.

Chapter 3

1. The descriptions in this chapter are based on interviews with overseas Vohras in the United Kingdom (in 2012 and 2016) and the United States (in 2015 and 2018), as well as some travel-along research among these interlocutors when they returned to Gujarat

during my stays there. The most in-depth conversations were had with elderly and middle-aged men and women, who had lived overseas for several years and were British or US citizens, or permanent residents. I collected some additional data on Australia through a survey (carried out by a research assistant) among Muslims from the Charotar region, but I omitted these data from the book because I did not visit Australia myself.

2. For an analysis of these experiences of return, in comparison with the perspectives of overseas Patels, see Sanderien Verstappen and Mario Rutten (2015, 243–44).

3. Of these twenty-six families with children abroad, nineteen were recorded as being Vohra (the surname was not recorded in all households). Seventeen migrants were said to have had obtained permanent residency abroad.

4. Whereby "aliens who are the spouses and unmarried minor children of U.S. citizens and the parents of adult U.S. citizens" can apply for legal immigration, according to the Legal Immigration Preference System (Wassem 2009).

5. These estimates are based on interviews. During the 2015 Vohra Families Reunion in Delaware, 350 attendees were registered from Maryland, Connecticut, New Jersey, Pennsylvania, Illinois, and other states in the United States, and four from abroad (including myself). In conversations with me, various attendees suggested estimates of the number of Vohras in the United States and Canada.

6. Mumbai has long been an important destination for migration for Gujaratis in India, including the Vohras. As early as the 1930s, the Vohras of Charotar were organizing themselves as a community in the city. In the community directory produced by the Mumbai Charotar Sunni Vohra Society in 1999, 264 Vohra households were listed as residents of Mumbai. Some used the city as a stepping-stone to destinations farther away, such as the United Kingdom or the United States.

7. In an address list produced for internal usage in the UK Vohra Community Association (accessed in 2012), 114 Vohra households are listed.

8. These young people had made use of the opportunities for students to migrate to the United Kingdom, which had opened up as a result of the liberalization and internationalization of education. For further insights into the living conditions of youth from Gujarat who migrate to the United Kingdom on student visas, I refer to my film *Living Like a Common Man* (Verstappen, Rutten and Makay 2011) and related article (Rutten and Verstappen 2014). Post-Brexit, young people's interest in migration to the United Kingdom had initially dwindled, but in 2017–2018, the number of student visas and work permits granted to Indian nationals in the United Kingdom rose again (Bhattacharya 2019).

9. For an overview of research participants in the United Kingdom and United States, see table A.10. In London, I lived with a Vohra household for two months while conducting a survey (Survey B) among thirty-five Gujarati Muslims (almost all of them Vohras) living in the United Kingdom. Survey B contained closed and open questions that primarily focused on social and economic links of overseas Gujarati Muslim families with central Gujarat. The interviews took place in the homes of interlocutors in London, Leicester, Newcastle, Crawley, and Guildford. In the United States, I conducted interviews and recorded a film during a community event organized by the Vohra Association

of North America (previously the Muslim Vohra Association). The footage I recorded in 2015 and 2018 resulted in a film (*Everybody Needs a Tribe,* 2019) and informs the analysis in this book, with some quotations included in an anonymized form.

10. Elsewhere, I have written in more detail about the donations of overseas Gujarati Muslims to initiatives, specifically in the field of education for Muslims in central Gujarat (Verstappen 2018b).

11. Elsewhere I have written about this shift in more detail (Verstappen 2005, in Dutch).

12. Pieter Friedrich, "How India's Ruling Party Mobilizes Indian-Americans to Win Elections," *The Citizen*, April 8, 2019.

13. For discussions on religious nationalism in relation to overseas Indians, see Peter van der Veer (2002), Bidisha Biswas (2010), Prema Kurien (2003), and Ingrid Therwath (2012).

14. Elsewhere I have written about this in more detail (Verstappen 2018b).

15. This multilayered perception of the state was also observed among Gujarati Muslims in Ahmedabad by Rubina Jasani (2011).

16. Theodore Schleifer, "Donald Trump: 'I think Islam Hates Us,'" *CNN*, March 10, 2016 (https://www.cnn.com/2016/03/09/politics/donald-trump-islam-hates-us).

17. "Donald Trump says 'I love Hindu', Promises Closer Links to India if Elected," *The Telegraph*, October 16, 2016 (https://www.telegraph.co.uk/news/2016/10/16/donald-trump-promises-closer-links-to-india-if-elected/).

18. "Raveesh Kumar, official spokesperson of the Ministry of External Affairs in the Government of India, quoted in Sriram Lakshman (2019), "U.S. Report on Religious Freedom Notes Mob Attacks in India." *The Hindu*, June 22. For an earlier example, see Kallol Bhattacherjee (2016), "Religious Intolerance is 'Aberration', India tells the US." *The Hindu*, February 29."

19. My research has focused on the first generation. When I talked with members of the second generation, often briefly before or after the interviews with their parents, they shared experiences of discrimination in the British labor market or at school and suggested that Muslims around the world were under pressure.

20. Within assimilationist interpretations of integration, efforts to forge transnational relations with the homeland have often been regarded as a desire to separate oneself from the dominant society; however, transnational scholars argue that transnationalism can be an essential aspect of the integration process (for a discussion, see Cağlar 2006, 2–3; Kivisto 2001). Migration scholars have demonstrated that it is often the more established migrants—those who have lived abroad for a long time—who are most active in forging transnational networks (Portes, Haller, and Guarnizo 2002) and migrant associations (Portes, Escobar, and Radford 2007, 276). Moreover, in countries such as the United Kingdom, the integration of migrants into the dominant society has been linked to attempts to organize people as ethnic or religious groups (Baumann 2003, 46–47).

21. While migration policies have become stringent in the United Kingdom, short-term family visitor visas for a maximum duration of six months have remained accessible to families who can support their relatives for the duration of their stay.

22. Rangin Tripathy, "So far, OCI card holders have enjoyed benefits. With CAA, India has put a price on the scheme," *Scroll.in*, June 6, 2020.

23. Almeida, Albertina. 2020. "The CAA's Provision for Cancelling OCI Is Aimed at Punishing Dissenters." *The Wire*, April 25.

24. For a more detailed description and analysis of this case study, see Sanderien Verstappen (2017).

25. For further discussions on land and real estate investments, see, among others, C. Ramachandraiah (2016), Llerena Searle (2016), and Michael Levien (2018).

Chapter 4

1. This record was established by a research assistant who went around Anand town on a motorcycle in 2012 and asked about all the mosques he knew of. In addition to the mosques, two *dargahs* were counted. Shia mosques were not taken into account.

2. In a previous version of this case study, I had anonymized Vasim and called him "Javed." In 2017, I gave him the story I had written about our encounters, and he read it. He thought I had represented him well, and positively—more positively even than what he thought of himself—and asked me to use his real name (Vasim) in future publications.

3. Both men and women travel. Men more often do so for economically dispersed activities, and women do so more often to maintain relations with kin. For a further description of female mobility, see chapter 1.

4. For scholarship about madrassas in India, see Arshad Alam (2011), Usha Sanyal and Sumbul Farah (2018), Robert Hefner and Muhammad Zaman (2007), and Ebrahim Moosa (2015).

5. This is somewhat different from findings in Andhra Pradesh (Mustafi 2013) and Kerala (F. Osella and C. Osella 2009).

6. The association of education with religious groups is a social consequence of the privatization of educational institutes. Gujarat has a long tradition of private participation in education, driven by philanthropic and civil society motives. The privatization of education after the 2000s, however, increased the influence of private organizations in educational institutes. Simultaneously, private education turned into a money-making endeavor, with private institutes demanding high monthly fees and additional "donations" at the time of enrolment (Iyengar 2012). These developments have created a three-tier system, where the poor are dependent on poorly functioning government schools, the middle classes prefer private colleges, and the wealthy elites have monopolized exclusive forms of education in metropolitan cities. It is in the private colleges—which the children of middle-class families attend—that caste and community groups have become prominent organizers. This is clearly visible in Anand's educational landscape.

7. For a discussion of the difficulty of answering such questions, see Kirmani (2013, 134–35).

8. During 2011 and 2012, I frequently visited the school as part of my effort to get to know the neighborhood. This primary school, financed and organized by Muslims,

was one of the eight self-funded trusts in which I conducted interviews in Anand. The activities of these trusts included running primary schools, hospitals, and charitable initiatives to distribute allowances to poor, sick, or widowed Muslims.

9. Government-aided private schools are a form of public-private partnership in which the school management is left to private actors, in this case a Christian trust, while partial government support is provided. The salary of the teachers is fixed by the same regulations that govern public schools that are fully funded by the government.

10. The historical conversions rates used in this chapter are established on February 1, 2012.

Conclusion

1. Some of these conclusions have also been presented in my articles (Verstappen 2017, 2018a).

2. For previous discussions of small-town India, see, among others, Binod Agrawal (1971), Lauren Corwin (1977), F. M. Dahlberg (1974), Lalta Prasad (1985), and P. Rana and G. Krishan (1981).

3. The task of fact-checking and analyzing where stereotypes and biases come from have been taken up by many other scholars of Gujarat. My book has been a different kind of response, inspired by those in Anand who mostly ignore prevalent stereotypes and develop their own ways of understanding and discussing their daily problems.

4. Others have discussed the social and psychological processes through which people contemplate violence and violence-induced displacement (Appadurai 2006; Arendt 1962; Das 2007; Malkki 1992).

BIBLIOGRAPHY

Abu-Lughod, Lila. 1986. *Veiled Sentiments: Honor and Poetry in a Bedouin Society.* Berkeley: University of California Press.

Agrawal, Binod Chand. 1971. "Cultural Factors in Political Decision-Making: A Small Town Election in India." *Economic & Political Weekly* 6 (8): 495–502.

Ahmad, Irfan. 2009. *Islamism and Democracy in India: The Transformation of Jamaat-e-Islami.* Princeton: Princeton University Press.

Ahmed, Hilal. 2019. *Siyasi Muslims: A Story of Political Islams in India.* Gurgaon: Penguin India.

Alam, Arshad. 2011. *Inside a Madrasa: Knowledge, Power and Islamic Identity in India.* Delhi: Routledge.

Alexander, Claire, Joya Chatterji, and Annu Jalais. 2016. *The Bengal Diaspora: Rethinking Muslim Migration.* Oxford: Routledge.

Anderson, Benedict. 1998. "Long-Distance Nationalism." In *The Spectre of Comparisons: Nationalism, Southeast Asia and the World*, by Benedict Anderson, 58–74. London: Verso.

Appadurai, Arjun. 1996. *Modernity at Large: Cultural Dimensions of Globalization.* Minneapolis: University of Minnesota Press.

———. 2004. "The Capacity to Aspire: Culture and the Terms of Recognition." In *Culture and Public Action*, edited by Vijayendra Rao and Michael Walton, 59–84. Stanford: Stanford University Press.

———. 2006. *Fear of Small Numbers: An Essay on the Geography of Anger.* Durham: Duke University Press.

Arendt, Hannah. 1962. *Origins of Totalitarianism.* Cleveland: Meridian Books.

Axel, Brian Keith. 2002. "The Diasporic Imaginary." *Public Culture* 14 (2): 411–28.

Baas, Michiel. 2020. *Muscular India: Masculinity, Mobility, and the New Middle Class.* Chennai: Context.

Bal, Ellen, and Kathinka Sinha-Kerkhoff. 2005. "Muslims in Surinam and the Netherlands, and the Divided Homeland." *Journal of Muslim Minority Affairs* 25 (2): 193–217.

Ballard, Roger. 1990. "Migration and Kinship: The Differential Effect of Marriage Rules on the Processes of Punjabi Migration to Britain." In *South Asians Overseas: Migration and Ethnicity*, edited by C. Clarke, C. Peach, and S. Vertovec, 219–49. Cambridge: Cambridge University Press.

———. 2003. "A Case of Capital-Rich Under-Development: The Paradoxical Consequences of Successful Transnational Entrepreneurship from Mirpur." *Contributions to Indian Sociology* 37 (1–2): 25–57.

Banaji, Jairus, ed. 2013. *Fascism: Essays on Europe and India*. New Delhi: Three Essays Collective.

Banerjee, Dyotana, and Mona G. Mehta. 2017. "Caste and Capital in the Remaking of Ahmedabad." *Contemporary South Asia* 25 (2): 182–95.

Basant, Rakesh, and Abusaleh Sharif, eds. 2010. *Oxford Handbook of Muslims in India: Economic and Policy Perspectives*. New Delhi: Oxford University Press.

Basso, Keith H. 1996. *Wisdom Sits in Places: Landscape and Language among the Western Apache*. Albuquerque: University of New Mexico Press.

Bastia, Tanja, and Ronald Skeldon, eds. 2020. *Routledge Handbook of Migration and Development*. London: Routledge.

Baumann, G. 2003. *Contesting Culture: Discourses of Identity in Multi-Ethnic London*. Cambridge: Cambridge University Press.

Blank, Jonah. 2001. *Mullahs on the Mainframe: Islam and Modernity among the Daudi Bohras*. Chicago: University of Chicago Press.

Bedi, Tarini. 2016. *The Dashing Ladies of Shiv Sena: Political Matronage in Urbanizing India*. Albany, NY: SUNY Press.

Berenschot, Ward J. 2011. *Riot Politics: Hindu–Muslim Violence and the Indian State*. London: Hurst and Company.

Berenschot, Ward, and Sarthak Bagchi. 2020. "Comparing Brokers in India: Informal Networks and Access to Public Services in Bihar and Gujarat." *Journal of Contemporary Asia* 50 (3): 457–77.

Bertocci, Peter J. 1975. "Microregion, Market Area and Muslim Community in Rural Bangladesh." *Bangladesh Development Studies* 3 (3): 349–66.

Bhachu, Parminder. 1986. *Twice Migrants: East African Sikh Settlers in Britain*. London: Routledge.

Bhatt, Chetan. 2001. *Hindu Nationalism: Origins, Ideologies and Modern Myths*. Oxford: Berg.

Biswas, Bidisha. 2010. "Negotiating the Nation: Diaspora Contestations in the USA about Hindu Nationalism in India." *Nations and Nationalism* 16 (4): 696–714.

Bobbio, Tommaso. 2015. *Urbanisation, Citizenship and Conflict in India: Ahmedabad 1900–2000*. Oxon: Routledge.

Bourdieu, Pierre. 1986. "The Forms of Capital." In *Handbook of Theory and Research in the Sociology of Education,* edited by J. G. Richardson, 241–58. New York: Greenwood Press.

Brass, Paul. 2003. *The Production of Hindu–Muslim Violence in Contemporary India*. Seattle: University of Washington Press.

Breman, Jan. 2002. "Communal Upheaval as Resurgence of Social Darwinism." *Economic & Political Weekly* 37 (16): 1485–88.

———. 2004. *The Making and Unmaking of an Industrial Working Class: Sliding Down the Labour Hierarchy in Ahmedabad, India*. New Delhi: Oxford University Press.

Brubaker, Rogers. 2005. "The 'Diaspora' Diaspora." *Ethnic and Racial Studies* 28 (1): 1–19.
Cağlar, Ayse. 2006. "Hometown Associations, the Rescaling of State Spatiality and Migrant Grassroots Transnationalism." *Global Networks* 6 (1): 1–22.
Cağlar, Ayse, and Nina Glick Schiller. 2015. "A Multiscalar Perspective on Cities and Migration. A Comment on the Symposium." *Sociologica* 2: 1–9.
———. 2018. *Migrants and City-Making: Dispossession, Displacement, and Urban Regeneration*. Durham and London: Duke University Press.
Census of India. 1981. Office of the Registrar General and Census Commissioner, Ministry of Home Affairs, Government of India, New Delhi.
———. 1991. Office of the Registrar General and Census Commissioner, Ministry of Home Affairs, Government of India, New Delhi.
———. 2001. Office of the Registrar General and Census Commissioner, Ministry of Home Affairs, Government of India, New Delhi.
———. 2011. Office of the Registrar General and Census Commissioner, Ministry of Home Affairs, Government of India, New Delhi.
Chandrani, Yogesh Rasiklal. 2013. "Legacies of Colonial History: Region, Religion and Violence in Postcolonial Gujarat." PhD diss., Colombia University.
Chaturvedi, Vinayak. 2007. *Peasant Pasts: History and Memory in Western India*. Berkeley: University of California Press.
Chatterjee, Anasua. 2017. *Margins of Citizenship: Muslim Experiences in Urban India*. London: Routledge.
Chaudhury, Anasua Basu Ra. 2007. "Sabarmati: Creating a New Divide?" *Economic & Political Weekly* 42 (8): 697–703.
Clifford, James. 1994. "Diasporas." *Cultural Anthropology* 9 (3): 302–38.
Cohen, Anthony. P. 2000. *The Symbolic Construction of Community*. Hove: Psychology Press.
Cohen, Robin. 1996. "Diasporas and the Nation-State: From Victims to Challengers." *International Affairs* 72 (3): 507–20.
Cohn, Bernard S. 1987. "Regions Subjective and Objective: Their Relation to the Study of Modern Indian History and Society." In *An Anthropologist among the Historians and Other Essays*, edited by Bernhard Cohn, 1–17. Oxford: Oxford University Press.
Corwin, Lauren Anita. 1977. "The Rural Town: Minimal Urban Center." *Urban Anthropology* 6 (1): 23–43.
Cross, Jamie. 2014. *Dream Zones: Capitalism and Development in India*. London: Pluto Press.
Dahlberg, F. M. 1974. "The Provincial Town." *Urban Anthropology* 3 (2): 171–83.
Das, Veena. 2007. *Life and Worlds: Violence and the Descent into the Ordinary*. Berkeley: University of California Press.
de Certeau, Michel 1984. *The Practice of Everyday Life*. Translated by Steven Rendall. Berkeley: University of California Press.
Dekkers, Natascha, and Mario Rutten. 2018. "Reciprocity and Contestation: Diaspora Philanthropy in Central Gujarat." In *Provincial Globalization in India: Transregional*

Mobilities and Development Politics, edited by Carol Upadhya, Mario Rutten, and Leah Koskimaki, 24–45. Oxon: Routledge.

Deshpande, Satish. 1998. "Hegemonic Spatial Strategies: The Nation-Space and Hindu Communalism in Twentieth-Century India." *Public Culture* 10 (2): 249–83.

Dhattiwala, Raheel. 2013. *Hindu-Muslim Violence in Gujarat, 2002: Political Logic, Spatial Configuration, and Communal Cooperation*. PhD Thesis, University of Oxford.

———. 2017. "Mapping the Self: Challenges of Insider Research in a Riot-Affected City and Strategies to Improve Data Quality." *Contemporary South Asia* 25 (1): 7–22.

———. 2019. *Keeping the Peace: Spatial Differences in Hindu–Muslim Violence in Gujarat in 2002*. Cambridge: Cambridge University Press.

Dhattiwala, Raheel, and Michael Biggs. 2012. "The Political Logic of Ethnic Violence: The Anti-Muslim Pogrom in Gujarat, 2002." *Politics & Society* 40 (4): 483–516.

Dickey, Sara. 2012. "The Pleasures and Anxieties of Being in the Middle: Emerging Middle-Class Identities in Urban South India." *Modern Asian Studies* 46 (3): 559–99.

Doron, Assa. 2016. "Unclean, Unseen: Social Media, Civic Action and Urban Hygiene in India." *South Asia: Journal of South Asian Studies* 39 (4): 715–39.

Dumont, Louis. 1980. *Homo Hierarchicus: The Caste System and Its Implications*. Chicago: University of Chicago Press.

Elliot, Alice, Roger Norum, and Noel B. Salazar, eds. 2017. *Methodologies of Mobility: Ethnography and Experiment*. New York: Berghahn Books.

Engineer, Asghar Ali. 1989. *The Muslim Communities of Gujarat: An Exploratory Study of Bohras, Khojas, and Memons*. Delhi: Ajanta Publications.

Enthoven, Reginald Edward. 1920. *The Tribes and Castes of Bombay* (Vol. 1). Bombay: Government Central Press.

Evans-Pritchard, E. 1976. *Witchcraft, Oracles, and Magic among the Azande*. Oxford: Clarendon Press.

Faist, Thomas. 2008. "Migrants as Transnational Development Agents: An Inquiry into the Newest Round of the Migration-Development Nexus." *Population, Space and Place* 14 (1): 21–42.

Faist, Thomas, Margit Fauser, Peter Kivisto, eds. 2011. *The Migration–Development Nexus: A Transnational Perspective*. London: Palgrave Macmillan.

Falzon, Mark-Anthony. 2004. "Paragons of Lifestyle: Gated Communities and the Politics of Space in Bombay." *City & Society* 16 (2): 145–67.

Feld, Steven, and Keith H. Basso. 1996. *Senses of Place*. Santa Fe: School of American Research Press.

Fernandes, Leela. 2004. "The Politics of Forgetting: Class Politics, State Power and the Restructuring of Urban Space in India." *Urban Studies* 41 (12): 2415–30.

Féron, Élise, and Bruno Lefort. 2019. "Diasporas and Conflicts: Understanding the Nexus." *Diaspora Studies* 12 (1): 34–51.

Gardner, Katy. 2001. *Global Migrants, Local Lives: Travel and Transformation in Rural Bangladesh*. Oxford: Oxford University Press.

———. 2018. "'Our Own Poor': Transnational charity, development gifts, and the politics of suffering in Sylhet and the UK." *Modern Asian Studies* 52 (1): 163–85.
Gayer, Laurent, and Christophe Jaffrelot, eds. 2012. *Muslims in Indian Cities: Trajectories of Marginalisation*. Noida: HarperCollins.
Geertz, Clifford 1998. Deep Hanging Out. *New York Review of Books* 45 (16): 69–72.
Geschiere, Peter. 2009. *The Perils of Belonging: Autochthony, Citizenship, and Exclusion in Africa and Europe*. Chicago: University of Chicago Press.
Ghassem-Fachandi, Parvis. 2008. "Bridge over the Sabarmati: An Urban Journey into Violence and Back." *Journeys* 9 (1): 68–94.
———. 2010. "On the Political Use of Disgust in Gujarat." *South Asian History and Culture* 1 (4): 557–76.
———. 2012. *Pogrom in Gujarat: Hindu Nationalism and Anti-Muslim Violence in India*. Princeton: Princeton University Press.
Ghertner, Asher. 2015. *Rule by Aesthetics: World Class City Making in Delhi*. New York: Oxford University Press.
Gidwani, Vinay. 2008. *Capital Interrupted: Agrarian Development and the Politics of Work in India*. Minneapolis: University of Minnesota Press.
Gielis, R. 2009. "A Global Sense of Migrant Places: Towards a Place Perspective in the Study of Migrant Transnationalism." *Global Networks* 9 (2): 271–87.
Global IDP. 2002. *Profile of Internal Displacement: India* (2002). Geneva: Norwegian Refugee Council.
Glick Schiller, Nina. 2020. "Theorising Changing Conditions and Ongoing Silences." *Routledge Handbook of Migration and Development*, edited by Tanja Bastia and Ronald Skeldon, 32–42. London: Routledge.
Glick Schiller, Nina, Linda Basch, and Cristina Blanc-Szanton. 1992. "Transnationalism: A New Analytic Framework for Understanding Migration." *Annals of the New York Academy of Sciences* 645 (1): 1–24.
———. 1995. "From Immigrant to Transmigrant: Theorizing Transnational Migration." *Anthropological Quarterly* 68 (1): 48–63.
Goldman, Michael, and Wesley Longhofer. 2009. "Making World Cities." *Contexts* 8 (1): 32–36.
Gottschalk, Peter. 2000. *Beyond Hindu and Muslim: Multiple Identity in Narratives from Village India*. New York: Oxford University Press.
Guha, Puja and Biplab Dhak. 2013. *District-Level Survey of International Migration and Reverse Flows in Central Gujarat, India: Anand and Kheda*. Research Report 7 of the Provincial Globalisation Research Program. Bangalore and Amsterdam: National Institute of Advanced Studies and University of Amsterdam.
Gupta, Akhil, and James Ferguson. 1997. "Discipline and Practice: 'The Field' as Site, Method, and Location in Anthropology." In *Anthropological Locations: Boundaries and Grounds of a Field Science*, edited by Akhil Gupta and James Ferguson, 1–46. Berkeley: University of California Press.
Gupta, Dipankar. 2009. *The Caged Phoenix: Can India Fly?* India: Penguin Books.

Gupta, Radhika. 2015. "There Must Be Some Way Out of Here: Beyond a Spatial Conception of Muslim Ghettoization in Mumbai?" *Ethnography* 16 (3): 352–70.
de Haas, Hein. 2010. "Migration and Development: A Theoretical Perspective." *International Migration Review* 44 (1): 227–64.
Habitat International Coalition. 2014. "Acts of Commission, Acts of Omission. Housing and Land Rights and the Indian State: A Report to the United Nations Committee on Economic, Social and Cultural Rights." Habitat International Coalition, Housing and Land Rights Network.
Hannerz, Ulf. 2003. "Being There . . . and There . . . and There! Reflections on Multi-Site Ethnography." *Ethnography* 4 (2): 201–16.
Hansen, Thomas Blom. 1999. *The Saffron Wave: Democracy and Hindu Nationalism in Modern India*. Princeton: Princeton University Press.
———. 2019." Economies of Segregation." *Contemporary South Asia* 27 (2): 290–92.
Hardiman, David. 1981. *Peasant Nationalists of Gujarat: Kheda District 1917–1934*. Delhi: Oxford University Press.
Harney, Nicholas DeMaria. 2006. "The Politics of Urban Space: Modes of Place-Making by Italians in Toronto's Neighbourhoods." *Modern Italy* 11 (1): 25–42.
Hastrup, Kirsten. 2013. "Scales of Attention in Fieldwork: Global Connections and Local Concerns in the Arctic." *Ethnography* 14 (2): 145–64.
Heitmeyer, Carolyn. 2009a. "Identity and Difference in a Muslim Community in Central Gujarat, India, Following the 2002 Communal Violence." PhD diss., London School of Economics and Political Science.
———. 2009b. "'There Is Peace Here': Managing Communal Relations in a Town in Central Gujarat." *Journal of South Asian Development* 4 (1): 103–20.
———. 2011. "Religion as Practice, Religion as Identity: Sufi Dargahs in Contemporary Gujarat." *Journal of South Asian Studies* 34 (3): 485–503.
Hefner, Robert W. and Muhammad Qasim Zaman. 2007. *Schooling Islam: The Culture and Politics of Modern Muslim Education*. Princeton: Princeton University Press.
Hirway, Indira. 2012a. "Inclusive Growth under a Neo-Liberal Policy Framework." *Economic & Political Weekly* 47 (20): 64–72.
———. 2012b. "Is the Economic Growth in Gujarat Inclusive?" Paper presented at the seminar on understanding the growth story of Gujarat, Ahmedabad, May 7–8.
Hirway, Indira, Amita Shah, and Ghanshyam Shah. 2014. *Growth or Development: Which Way is Gujarat Going?* New Delhi: Oxford University Press.
Human Rights Watch. 2002. "'We Have No Orders to Save You': State Participation and Complicity in Communal Violence in Gujarat." *Human Rights Watch India* 14 (3C), April.
———. 2003. "Compounding Injustice: The Government's Failure to Redress Massacres in Gujarat." *Human Rights Watch* 15 (3C), July.
Ibrahim, Farhana. 2008. *Settlers, Saints and Sovereigns: An Ethnography of State Formation in Western India*. London: Routledge.
———. 2011. "Re-making a Region: Ritual Inversions and Border Transgressions in Kutch." *South Asia: Journal of South Asian Studies* 34 (3): 439–59.

———. 2018. "Wedding Videos and the City: Neighbourhood, Affect and Community in the Aftermaths of the Gujarat Earthquake of 2001." *South Asia: Journal of South Asian Studies* 41 (1): 121–36.

Inda, Jonathan Xavier, and Renato Rosaldo. 2008. *The Anthropology of Globalization: A Reader*. Malden, MA: Blackwell.

Ingold, Tim. 2005. *The Perception of the Environment: Essays in Livelihood, Dwelling and Skill*. London: Routledge.

Iyengar, Sudarshan. 2012. "Education in Gujarat: A Review." In *Growth or Development: Which Way is Gujarat Going?*, edited by Indira Hirway, Amita Shah, and Ghanshyam Shah, 477–516. New Delhi: Oxford University Press.

Jaffrelot, Christophe. 2012. "Gujarat 2002: What Justice for the Victims?: The Supreme Court, the SIT, the Police and the State Judiciary." *Economic & Political Weekly* 47 (8): 77–89.

Jaffrelot, Christophe, and Charlotte Thomas. 2012. "Facing Ghettoisation in 'Riot-City': Old Ahmedabad and Juhapura between Victimisation and Self-Help." In *Muslims in Indian Cities: Trajectories of Marginalisation*, edited by Laurent Gayer and Christophe Jaffrelot, 43–80. Noida, India: HarperCollins.

Jain, R. K. 1993. *Indian Communities Abroad: Themes and Literature*. New Delhi: Manohar.

Jamil, Ghazala. 2017. *Accumulation by Segregation: Muslim Localities in Delhi*. New Delhi: Oxford University Press.

———. 2019. "Addressing Silence through an Emancipatory Reading." *Contemporary South Asia* 27 (2): 300–303.

Janvikas. 2012. *Gujarat's Internally Displaced: Ten Years Later. The 2012 Survey of Gujarat's IDP Colonies*. Ahmedabad: Janvikas.

Jasani, Rubina. 2008. "Violence, Reconstruction and Islamic Reform: Stories from the Muslim 'Ghetto.'" *Modern Asian Studies* 42 (2–3): 431–56.

———. 2010. "A Potted History of Neighbours and Neighbourliness in Ahmedabad." In *The Idea of Gujarat: History, Ethnography and Text*, edited by Edward Simpson and Aparna Kapadia, 153–67. New Delhi: Orient Blackswan.

———. 2011. "A Game of Hide and Seek: Gendered Ethnographies of the Everyday State after Communal Violence in Ahmedabad, Western India." *Contemporary South Asia* 19 (3): 249–62.

Jeffrey, Craig. 2001. "'A Fist Is Stronger than Five Fingers': Caste and Dominance in Rural North India." *Transactions of the Institute of British Geographers* 26 (2): 217–36.

———. 2010. *Timepass: Youth, Class, and the Politics of Waiting in India*. Stanford: Stanford University Press.

Jeffrey, Craig, Patricia Jeffery, and Roger Jeffery. 2004. "'A Useless Thing!' or 'Nectar of the Gods?' The Cultural Production of Education and Young Men's Struggles for Respect in Liberalizing North India." *Annals of the Association of American Geographers* 94 (4): 961–81.

———. 2008. *Degrees without Freedom?: Education, Masculinities, and Unemployment in North India*. Stanford: Stanford University Press.

Kearney, M. 1995. "The Local and the Global: The Anthropology of Globalization and Transnationalism." *Annual Review of Anthropology* 24 (1): 547–65.

Kenny, Judith T. 1995. "Climate, Race, and Imperial Authority: The Symbolic Landscape of the British Hill Station in India." *Annals of the Association of American Geographers* 85 (4): 694–714.

King, Russell, and Ronald Skeldon. 2010. "'Mind the Gap!' Integrating Approaches to Internal and International Migration." *Journal of Ethnic and Migration Studies* 36 (10): 1619–46.

Kivisto, Peter. 2001. "Theorizing Transnational Immigration: A Critical Review of Current Efforts." *Ethnic and Racial Studies* 24 (4): 549–77.

Koch, Julia. 2017. "South Asian Muslim Women on the Move: Missionaries in South Africa." *South Asian Diaspora* 9 (2): 129–46.

Koinova, Maria. 2011. "Diasporas and Secessionist Conflicts: The Mobilization of the Armenian, Albanian and Chechen Diasporas." *Ethnic and Racial Studies* 34 (2): 333–56.

Kundu, Amitabh, and Lopamudra Ray Saraswati. 2012. "Migration and Exclusionary Urbanisation in India." *Economic & Political Weekly* 47 (26–27): 219–27.

Kurien, Prema A. 2002. *Kaleidoscopic Ethnicity: International Migration and the Reconstruction of Community Identities in India*. New Brunswick, NJ and London: Rutgers University Press.

———. 2003. "To Be or Not To Be South Asian: Contemporary Indian American Politics." *Journal of Asian American Studies* 6 (3): 261–88.

Laul, Revati. 2018. *The Anatomy of Hate*. Chennai: Context.

Levien, Michael. 2018. *Dispossession without Development: Land Grabs in Neoliberal India*. New York: Oxford University Press.

Levitt, Peggy. 2001. *The Transnational Villagers*. Berkeley: University of California Press.

Levitt, Peggy, and Deepak Lamba-Nieves. 2010. "Social Remittances Revisited." *Journal of Ethnic and Migration Studies* 37 (1): 1–22.

Levitt, Peggy, and Sanjeev Khagram. 2007. "Constructing Transnational Studies: Introduction." In *The Transnational Studies Reader: Intersections and Innovations*, edited by Sanjeev Khagram and Peggy Levitt, 1–15. London: Routledge.

Lokhande, Sanjeevini Badigar. 2015. *Communal Violence, Forced Migration and the State: Gujarat since 2002*. Delhi: Cambridge University Press.

Low, Setha. 2017. *Spatializing Culture: The Ethnography of Space and Place*. London: Routledge.

Ludden, David. 1994. "History Outside Civilization and the Mobility of South Asia." *South Asia* 17 (1): 1–23.

———. 2005. "Development Regimes in South Asia History and the Governance Conundrum." *Economic and Political Weekly* 40 (37): 4042–51.

Mahadevia, Darshini. 2007. "A City with Many Borders—Beyond Ghettoisation in Ahmedabad." In *Indian Cities in Transition*, edited by Annapurna Shaw, 341–89. Chennai: Orient Longman.

Mahammad, Master Karim. 1954. "Muslims in Charotar." In *Charotar Sarvasangra (1954)*, edited by Purushotam C. Shah and Chandrakandh F. Shah, 8–13. Nadiad, India: Parekh Kevdachand Kanjibhai and Sons.

Mander, Harsh. 2010. "Conflict and Suffering: Survivors of Carnages in 1984 and 2002." *Economic & Political Weekly* 45 (32): 57–65.

Marcus, George E. 1995. "Ethnography in/of the World System: The Emergence of Multi-Sited Ethnography." *Annual Review of Anthropology* 24 (1): 95–117.

Marcuse, Peter. 1997. "The Enclave, the Citadel, and the Ghetto: What Has Changed in the Post-Fordist City." *Urban Affairs Review* 33 (2): 228–64.

Marshall, P. J. 2000. "The White Town of Calcutta under the Rule of the East India Company." *Modern Asian Studies* 34 (2): 307–31.

Massey, Doreen. 1994. *Space, Place, and Gender*. Cambridge: Polity Press.

Mehta, Makrand. 2001. "Gujarati Business Communities in East African Diaspora: Major Historical Trends." *Economic & Political Weekly* 36 (20): 1738–47.

Mehta, Mona G. 2015. "Partisan Dreams, Fractured Homeland: Gujarati Diaspora Politics in America." In *Pluralism and Democracy in India: Debating the Hindu Right*, edited by W. Doniger and M. C. Nussbaum, 327–45. Oxford: Oxford University Press.

Merchant, Amrapali M. 1999. *Fruits of Perseverance and Hard Work: The Establishment of Vallabh Vidyanagar*. Vallabh Vidyanagar: Sardar Patel University.

Mosse, David. 2013. "The Anthropology of International Development." *Annual Review of Anthropology* 42: 227–46.

Kapur, D. 2010. *Diaspora, Development, and Democracy: The Domestic Impact of International Migration from India*. New Delhi: Oxford University Press.

Karve, Irawati. 1994. "The Kinship Map of India." In *Family, Kinship, and Marriage in India*, edited by Patricia Uberoi, 50–73. Delhi: Oxford University Press.

Kirmani, Nida. 2008. "Competing Constructions of 'Muslim-ness' in the South Delhi Neighborhood of Zakir Nagar." *Journal of Muslim Minority Affairs* 28 (3): 355–70.

———. 2013. *Questioning the Muslim Woman: Identity and Insecurity in an Urban Indian Locality*. New Delhi: Routledge.

Kumar, Megha. 2016. *Communalism and Sexual Violence in India: The Politics of Gender, Ethnicity, and Conflict*. London: I. B. Tauris.

Malkki, Liisa. 1992. "National Geographic: The Rooting of Peoples and the Territorialization of National Identity among Scholars and Refugees." *Cultural Anthropology* 7 (1): 24–44.

Michaelson, Maureen. 1979. "The Relevance of Caste among East African Gujaratis in Britain." *Journal of Ethnic and Migration Studies* 7 (3): 350–60.

Misra, Satish C. 1964. *Muslim Communities in Gujarat: Preliminary Studies in Their History and Social Organization*. London: Asia Publishing House.

Mistry, Malika B. 1992. "Muslims in India: A Demographic and Socio-economic Profile." *Journal of Muslim Minority Affairs* 25 (3): 399–422.

Moosa, Ebrahim. 2015. *What is a Madrasa?* Chapel Hill: University of North Carolina Press.

Mustafi, Sulagna. 2013. "Shaping of the 'Modern Islamic Woman' in Coastal Karnataka, India: Transnational Experiences and English Education amongst the Beary Muslim Community." Paper presented at the First Annual Muslim South Asia Graduate Research Conference at SOAS, London, October 28.

Nandy, Ashish. 1998. "Indian Popular Cinema as a Slum's Eye View of Politics." In *The Secret Politics of Our Desires: Innocence, Culpability, and Indian Popular Cinema*, edited by Ashish Nandy, 1–18. London: Palgrave Macmillan.

Orjuela, Camilla. 2008. "Distant Warriors, Distant Peace Workers? Multiple Diaspora Roles in Sri Lanka's Violent Conflict." *Global Networks* 8 (4): 436–52.

———. 2018. "Mobilising Diasporas for Justice. Opportunity Structures and the Presencing of a Violent Past." *Journal of Ethnic and Migration Studies* 44 (8): 1357–73.

Osella, Caroline, and Filippo Osella. 2006. "Once upon a Time in the West? Stories of Migration and Modernity from Kerala, South India." *Journal of the Royal Anthropological Institute* 12 (3): 569–88.

———. 2008. "Food, Memory, Community: Kerala as both 'Indian Ocean' Zone and as Agricultural Homeland." *South Asia: Journal of South Asian Studies* 31 (1): 170–98.

Osella, Filippo. 2014. "The (Im)morality of Mediation and Patronage in South India and the Gulf." In *Patronage as Politics in South Asia*, edited by Anastasia Piliavsky, 365–93. Cambridge: Cambridge University Press.

Osella, Filippo, and Caroline Osella. 2000. "Migration, Money and Masculinity in Kerala." *Journal of the Royal Anthropological Institute* 6 (1): 117–33.

———. 2008a. "Introduction: Islamic Reformism in South Asia." *Modern Asian Studies* 42 (2–3): 247–57.

———. 2008b. "Islamism and Social Reform in Kerala, South India." *Modern Asian Studies* 42 (2–3): 317–46.

———. 2009. "Muslim Entrepreneurs in Public Life between India and the Gulf: Making Good and Doing Good." *Journal of the Royal Anthropological Institute* 52 (S1): S202–21.

———. 2011. "Migration, Neoliberal Capitalism, and Islamic Reform in Kozhikode (Calicut), South India." *International Labor and Working-Class History* 79 (1): 140–60.

Pandey, Gyanendra. 1999. "Can a Muslim be an Indian?" *Comparative Studies in Society and History* 41 (4): 608–29.

———. 2001. *Remembering Partition*. Cambridge: Cambridge University Press.

Patel, Parvin J., and Mario Rutten. 1999. "Patels of Central Gujarat in Greater London." *Economic & Political Weekly* 34 (16–17): 952–54.

Patel, Sujata. 2006. "Urban Studies: An Exploration in Theories and Practices." In *Urban Studies*, edited by Sujata Patel and Kushal Deb, 1–38. New Delhi: Oxford University Press.

Piliavsky, Anastasia. 2014. *Patronage as Politics in South Asia*. Cambridge: Cambridge University Press.

Pink, Sarah. 2008. "An Urban Tour: The Sensory Sociality of Ethnographic Place-Making." *Ethnography* 9 (2): 175–96.
Pinney, Christopher. 1997. *Camera Indica: The Social Life of Indian Photographs*. London: Reaktion Books.
Pocock, David F. 1955. The Movement of Castes. *Man* 55 (6): 71–72.
———. 1972. *Kanbi and Patidar: A Study of the Patidar Community of Gujarat*. Oxford: Clarendon Press.
———. 1973. *Mind, Body and Wealth: A Study of Belief and Practice in an Indian Village*. Totowa, NJ: Rowman and Littlefield.
Portes, Alejandro. 2001. "Introduction: The Debates and Significance of Immigrant Transnationalism." *Global Networks* 1 (3): 181–94.
Portes, Alejandro, Cristina Escobar, and Alexandria Walton Radford. 2007. "Immigrant Transnational Organizations and Development: A Comparative Study." *International Migration Review* 41 (1): 242–81.
Portes, Alejandro, William J. Haller, and Luis Eduardo Guarnizo. 2002. "Transnational Entrepreneurs: An Alternative Form of Immigrant Economic Adaptation." *American Sociological Review* 67 (2): 278–98.
Pradhan, Basanta K., P. K. Roy, M. R. Saluja, and Shanta Venkatram. 2000. "Rural-Urban Disparities: Income Distribution, Expenditure Pattern and Social Sector." *Economic and Political Weekly* 35 (28–29): 2527–39.
Prasad, Lalta. 1985. *The Growth of a Small Town: A Sociological Study of Ballia, U.P.* New Delhi: Naurang Rai.
Punathil, Salah. 2016. "From Ethnic Enclave to Ghetto: Violence and Identity among Muslims in South Kerala." *Contributions to Indian Sociology* 50 (2): 187–213.
———. 2018. *Interrogating Communalism: Violence, Citizenship, and Minorities in South India*. London: Routledge.
Rajagopal, Arvind. 2010. "Special Political Zone: Urban Planning, Spatial Segregation and the Infrastructure of Violence in Ahmedabad." *South Asian History and Culture* 1 (4): 529–56.
Rajyagor, S. B. 1977. *Gazetteer State Gazetteers, Kheda District*. Ahmedabad: Government of Gujarat.
Ramachandraiah, C. 2016. "Making of Amaravati: A Landscape of Speculation and Intimidation." *Economic & Political Weekly* 51 (17): 68–75.
Rana, P., and G. Krishan. 1981. "Growth of Medium Sized Towns in India." *GeoJournal* 5 (1): 33–39.
Rao, Nikhil. 2013. *House, But No Garden. Apartment Living in Bombay's Suburbs*. Minneapolis: University of Minnesota Press.
Ring, Laura. 2006. *Zenana: Everyday Peace in a Karachi Apartment Building*. Bloomington: Indiana University Press.
Risley, H. H. 1891. *The Tribes and Castes of Bengal*. Calcutta. Quoted in Pinney 1997, 62–63.

Robinson, Rowena. 2005. *Tremors of Violence: Muslim Survivors of Ethnic Strife in Western India*. New Delhi: Sage.

Rodman, Margaret C. 2003. "Empowering Place: Multilocality and Multivocality." In *The Anthropology of Space and Place. Locating Culture*, edited by Setha M. Low and Denise Lawrence-Zúñiga, 204–223. Malden, MA: Blackwell.

Roohi, Sanam. 2016. "Giving back: Diaspora philanthropy and the transnationalisation of caste in Guntur (India)." PhD diss., Amsterdam Institute for Social Science Research (AISSR), University of Amsterdam.

Rutten, Mario. 1995. *Farms and Factories: Social Profile of Large Farmers and Rural Industrialists in West India*. Delhi: Oxford University Press.

———. 2007. *"Leuke Vakantie Gehad?" Verhalen over Antropologisch Veldwerk*. Amsterdam: Aksant.

Rutten, Mario, and Pravin J. Patel. 2003. "Indian Migrants in Britain. Mirror Image of Social Linkages between Gujarat and London." *Asia Europe Journal* 1 (3): 403–17.

———. 2004. "Family Linkages between India and Britain: Views from Gujarat and London." In *Asia in Europe, Europe in Asia*, edited by Srilata Ravi, Beng-Lan Goh, and Mario Rutten, 242–66. Singapore: Institute of Southeast Asian Studies and International Institute for Asian Studies.

Rutten, Mario, and Sanderien Verstappen. 2014. "Middling Migration: Contradictory Mobility Experiences of Indian Youth in London." *Journal of Ethnic and Migration Studies* 40 (8): 1217–35.

Säävälä, Minna. 2001. "Low Caste but Middle-Class: Some Religious Strategies for Middle-Class Identification in Hyderabad." *Contributions to Indian Sociology* 35 (3): 293–318.

Sachar, Rajindar, Saiyid Hamid, T. K. Oommen, M. A. Basith, Rakesh Basant, Akhtar Majeed, and Abusaleh Shariff. 2006. *Social, Economic and Educational Status of the Muslim Community of India*. New Delhi: Prime Minister's High Level Committee, Cabinet Secretariat, Government of India.

Safran, William. 1991. "Diasporas in Modern Societies: Myths of Homeland and Return." *Diaspora* 1 (1): 83–99.

Salazar, Noel B. 2017. "Key Figures of Mobility: An Introduction." *Social Anthropology* 25 (1): 5–12.

Sanyal, Usha, and Sumbul Farah. 2018. "Discipline and Nurture: Living in a Girls' Madrasa, Living in Community." *Modern Asian Studies* 53 (2): 411–50.

Sassen, Saskia. 2001. *The Global City: New York, London, Tokyo*. Princeton: Princeton University Press.

Scrase, Timothy J., Mario Rutten, Ruchira Ganguly-Scrase, and Trent Brown. 2015. "Beyond the Metropolis—Regional Globalisation and Town Development in India: An Introduction." *South Asia: Journal of South Asian Studies* 38 (2): 216–29.

Searle, Llerena Guiu. 2016. *Landscapes of Accumulation: Real Estate and the Neoliberal Imagination in Contemporary India*. Chicago: University of Chicago Press.

Shaban, Abdul, ed. 2012a. *Lives of Muslims in India: Politics, Exclusion and Violence*. New Delhi: Routledge.

Shaban, Abdul. 2012b. "Ethnic Politics, Muslims and Space in Contemporary Mumbai." In *Lives of Muslims in India: Politics, Exclusion and Violence*, edited by Abdul Shaban, 208–25. New Delhi: Routledge.

Shah, Ghanshyam. 1998. "The BJP's Riddle in Gujarat: Caste, Factionalism and the Hindutva." In *The BJP and the Compulsions of Politics in India*, edited by Christophe Jaffrelot, 243–66. Delhi: Oxford University Press.

Shah, Purushotam C., and Chandrakandh F. Shah. 1954. *Charotar Sarvasangra*. Nadiad, India: Parekh Kevdachand Kanjibhai and Sons.

Shani, Ornit. 2007. *Communalism, Caste and Hindu Nationalism: The Violence in Gujarat*. Cambridge: Cambridge University Press.

Sheikh, Samira. 2010. *Forging a Region: Sultans, Traders, and Pilgrims in Gujarat, 1200–1500*. Oxford: Oxford University Press.

Sheller, Mimi, and John Urry. 2016. "The New Mobilities Paradigm." *Environment and Planning A: Economy and Space* 38 (2): 207–26.

Simpson, Edward. 2003. "Migration and Islamic Reform in a Port Town of Western India." *Contributions to Indian Sociology* 37 (1–2): 83–108.

———. 2006. *Muslim Society and the Western Indian Ocean: The Seafarers of Kachchh*. Oxford: Routledge.

———. 2010a. "Introduction: The Parable of the Jakhs." In *The Idea of Gujarat: History, Ethnography and Text*, edited by Edward Simpson and Aparna Kapadia, 1–19. Hyderabad: Orient Blackswan.

———. 2010b. "Making Sense of the History of Kutch." In *The Idea of Gujarat: History, Ethnography, and Text*, edited by Edward Simpson and Aparna Kapadia, 66–83. Hyderabad: Orient Blackswan.

———. 2013. *The Political Biography of an Earthquake: Aftermath and Amnesia in Gujarat, India*. London: Hurst.

Simpson, Edward, and Aparna Kapadia. 2010. *The Idea of Gujarat: History, Ethnography and Text*. Hyderabad: Orient Blackswan.

Simpson, Edward, and Kai Kresse. 2007. *Struggling with History: Islam and Cosmopolitanism in the Western Indian Ocean*. London: Hurst.

Simpson, Edward, Alice Tilche, Tommaso Sbriccoli, and Patricia Jeffery. 2018. "A Brief History of Incivility in Rural Postcolonial India: Caste, Religion, and Anthropology." *Comparative Studies in Society and History* 60 (1): 58–89.

Skinner, G. William. 1964. "Marketing and Social Structure in Rural China: Part I." *Journal of Asian Studies* 24 (1): 3–43.

Spodek, Howard. 1972. "'Injustice to Saurashtra': A Case Study of Regional Tensions and Harmonies in India." *Asian Survey*, 12 (5): 416–28.

———. 1976. *Urban–Rural Integration in Regional Development: A Case Study of Saurashtra, India, 1800–1960*. Chicago: University of Chicago Press.

———. 2010. "In the Hindutva Laboratory: Pogroms and Politics in Gujarat, 2002." *Modern Asian Studies* 44 (2): 349–99.

———. 2013. "Local Meets Global: Establishing New Perspectives in Urban History—Lessons from Ahmedabad." *Journal of Urban History* 39 (4): 749–66.

Srivastava, Sanjay. 2015. *Entangled Urbanism: Slum, Gated Community, and Shopping Mall in Delhi and Gurgaon.* New Delhi: Oxford.
Sud, Nikita. 2014. "The Men in the Middle: A Missing Dimension in Global Land Deals." *Journal of Peasant Studies* 41 (4): 593–612.
Sud, Nikita, and Harald Tambs-Lyche. 2011. "Introduction: Religion in the Making of a Region." *South Asia: Journal of South Asian Studies* 34 (3): 319–32.
Susewind, Raphael. 2013. *Being Muslim and Working for Peace.* Delhi: Sage.
———. 2015. "Spatial Segregation, Real Estate Markets and the Political Economy of Corruption in Lucknow, India." *Journal of South Asian Development* 10 (3): 267–91.
———. 2017. "Muslims in Indian Cities: Degrees of Segregation and the Elusive Ghetto." *Environment and Planning A: Economy and Space* 49 (6): 1286–1307.
Sutoris, Peter. 2016. *Visions of Development: Films Division of India and the Imagination of Progress, 1948–75.* London: Hurst.
Tacoli, Cecilia. 1998. "Rural-urban interactions: a guide to the literature." *Environment and Urbanization* 10: 147–66.
Tambs-Lyche, Harald. 1980. *London Patidars: A Case Study in Urban Ethnicity.* London: Routledge.
———. 1997. *Power, Profit, Poetry: Traditional Society in Kathiawar, Western India.* New Delhi: Manohar.
Taylor, Steve. 2013. "Searching for Ontological Security: Changing Meanings of Home amongst a Punjabi Diaspora." *Contributions to Indian Sociology* 47 (3): 395–422.
Taylor, Steve, Manjit Singh, and Deborah Booth. 2007. "Migration, Development and Inequality: Eastern Punjabi Transnationalism." *Global Networks* 7 (3): 328–47.
Thakar, Shri Umyashankar Jivanlal. 1954. "Anand Town." In *Charotar Sarvasangra*, edited by Purushotam C. Shah and Chandrakandh F. Shah, 8–13. Nadiad, India: Parekh Kevdachand Kanjibhai and Sons.
Therwath, Ingrid. 2012. "Cyber-hindutva: Hindu Nationalism, the Diaspora and the Web." *Social Science Information* 51(4), 551–77.
Tilche, Alice. 2016. "Migration, Bachelorhood and Discontent among the Patidars." *Economic & Political Weekly* 51 (26–27): 17–24.
Tilche, Alice, and Edward Simpson. 2017. "On Trusting Ethnography: Serendipity and the Reflexive Return to the Fields of Gujarat." *Journal of the Royal Anthropological Institute* 23 (4): 690–708.
———. 2018. "Marriage and the Crisis of Peasant Society in Gujarat, India." *Journal of Peasant Studies* 45 (7): 1518–38.
Tsing, Anna. L. 2005. *Friction: An Ethnography of Global Connection.* Princeton: Princeton University Press.
Turèl, Thijs. 2007. "Community Upliftment through Self-Sustenance: The Impact of the 2002 Riots on Ahmedabad's Muslim Community's Choice between Political and Self-Sustenance Strategies to Improve Access to State Services." Master's thesis, University of Amsterdam.
Unni, Jeemol, and Ravikiran Naik. 2012. "Gujarat's Employment Story: Growth with Informality." In *Growth or Development: Which Way is Gujarat Going?*, edited by

Indira Hirway, Amita Shah, and Ghanshyam Shah, 270–300. New Delhi: Oxford University Press.

Upadhya, Carol. 2016. *Reengineering India: Work, Capital, and Class in an Offshore Economy*. Delhi: Oxford University Press.

———. 2017. "Amaravati and the New Andhra: Reterritorialization of a Region." *Journal of South Asian Development* 12 (2): 177–202.

———. 2018. "'Love for Land': Transregional Property Investments in Andhra." In *Provincial Globalization in India: Transregional Mobilities and Development Politics*, edited by Carol Upadhya, Mario Rutten, and Leah Koskimaki. Oxon: Routledge.

Upadhya, Carol, and Mario Rutten. 2012. "Migration, Transnational Flows, and Development in India. A Regional Perspective." *Economic & Political Weekly* 47 (19): 54–62.

Upadhya, Carol, Mario Rutten, and Leah Koskimaki, eds. 2018. *Provincial Globalization in India: Transregional Mobilities and Development Politics*. Oxon: Routledge.

Urry, John. 2016. *Mobilities: New Perspectives on Transport and Society*. London: Routledge.

Vahora, Ismailbhai Sabanbhai. n.d. *Vahora Darshan*. Unpublished manuscript, Mumbai.

van der Veer, Peter. 1994. *Religious Nationalism: Hindus and Muslims in India*. Berkeley: University of California Press.

———. 2002. "Transnational Religion: Hindu and Muslim Movements." *Global Networks* 2 (2): 95–109.

van Naerssen, Ton, Ernst Spaan, and Annelies Zoomers, eds. 2008. *Global Migration and Development*. New York: Routledge.

van Schendel, Willem. 1982. "Regions from Below: An Exploration in Rural Bangladesh." In *Focus on the Region in Asia*, edited by O. van den Muijzenberg, P. Streefland, and W. Wolters, 39–57. Rotterdam: Erasmus University.

Varadarajan, Siddharth, ed. 2002. *Gujarat: The Making of a Tragedy*. New Delhi: Penguin.

Varrel, Aurélie. 2012. "NRIs in the City: Identifying International Migrants' Investments in the Indian Urban Fabric." *Samaj* 6 (doi.org/10.4000/samaj.3425).

Varshney, Ashutosh. 2002. *Ethnic Conflict and Civic Life: Hindus and Muslims in India*. New Haven: Yale University Press.

Verstappen, Sanderien. 2005. *Jong in Dollywood: Hindostaanse Jongeren en Indiase Films*. Amsterdam: Het Spinhuis.

———. 2017. Mobility and the Region: Pathways of Travel within and beyond Central Gujarat. *Journal of South Asian Development* 12 (2), 112–35.

———. 2018a. "Communal Living: Religion, Class, and the Politics of Dwelling in Small-town Gujarat." *Contributions to Indian Sociology* 52 (1), 53–78.

———. 2018b. "Frustrations and Alliances: The Politics of Migrant Funding for Muslim Education in Central Gujarat." In *Provincial Globalization in India: Transregional Mobilities and Development Politics*, edited by Carol Upadhya, Mario Rutten, and Leah Koskimaki. 67–85. Oxon: Routledge.

Verstappen, Sanderien, and Mario Rutten. 2015. "A Global Town in Central Gujarat, India: Rural–Urban Connections and International Migration." *South Asia: Journal of South Asian Studies* 38 (2): 230–45.

Verstappen, Sanderien, Mario Rutten, and Isabelle Makay (dir.). *Living Like a Common Man*. 2011; The Netherlands: University of Amsterdam, 2011.

Vertovec, Steven. 1999. "Conceiving and Researching Transnationalism." *Ethnic and Racial Studies* 22 (2): 447–62.

Vullnetari, Julie. 2020. "The Interface between Internal and International Migration." *Routledge Handbook of Migration and Development*, edited by Tanja Bastia and Ronald Skeldon, 54–63. London: Routledge.

Wacquant, Loic. 2008. *Urban Outcasts: A Comparative Sociology of Advanced Marginality*. Cambridge: Polity.

Wassem, Ruth Ellen. 2009. "U.S. Immigration Policy on Permanent Admissions (3)," Congressional Research Service, March.

Wilding, R. 2007. "Transnational Ethnographies and Anthropological Imaginings of Migrancy." *Journal of Ethnic and Migration Studies* 33 (2): 331–48.

Wilkinson, Steven. 2008. "Which Group Identities Lead to Most Violence? Evidence from India." In *Order, Conflict, and Violence*, edited by Statis Kalyvas, Ian Shapiro, and Tarek Masoud, 271–300. Cambridge: Cambridge University Press.

Wimmer, Andreas, and Nina Glick Schiller. 2002. "Methodological Nationalism and Beyond: Nation–State Building, Migration and the Social Sciences." *Global Networks* 2 (4): 301–34.

Wogan, Peter. 2004. "Deep Hanging out: Reflections on Fieldwork and Multisited Andean Ethnography." *Identities: Global Studies in Culture and Power* 11 (1): 129–39.

Wolf, Eric R. 1982. *Europe and the People without History*. Berkeley: University of California Press.

Xavier, Constantino. 2011. "Experimenting with Diasporic Incorporation: The Overseas Citizenship of India." *Nationalism and Ethnic Politics* 17 (1): 34–53.

Xiang, Biao. 2013. "Multi-Scalar Ethnography: An Approach for Critical Engagement with Migration and Social Change." *Ethnography* 14 (3): 282–99.

INDEX

Page references in *italics* refer to illustrations.

accumulation, Marxist, 93
Ahmedabad (Gujarat): anti-Muslim violence in, 11, 48; commemoration activities in, 145n6; Muslim ghettoization in, 7, 142nn2–3; residential segregation in, 69; spatial marginalization in, 117; wealthy/poor proximity in, 109
Alexander, Claire, 61
Amsterdam Institute for Social Science Research (AISSR), 142n8
Amul Dairy Co-Operative (Anand), 57, 147n27
Anand (Gujarat), *x*; as administrative center, 55–56, 58; alliance narratives of, 41; Anand-Vidyanagar Road, ix; during anti-Muslim violence, ix, 18, 46–47, 52–54, 95, 117; as aspirational place, 14, 121, 122; Azad Chowk area, 56; BJP party in, 111; center-making in, 4, 9–12; Charotar conferences at, 25; Christian relocation from, 62–63, 65; closed houses of, 70–71, 75; commercial areas of, 56; Congress party in, 65, 111; construction industry in, ix–x, 3; during Covid-19 lockdown, 95; cross-community relations in, 53, 89; dynamism of, 88; educational institutions of, 45, 55, 57–58, 106, 147n28; globalization of, 112; Gujarati Muslims' return to, 4, 14, 70–71; Hindu areas of, x, 119; Hindu departures from, 55; Hindu-Muslim border of, 3–4, 9; Hindu-Muslim ratio in, 47, 65; Hindu-Muslim relations in, 108; infrastructure concerns of, 110–11; interreligious relations in, 108; Ismail Nagar area, 52, 56–57; land brokers of, 88-93; land prices in, 72, 102; land transfers around, 89, 90; liberation from village life in, 8; as lucky space, 4, 8, 60, 119; madrassa of, 57–58, 106; manufacturing at, 55; map of, *xiv*; minority populations of, 18; mobility in, 8–9, 13, 48, 69, 100, 101, 105–11, 121; mosques of, 48, 56, 97–98, 150n1; Muslim associations of, xi–xii; as Muslim center, 9, 70; national highways system to, 58; old town, 56; 100 Feet Road, 3–4, 23, 64, 65, 71; outskirts of, *56*; overseas relocations to, 14, 70–71; overseas remittances to, 12, 80; overseas residents' homes in, 71–74, 92, 121; overseas Vohras' investment in, 72, 73, 77; Patidar landowners, 91–92; Patidars of, 17, 89; as place of privilege, 60; population by religious community, 129–31; population size, 56, 133; post-violence emergence of, 48, 70; primary education in, 150n6; refugees from Ode to, 3, 47; refugees in, 3, 47, 54, 79, 80, 117, 146n22; as regional market, 122; relief societies of, 54, 73, 80; religious discrimination in,

169

Anand (Gujarat) (continued)
83; residential segregation in, 9, 22, 36, 61–65, 71, 92, 95, 119; rickshaw travel in, *104*, 119; rupture narratives of, 41; rural-urban connectivity of, 10, 100–105; rural-urban relocations to, 8–9, 14, 18–19, 41, 45, 47–48, 53–55, 90–91; safety in, 48, 52–54, 73, 117; Saiyeds of, 97, 98; service sector employees in, 99, 104; Shia communities of, 97; shop owners in, 134; as site of significance, 81; social mobility of, 8–9, 14, 48; social-political communities of, 120; social realms of, 119; student hostels of, 25; town planning in, 118; transnational development in, 88; transnational links of, 112; transnational visitors to, 71–74, 86–87, 92, 120; transportation network of, 118–19; "Urban Agglomerate" of, 56; urbanization in, 55–59; urban professionals of, 55; as vacation destination, 3; visa consultancy agents, 112; as Vohra hub, 9, 90–91, 121–23; Vohra landowners of, 91; in Vohra regional imagination, 43. *See also* middle class, Muslim (Anand); Muslims, Anand; neighborhoods, Muslim (Anand); Vohras, Anand

Andhra Pradesh: transnational caste claims in, 42; transnational land investments in, 93

anthropology: modes of construction, 20; multisited fieldwork in, 19, 20; of reorientation, 13–14, 126; scale in, 21

Appadurai, Arjun, 20

Arsad marriage circle, 29, 32–33; endogamous, 34, 124; relation with Makeriya circle, 100; status of, 35

asmita (Gujarati pride), 5, 37–38

Australia, overseas Vohras in, 74, 75, 113–14, 141n5, 148n1

autochthony, globalization and, 143n10

Bajrang Dal (VHP party), 49

Baruch (Muslim community, Gujarat), 15; overseas migration from, 74

belonging, regional: transnational politics of, 93; Vohras', 40, 43–44

Bertocci, Peter, 143n1

Bhaikaka (hero-engineer), x; memorialization of, 57

Bharatiya Janata Party (BJP), 38; in Anand, 111; in elections of 2002, 50; in Gujarati government, 82; Hindu nationalist agenda of, 51; Patidars in, 90

Bhatt, Vinod, 64

Bhuj (Kitch), residential segregation in, 115

Bobbio, Tommaso, 142n3

Bombay, colonial: middle-class suburb of, 119–20; Vohras of, 26. *See also* Mumbai

Boriavi (Gujarat), overseas Vohras from, 72

business families, economic subsidies for, 112

business families, Vohra, 30, 41, 59; in Hindu-dominated environment, 31, 103; linkages to land, 104; of Majestic Housing Society, 99–100; relations outside Vohra community, 125; rural-urban linkages of, 101

caste: among South Asian Muslims, 96; colonial categories of, 26; in community formation, 42; dynamics of exclusion, 117; in Gujarat social fabric, 38; importance in migration, 77; marriage within, 17, 34; oppression, 29; in Patidar internal politics, 124; regional orientation in, 13, 92; regrouping by, 6; transnational, 42; in village oppression, 62 center-making: in Anand, 4, 9–12; following anti-Muslim violence, 116; mobile research on, 9; neighborhood understanding of, 10; role of transnational migrants in, 12; spatial transformation in, 11

Chanawallah family (Vohras), 30; narratives of, 40

Chandrani, Yogesh Rasiklal, 38

Charotar microregion (Gujarat), *xiii*; agriculture of, 24–25; displacement of Muslims in, 44; geography of, 24; Islamic reform in, 98; migration from, 75, 76; Muslims' perspectives of, 13; Patidar influence in, 41–44; periurban growth in, 102–3; regional economy of, 24–25; Vohras' conception of, 40, 42; Vohras' relations to, 43–44, 100, 125; zones of opportunity in, 102. *See also* Vohras

Charotar Muslim Anjuman (association of Charotar Muslims, Karachi), 27

Charotar Sunni Vahora Anjuman (assembly), 25

Charotar Sunni Vahora Sudharak Mandalnu Mukapatr (Pamphlet for the Reformation of the Charotar Sunni Vohra Community), 27

Charotar Sunni Vahora Young Men's Association, 25, 26

Charotar Sunni Vohra Panchayat (village council, Petlad), 25

Charotar Sunni Vohra Samaj (community association), 23, 27, 81; in Mumbai, 27, 148n6

Charotar Sunni Vohra Tarahija Mandal association (Chaklasi), 26

Chatterjee, Anasua, 7

Chatterji, Joya, 61

Chaud family, business orientation of, 59

Chaud marriage circle, 29, 32–33; endogamous, 124; status of, 33, 35, 100

Chikhodra (Gujarat), Muslims of, 31

Chinakaka (BJP party worker), on infrastructure, 110

Christians: departure from Muslim neighborhoods, 117–18; relocation of, 62–63, 65; schools of, 107

cinema, Hindi: portrayal of overseas Indians in, 82, 149n11

cities, Indian: debates about Muslims in, 123; diversity of perspectives in, 127; Hindu-Muslim segregation in, 118; spatial divisions of, 108–9, 116–17; unequal access to, 60

cities, South Asian: walls of, 116

Citizenship Amendment Act (India, 2019), 87–88, 127

community: anthropological study of, 13–14; bureaucratic practices affecting, 7; in caste formation, 42; education as symbol of, 99; meanings attached to, 13

community, transnational: of India, 81; structures of, 80–81; Vohras', 20, 74. *See also* Gujarati Muslims, overseas; Vohras, overseas

Congress Party: in Anand, 65, 111; in Gujarat, 84

Covid-19 lockdown, Anand during, 95

Dalits, educational aspirations of, 60

Daneta Jatts (Kutch Muslims), critique of the notion of Gujarat, 39, 40

Daudi Bohras, Shia: of Anand, 143n11; communities of, 15, 28; urban, 28

Delhi, rural-urban migrants to, 92

Dewataja marriage circle, 27; status of, 35

Dharalas (peasant community, Gujarat), exploitation of, 17

Dhattiwala, Raheel, 52

diaspora: incorporation into India, 81; studies of, 11, 88. *See also* community, transnational; migrants, transnational; migration

displacement: following anti-Muslim violence, 49, 61, 71, 91, 124, 125, 127; to marginalized spaces, 116; reorientation following, 126; violence-induced, 151n4. *See also* refugees, Muslim; relocation, rural-urban
Dudhwala family (Vohras), 30, 33

East Africa: Anand residents from, 70; anti-Indian sentiment in, 75; Patidar migration to, 60, 75; Vohra migration to, 76–77
education: aspirations for, 58–59, 60, 99–100, 105–8; association with religious groups, 150n6; ceremonial interactions in, 110; Christian, 62, 107; cost of, 110, 150n6; free, 110; Hindu-majority spaces for, 107; importance for Vohras, 100; madrassa, 57–58, 106; middle-class patronage of, 109; mobility for, 106–8; Muslim-Hindu relations and, 106; overseas visas for, 111–12; primary, 109, 150n8; private, 113, 150n6, 151n9; for refugees, 107; role in social status, 106; secure employment in, 114; service families' focus on, 104; social/cultural capital through, 106; student mobility in, 107; as symbol of community, 99; trusts for, 109–10, 151n9
Elecon industrial enterprise (Anand), 57
endogamy, in Vohra marriage circles, 34, 124
Engineer, Asghar Ali, 28

Fruitwala family (Vohras), 30

Gamdi (Anand suburb): Christian relocation from, 62–63; Christian schools in, 107; Hindu population of, 147n31; infrastructure problems of, 63–64, 65; missionary activity at, 62; neighborhood classification of, 63

Ganesh Chokdi (Anand), housing of, 64
Garasia Jatta (Kutch Muslims): *Gujaratni asmita* and, 39; similarity to Hindus, 39–40
Gardner, Katy, 142n6
Gayer, Laurent, 52
Geschiere, Peter, 143n10
ghetto: negative connotations of, 118; sociological concept of, 116; as symbol of marginalization, 118; understanding of, 8, 142n3
ghettoization: Euro-American connotations of, 8; intermixtures within, 8; residential segregation as, 117; in urban studies, 121–22. *See also* housing societies; neighborhoods
ghettoization, Muslim, 6–7, 10; of Ahmedabad, 7, 142nn2–3; reproduction of stereotypes, 8
globalization: of Anand, 112; autochthony and, 143n10; of Patel caste networks, 42; scale of, 21
Godhra Station fire (2002), 145n13; fatalities related to, 50, 145n5
governance, scale in, 21
Gujarat, *xiii*; agricultural decline in, 60; anti-Muslim violence in, 5, 141n1; BJP government, 82; community dynamics of, 13; community in, 13; Congress Party in, 84; consequences of communal violence in, 127; conversion to Sunni Islam in, 28; current configuration of, 39; discourse of development in, 12; educational institutions of, 57–58; Hindu nationalism in, 5, 14; "idea of," 38–39; infrastructure development of, 58; labor discrimination in, 114; neoliberal economic policies of, 50, 112, 113; overseas visitors to, 85–88; population by religious community, 130–31; private education in, 113, 150n6, 151n9; public sector

employment in, 112; real estate business in, 88–93; refugee camps, 54, 67; regional centers of, 122; regional identity in, 123–24, 125; residential segregation in, 12, 69, 71; rural-urban land conversions in, 88–93; safe/unsafe divisions of, 47; secure employment in, 58, 113–14; spatial reorientation in, 77; status competition in, 97; transnational migration of, 11, 112, 125, 148n6; urbanization in, 12; urban/transnational networks of, 21

Gujarat, Government of: opportunities for overseas Indians, 70, 71, 82; "Status Report of the Displaced Families in Gujarat," 147n29

Gujarat High Court, verdicts of, 51

Gujarati Muslims: Ashraf/non-Ashraf groups, 29; community identity among, 96; descent of, 29; discursive exclusion of, 6; displacement in Charotar, ix, 3, 41, 43, 44, 61, 71, 74, 91; labor discrimination against, 114; loss of trust, 5; migration to Mumbai, 148n6; minority status of, 83; negative stereotypes of, 5, 9, 151n3; networks of, 19; nonbinary identity of, 123; perception of state, 149n15; population size, 18; recovering of agency, 6; regional identities of, 123–24, 125; religious identities of, 6; remaining in villages, 65–68; rural-to-urban distributions of, 47; rural-to-urban relocations, 18–19, 55-58; seafaring, 15; self-representation of, 123–24; socioeconomic exchange affecting, 126. *See also* Muslims, Anand; Vohras

Gujarati Muslims, overseas: as agents of development, 12, 71; Anand as home base for, 93; aspirations of, 94; businesses in Anand, 86, 88–90; from coastal communities, 74; discrimination in UK, 149n19; donations to Muslim initiatives, 149n10; educational visas for, 111–12; first generation, 84, 85, 149n19; government initiatives for, 82; homeland orientations of, 11, 93, 94; land-owning status of, 89; on mistreatment of minorities, 81; OCI status among, 85; opportunities in Gujarat, 70, 71; Patidar friendship of, 89–90; post-Brexit migration, 148n8; privileges in homeland, 87; relocations to Anand, 4, 14, 70–71; remittances to Anand, 12, 82; role in development, 12; socioeconomic links to Gujarat, 148n8; in the United Kingdom, xi, 9, 11, 83–84, 141n2, 148nn8–9; in the United States, xi; visits to Anand, 71–74, 86–87

Gujaratis: nonresident (NRGs), initiatives for, 82; as synonymous with Hindus, 38

Gujaratni asmita (Gujarati pride), 37–39; in anti-Muslim violence, 38; Garasia Jatta and, 39; Hindu celebrations of, 39–40; in popular culture, 38

Heitmeyer, Carolyn, 27, 28, 144n12; on Sultanpur Vohras, 41; on Vohra marriage system, 32, 35

hill stations, Indian, 117

Hindu-Muslim binary: in India, 38, 87, 123; overseas Indians and, 87

Hindu-Muslim relations, 52, 119; in Anand, 41, 108; education and, 106; middle class Muslims', 106; spatiality in, 22, 46, 49; in Sultanpur, 41; in Sundarana, 40–41; in Umreth, 103; Vohra business families', 31, 103

Hindus: as agents of development, 12; claims over village spaces, 43;

Hindus (continued)
  departure from Muslim neighborhoods, 55, 64–65, 117–18; dominant spaces of, 31, 103, 107–8; housing societies of, 64; rural spaces of, 4; as synonymous with Gujaratis, 38; vegetarianism, 5, 51; Vohra similarity to, 29, 40, 41, 43
Hindutva ideology: in anti-Muslim violence, 49–50; organizations associated with, 59, 145n10; overseas Vohras on, 71. *See also* nationalism, Hindu
homeland: in migration, 11, 90, 149n20; overseas Gujarati Muslims' privileges in, 87; overseas Gujarati orientations to, 11, 93, 94; overseas Vohras' narratives of, 82, 85, 88; reorientation within, 77
housing societies, Anand: during anti-Muslim violence, 117; builders of, 146n24; Christian, 63; for displaced persons, 91; formerly Hindu, 45; Hindu, 64; international migration in, 135; Ismail Nagar, 56–57; as middle-class spaces, 96–100; Mogri-Sisva, 54; of Muslim neighborhoods, xi, 4, 32, 52, 141n3; Nutan Nagar, 52, 56–57, 147n27; post-violence, 48; professionals living in, 59; for refugees, 80; rural-urban relocation to, 120; transnational connections of, 75. *See also* Majestic Housing Society; neighborhoods
hub: Anand as, 9, 90–91, 121–23; neighborhoods as, 122

Ibrahim, Farhana, 38, 39
I. J. Kapurwala Commercial School (Anand), 25
India: capitalist accumulation in, 92; colonial classifications for, 26; colonial "white" towns of, 117; decline of rural economy, 60; development in, 143n9; discrimination against minorities, 82–85; encouragement of remittances, 82; free speech in, 88; gated communities of, 117; Government of, 82, 84; Hindu-Muslim binary in, 38, 87, 123; Hindu-Muslim segregation in, 7, 119; incorporation of diaspora into, 81; madrassas, 150n4; neoliberal economy of, 7, 81–82; networks of, 122; opportunities for overseas Muslims, 70, 71; pluralistic image of, 85; regimes of migration in, 93; residential segregation in, 6, 7, 92, 115; small-town aspirations in, 14; small-town transformations in, 17–18; suppression of minority voices, 4; transnational community of, 81; urbanization in, 17, 18; urban space of, 108; urban studies in, 6. *See also* cities, Indian; Gujarat; Muslims, Indian; villages, Indian
Indians, overseas: banking in India, 82; effect of OCI amendments on, 88; Hindu-Muslim binary and, 87; real estate investments of, 93; rights of, 82; self-presentation by, 87. *See also* Gujarati Muslims, overseas; Vohras, overseas
Islam: mystic versus reformist, 98; reform movements, 96, 98–99; Shia, 97; Sunni, 97
Islamophobia, 83

Jaffrelot, Christophe, 53, 146n14
Jalais, Annu, 61
Jamil, Ghazala, 7, 92, 93
Janvikas, 147n25
Juhapura (Ahmedabad), 109, 142n3

Kanbis (agricultural caste), 26. *See also* Patidars (Patels, Charotar region)
Karamsad village, farmers of, 57

Kheda (former administrative district, Gujarat), 24
kinship, regional geography of, 36
Kirmani, Nida, 7
Kundu, Amitabh, 60
Kutch (Muslim community, Gujarat), 15; anti-Muslim violence in, 142n5; incorporation into Gujarat, 39; overseas migration from, 74; trade with Sindh, 39

Limbuwallah family (Vohras), 30
Living Like a Common Man (film, 2011), 148n8
Lokhande, Sanjeevini, 147n29

madrassas, 150n4; of Anand, 57–58, 106
Majestic Housing Society (Anand): business families of, 99–100; call for prayer in, 96; household occupations of, 134; middle class of, 96–100; mixed economic strategies of, 100; service sector employees in, 99; Tablighis of, 97. *See also* housing societies, Anand
majoritarianism (Hindu nationalism), 4, 51, 118
Makeriya marriage circle, 27; in Anand, 59; relation with Arsad circle, 100; status of, 35
Makeriyas, education of, 35–36, 59
Marcus, George E., 20
marriage circles, Vohra, 22, 23, 27; Arsad, 29, 32–33, 34, 35, 100, 124; *ataks* (subgroups) of, 33; Chaud, 29, 32–33, 35, 100, 124; concept of region in, 33; Dewataja, 27, 35; *ekla kutumb* (single-family), 33–34; endogamous, 32, 124; exogamy in, 36–37; formalization of, 124; hierarchy in, 33–34, 37, 144n10; hypergamy in, 33, 35; Makeriya, 27, 35, 59; matchmaking in, 32; membership in, 124; names of, 32; Patidar marriage and, 40; patrilocality in, 36, 125; regional, 36; schematic representation of, 34; status in, 29; unity through, 33; village-based, 31–37, 43
marriage system, Patidar: hierarchy in, 35, 124; hypergamous, 144n10; origins of, 144n10; village-based, 34–35; Vohra marriage and, 40
marriage systems, South Asian, 36
Mecca (Saudi Arabia), community-making of, 8
Merchant, Amrapali, ix–x, 141n1
microregions, 143n1; construction of, 23–24. *See also* Charotar microregion (Gujarat)
middle class, Indian: gated communities of, 108; social capital of, 108; social networks of, 95
middle class, Indian Muslim, x, 141n3; appeal of reform to, 98; aspirations of, 14, 95, 150n6; educational aspirations of, 99–100, 105–8; exclusion of, 120–21; income of, 113–14; philanthropy of, 109; private education for, 150n6; proximity to the poor, 109; transnational aspirations of, 112
middle class, Muslim (Anand): class aspirations of, 105; employment opportunities for, 112; entrepreneurs, 105; future prospects of, 112–14; income of, 113; Islamized, 99; of Majestic Housing Society, 96–100; marginal spaces of, 116; patronage of education, 109; professionals, 105; relations with Hindus, 106; retention of connections, 115; secure employment for, 113–12; transnational aspirations of, 111–15; view of Muslim neighborhoods, 120. *See also* Muslims, Anand; Vohras, Anand

migrants, transnational: as agents of development, 11, 142n7; homeland relations of, 11; mapping practices for, 142n6; political viewpoints of, 11; role in center-making, 12. *See also* mobility, transnational

migrant-sending regions: economic inequality in, 142n7; regional-level politics in, 123; spatial transformations in, 11

migration: crosscutting social networks of, 20; homeland in, 11, 90, 149n20; importance of caste in, 77; multifaceted process of, 9; multistranded social relations of, 19; neoliberal regimes of, 71; "transnational optic" of, 19; transnational pattern shifts in, 112. *See also* mobility; relocation

Misra, Satish, 28

mobility: in Anand, 69, 95, 105–11; of Anand Vohras, 121; effect of residential segregation on, 115; gender and, 150n3; for good works, 108–11; in Hindu dominated spaces, 107–8; inequality in, 115; as middle-class trademark, 115; safety in, 107; in South Asia, 19; stagnation and, 115; varying capacities for, 115; village patterns of, 122; Vohra regional conceptualization of, 125–26

mobility, rural-urban: across continuum, 126; in Anand, 101; in response to regional politics, 123. *See also* relocation, rural-urban

mobility, social: in Anand, 8–9, 14, 48; beyond social barriers, 95; capital in, 60; for education, 106–8; from Muslim neighborhoods, 95; research on, 19–20

mobility, transnational: aspirations for, 111–15; of Indian Muslims, 10, 95; in response to regional politics, 123. *See also* migrants

Modi, Narendra, 114; aid to non-resident Muslims, 87; on anti-Muslim violence, 50, 145nn9,11–12, 146n18; economic agenda of, 51; re-election of, 51; Zee TV interview, 50, 145n12

Mogri, refugees to Anand from, 54

mohalla (neighborhood), 142n4

mollahs, name-giving by, 33

Mosse, David, 142n6

Mumbai: Anand residents from, 70; Charotar Sunni Vohra Society, 27, 148n6; cost of living in, 73; Gujarati migrants to, 148n6; land prices in, 72; Vohra households in, 148n6. *See also* Bombay

"Muslim Lives Matter" (social media campaign), 88

Muslims, Anand: access to Hindu-majority spaces, 119; access to public roads, 118; alliance with Hindus, 52; Ashraf/non-Ashraf hierarchy among, 96–97; in Census of 2001, 47; connection to Hindu society, 119; economic opportunities for, 55; educational aspirations, 58–59, 99; estrangement from Anand, 118; feelings of being well, 119; financial concerns of, 112–14; of Gamdi suburb, 62–63; in Hindu-dominated spaces, 108; on Islamic schooling, 106; length of residence in, 48; mobility practices of, 100; moves within, 47; networks of, xi, 9, 10; population size, 18; regional/transnational networks of, 9; relations with state, 127; residential norms of, 61; response to violence, 52; self-perceptions of, 123; self-transformation among, 14; social boundaries for, 100; social identities of, 9; social life of, xi–xii; social mobility of, 8–9, 14, 48; social unacceptability of, 62; stable employment for, 120; Sunnis,

97; Tablighis, 97–99, 103; teachers, 58; transnational life of, xii, 88, 112; in transportation sector, 58; urbanization of, 18; white-collar employment for, 58–59. *See also* Gujarati Muslims; Hindu-Muslim relations; middle class, Muslim (Anand); Vohras, Anand

Muslims, Indian: Ashraf/non-Ashraf, 96–97; coerced displacement of, 61; cross-class solidarity among, 109; displacement to marginal spaces, 116; educational aspirations of, 60; exclusion of, 5, 81, 120–21; exclusions from citizenship concepts, 87; generic categories of, 6; incentives for land investment, 92; intermarriage between communities, 32; marginalization of, 5, 6, 7, 61, 116; metrocentric focus on, 10–11; middle-class aspirations of, 14, 95; nationalist depictions of, 4–5; regional orientations of, 13, 123–27; religious status among, 98; representation as outsiders, 4, 6, 82; self-representations of, 5–6; threats to territorial integrity, 123; translocal understandings of, 10; transnational mobility of, 10, 95; wealth/poor proximity of, 109. *See also* Gujarati Muslims; Vohras

Muslims, South Asian: class status among, 96

Muslim Vohra Association (United States), 27

Muzfarshah I, Sultan: conversions under, 28

Narmad, "Gujarat Koni?," 38
National Institute of Advanced Studies (NIAS, Bangalore India), 142n8
nationalism, Hindu: anti-Muslim violence in, 3; of BJP, 51; effect on Vohras, 17; as fascism, 52; in Gujarat, 5, 14; *Gujaratni asmita* in, 37–39; majoritarian, 4, 51, 118; Muslims as outsiders in, 4–5. *See also* Hindutva ideology

nationalism, Indian: contemporary concepts of, 81; internationalizing of, 82

neighborhoods: everyday practices of, 21; geographic zones of, 21; as hubs, 122; multistranded social fields of, 20; translocal, 10. *See also* ghettoization; housing societies; segregation, residential; suburb

neighborhoods, Muslim: daily life in, 10, 19; multiscalar perspective on, 122; networks of, 10; as "open air prisons," 115; role of state in, 7; stigma of living in, 7

neighborhoods, Muslim (Anand), x–xii; ghetto/suburb aspects of, 116–21; Hindus' departure from, 64–65, 117–18; infrastructure of, 63, 110, 115, 118; lack of representation in, 65; limited services for, 62; marginalization of, 122; mobility from, 95; non-Muslim departures from, 117–18; organizations of, xi–xii, 141n4; power structures of, 110–11, 122; as privileged spaces, 120; as regional center, 122; residents' perspectives on, 123; status differences in, 96–100; transnational networks of, xi; Vohras of, 3, 8, 13, 14–18, 121; as zone of awkward engagement, 93. *See also* housing societies, Anand

neoliberalism, 7; of Gujarat economic policies, 50, 112, 113; of migration regimes, 71; transnational migrants under, 81–82

Nicholas, Ralph W., 143n1

Nutan Nagar (Anand), housing society of, 52, 56–57, 147n27

Ode (Gujarat): anti-Muslim violence in, 46, 47, 51, 117; perpetrators of violence

Ode (Gujarat) (continued)
in, 146n17; rebuilding of, 146n23; refugees to Anand from, 3, 47
Overseas Citizenship of India (OCI), 81, 82, 94; amendments to (2019), 87–88, 127; free speech limitations of, 88; as marker of status, 86

Pakistan, anti-Hindu violence in, 49
Parmar, Mr. (Gamdi resident), 62–63
Partition of 1947, 46; communal violence at, 49; Vohras after, 25, 27, 124
pastoralists, Gujarati: state relations with, 39
Patel, Pravin, 75
Patel communities: agricultural, 30; educational aspirations of, 60; global caste networks of, 42. *See also* Patidars
Pathan, Minaz, xi, 141n3
Patidars (Patels, Charotar region): agricultural orientation of, 60; of Anand, 17, 89, 91–92; in BJP party, 90; caste-specific migration among, 125; colonial registration of, 26; conceptions of Charotar, 42; convictions for violence, 146n17; cross-border migrations of, 74; hierarchy among, 144n11; importance of village to, 42–43; influence in Charotar, 41–44; internal politics of, 17, 124; merchants, 41; migrants, 16; migration to East Africa, 60, 75; migration to the United Kingdom and the United States, 75; overseas Muslim associates of, 89–90; regional influence of, 16–17, 41–44; relations with villages, 125; relocation in Anand, 45; spatial imagination of, 42; transnational property claims of, 42; village-based marriage system of, 34–35; Vohras and, 40–43, 89, 91–92, 124. *See also* marriage system, Patidar

Patidars, overseas, 41; as "twice migrants," 75; in the United Kingdom, 74; in the United States, 74–75
place: anthropological perspectives of, 12–13; in reorientation, 13
place-making, practices of, 13
Pocock, David: on marriage systems, 35; Sundarana research of, 40, 144n12
power relations, scale in, 21
Provincial Globalisation, xv, 142n8

Rajyagor, S. B., 28
Rao, Nikhil, 119–20
real estate business (Gujarat): community politics in, 91; land brokerage in, 88–93; land ownership shifts in, 91; overseas Indians in, 93; transnational perspectives on, 93
reform, Islamic, 96, 98–99; rural-urban divide in, 99
refugee camps, 67; closure of, 54
refugees, Muslim: to Anand, 3, 47, 54, 80, 107, 117, 146n22; education for, 107; housing societies for, 80; from Ode, 3, 47; Vohras' aid to, 121
relocation, rural-urban, 18–19, 31, 54, 59–61; closure following, 7; cultural alienation in, 59; to Delhi, 92; earnings following, 59; economic, 61; following anti-Muslim violence, 46, 90–91; hierarchies in, 60; from Hindu-majority villages, 54; political aspects of, 61; profit generation in, 93; reasons for, 55; reproduction of privilege in, 60; Vohras', 31, 40, 73, 90–91, 92. *See also* displacement; mobility, rural-urban; refugees, Muslim; rural-urban linkages
relocation, rural-urban (to Anand), 8–9, 14, 18–19, 45, 47–48, 53–55, 65–68, 90–91; coerced *versus* voluntary, 61; to housing societies, 120; mobility

capital in, 60; reasons for, 57; from Tarapur, 105; urban segregation in, 62–65, 71
reorientation, 12–19, 123–27; from agriculture, 92; anthropology of, 13–14, 126; aspiration in, 13; class in, 13; economic practices of, 127; ethnography of, 12; following anti-Muslim violence, 94, 116; forces influencing, 126; long-term process of, 126; place in, 13; post-displacement, 126; rural-urban, 92, 126; social practices of, 127; spatial dimension of, 12, 13–14, 77, 127; translocal approach to, 126; transnational, 70, 74, 94, 126; within Vohra homeland, 77; Vohras' regional, 123–24
rural-urban land conversions (Gujarat), 88–93; speculation in, 90
rural-urban linkages: among service families, 104–5; among Vohras of Anand, 10, 100–105; of business families, 101; capital in, 105; Hindu-Muslim collaboration in, 103; mobility in, 101; segregation in, 115; social networks of, 101; of younger generation, 101. *See also* relocation, rural-urban
Rutten, Mario, xv, 11, 75, 142n8

Saiyeds (saints), of Anand, 97, 98
salwar kameez (dress), Gujarati women's, 107
samaj (community): in Anand, 15; importance of, 21
samuh lagna (group marriage, Vohra): celebration of, 23; reinvigoration of, 27. *See also* marriage circles, Vohra
Sangh Parivar organization: access to services through, 50; relation with anti-Muslim violence, 49
Saraswati, Lopamudra Ray, 60

Sarsa, Charotar conference (1940), 25
Savarkar, Vinayak Damodar, 49
scale: actor-centric approach to, 21; multiplicity of, 19, 21, 122; power relations in, 21
segregation, residential: in Anand, 9, 22, 46, 61–65, 71, 92, 95, 119; capitalist accumulation and, 92; causes of, 7, 46, 69; class status in, 62; connections with outside realms during, 69; estrangement in, 9, 115, 121; following anti-Muslim violence, 7, 22, 63–65; in Gujarat, 12; in India, 6, 92, 115, 118; intersecting connections of, 22; local-global linkages in, 115; meaning of mobility in, 95, 115; political economy of, 93; profit generation in, 93; in response to communal violence, 69; retention of connections in, 115; sense of closure in, 121; socioeconomic links in, 104. *See also* housing societies; neighborhoods
service families: focus on education, 104; rural-urban linkages among, 104–5
Shah, P. C. and C. G.: *Charotar Sarvasangra*, 76
Shias, of Anand, 97
Sindh traders, 39; alliances with Vohra, 53
Sisva, refugees to Anand from, 54
society: interwoven versus container model of, 19; nationalist descriptions of, 19; translocal understandings of, 10
South Asia: Islamic reform movements in, 98; marriage systems of, 36; mobility and exchange in, 19; transnational identities in, 123
space: effect of anti-Muslim violence on, 68–69; in Hindu-Muslim divide, 22, 46, 69; meanings imposed on, 9; Muslim discourse concerning, 8;

space (continued)
  religion-based regrouping in, 118;
  in reorientation, 12, 13–14, 77, 127;
  translocality of, 10, 20
space, Muslim: formation of, 4, 7, 67–69;
  perceptions of, x, 6, 9, 62–65
space, urban: bureaucratic practices
  affecting, 7; as Muslim, 4
Sreekumar, R. B., 145n7
suburb, in urban studies, 121–22
Sultanpur: Vohras of, 41, 58–59, 99;
  Vohra traders of, 33
Sunav (Gujarat), overseas Vohras from, 73
Sundarana: Hindu-Muslim relationships
  in, 40–41; Muslim relocations from,
  41; Vohras of, 40, 144n12
Sunni Charotar Vohras. *See* Vohras
Sunni Islam: in global discourses,
  97; in Gujarat, 28; Tablighi-Sunni
  divide in, 97
Sunnis, of Anand, 97
Supreme Court, Indian: on 2002
  violence, 50–51
Susewind, Raphael, 7, 92

Tablighi Jamaat (Islamic reform
  movement), 96; mosques of, 97–98
Tablighis, of Anand, 97–99, 103
Tanzania, Gujarati Muslims in, 73
Tarapur (Gujarat), relocation to
  Anand from, 105
Thakor, Asif, 141n4
Tilche, Alice, 40
Trump, Donald: anti-Muslim
  statements, 84

Umreth (Gujarat): development of, 102–
  3; real estate business in, 103
undhiyu (Gujarat dish), 45
United Kingdom: Anand residents from,
  70; Gujarati Muslims in, xi, 9, 11,
  83–84, 141n2, 148nn8–9; migration
  policies of, 149n21; overseas Vohras in,
  21, 70–81, 89, 148n7; religious tolerance
  in, 83–84; student visas for, 111
United Kingdom Vohra Association,
  27, 77–80; fundraising by, 78, 79–80;
  meeting in Leicester, 79, 80; relief
  committee, 79; social events of, 78, 80
United States: Anand residents from, 70;
  family-sponsored immigration system,
  77, 148n4; Muslims in, xi, 11, 84–85;
  Muslim Vohra Association, 27, 77, 78;
  tolerance for Muslims in, 87; Vohras
  in, 76, 77
Upadhya, Carol, xv, 142n8.
urbanization: middle-class strategies
  of, 120; of Muslim landowners,
  105; socioeconomic links in, 104;
  spatial imaginaries of, 118. *See also*
  cities, Indian; mobility, rural-urban;
  rural-urban linkages
Uttarayan festival, 45, 105
Uttarsanda, Charotar conference at
  (1926), 25

Vadodara, student hostel of, 25
Vahora, Ahmad (pseudonym), 71–73
Vahora, Haji Ismailbhai Sabanbhai,
  144nn4–5; *Vahora Darshan*, 26
Vahora, Samir (pseudonym), 86
Vahora, Shahinben (pseudonym), xi,
  31–32, 36, 98, 108
Vahora, Siraj (pseudonym), 105, 107,
  108, 109, 110
Vahora, Vasim, 150n2; attire of, 103; on
  Hindu-Muslim relations, 119; rural-
  urban linkages of, 101–5; Tablighi
  Jamaat activity, 103
Vahora, Zakiya (pseudonym), 95;
  mobility of family, 105–6
Vahora Sudharak (newspaper), 27
Vallabh Vidyanagar: anti-Muslim
  violence at, 117; attraction for

Muslims, 57–58; Hindu population of, 63; Hindu spaces of, 107; safety of, 107; town planning of, 63
Vallabh Vidyanagar campus (Sardar Patel University), x, 57, 58, 106–7; violence at, 52
van Schendel, Willem, 143n1
Varshney, Ashutosh, 53
vegetarianism, Hindu: Gujarati ideal of, 5; violence concerning, 51
VHP (Hindu organization), 49
villages, Indian: experiencing anti-Muslim violence, 3, 49, 145n7; income in, 59; lack of facilities, 68; land-owning elites of, 59–60; migrants' assets in, 69; mobility patterns of, 122; Muslim contentment with, 66–67; Muslims' fear in, 67–68; reasons for remaining in, 65–68; regional concept of, 124; rural-urban linkages of, 101; services for, 59; spatial organization of, 17; Vohras as minorities in, 125. *See also* rural-urban linkages
violence: social-spatial consequences of, 46, 116; societal transformations following, 4
violence, anti-Muslim: at Partition, 49; on roads, 122; in the United States, 84
violence, anti-Muslim (2002): in Ahmedabad, 11, 48; in Anand district, 132–33; Anand during, ix, 18, 46–47, 52–54, 95, 117; center-making following, 116; commemoration of, 54, 145n6; commemoration of Hindu "martyrs," 147n26; curfew during, 46, 95; defenses against, 47, 52; destruction of property during, 48; displacement following, 49, 61, 71, 91, 124, 125, 127; effecting Vohras, 17; effect of urbanization on, 69; eyewitnesses to, 52, 78–79; fatalities during, 46, 50, 79,

145n5; in Gujarat, 5, 141n1; *Gujaratni asmita* in, 38; in Hindu nationalism, 3; Hindutva ideology in, 49–50; in Kutch, 142n5; legitimization of, 5, 49; memory of, 102, 123; #NotInMyName protests, 51; in Ode, 3, 46, 47, 51, 117; official complicity in, 50; overseas response to, 79–80; persecutions following, 50–51; as pogrom, 48–52; police during, 49; political parties promoting, 49; rebuilding following, 146nn23–24; refugees following, 3, 5, 47; regional segregation following, 7, 22, 63–65; relief for, 54, 73, 79–81, 93, 147n25; religious identities in response to, 118; reorientation following, 94, 116; reporting on, 49; as revenge, 145n13; "riot" narrative of, 50; rural-urban relocation following, 46, 90–91; self-segregation following, 7; socio-spatial consequences of, 46, 116; spatial marginalization in, 117; Special Investigation Team (SIT) on, 51, 146nn15,18; threat of recurrence, 67–68; understanding of space in, 68–69; at Vallabh Vidyanagar campus, 52; villages experiencing, 49, 145n7; against women, 48–49. *See also* refugees, Muslim; relocation, rural-urban
visas, educational, 111–12
Vitthal Udyognagar Industrial Estate (Anand), 57
Vohra, Abdullahmia Hassan, 77
Vohra, Farida (pseudonym), 67–68
Vohra, Ibrahim (pseudonym), 66–68
Vohra, Idris (pseudonym): land brokerage activities, 88–93
Vohra, Salma (pseudonym), 66
Vohra, Yousuf (pseudonym), 73, 78–80
"Vohra": meaning of, 28; transliteration of, 143n2

Vohra Association of North America, 24, 27, 149n9
Vohra Families Reunion (Delaware, 2015), 148n5
Vohras: after Partition of 1947, 25, 27, 124; agricultural economy of, 15, 17; Anand as hub for, 9, 90–91, 121–23; Baruchi community, 15; belonging in Gujarat, 40, 43–44; Brahmin ancestry among, 29; business alliances with Hindus, 41; Charotar community, 15, 28; of colonial Bombay, 26; community books of, 27; community formation by, 26–28; community identity of, 123–24; community rural histories of, 28–31; conceptions of Charotar, 40, 42; conceptions of region, 13; dispersed kinship networks of, 125; diverse religious practices of, 15–16; educational institutions of, 25; effect of Hindu nationalism on, 17; engagement with rural economy, 100; equality among, 144n11; following independence, 25; as Gujarat community, 123; Gujarati language of, 41; Hindu ancestry of, 28–29, 97; history of, 26; importance of education to, 100; internal community hierarchy of, 100; Kadiwal community, 28; land brokers, 89; land owners, 30–31; migration to Pakistan, 25; of Mumbai, 148n6; narratives of agriculture, 29, 30, 40; narratives of aspiration, 122–23; narratives of community, 13, 17, 28–31, 40; narratives of conversion, 29, 31; narratives of economy, 30–31, 37; narratives of region, 14–15, 100; Patani community, 28; Patidars and, 40–43, 124; position in Charotar microregion, 43–44; positions of rupture, 41, 44; refugees, 3; regional communities of, 14–18, 20, 24–28; regional identity of, 23–24; regional orientations of, 123–25; relations with Charotar villages, 43, 125; religious leadership among, 97; reorientation from agriculture, 92; rupture of regional orientations, 125; rural-urban relocations, 31, 40, 73, 90–91, 92; safe spaces for, 4; similarities to Hindus, 29, 40, 41, 43; social networks of, 19, 37; status differences among, 29; of Sultanpur, 33, 41, 58–59, 99; of Sundarana, 40, 144n12; Surati community, 15, 28; trade activities, 28, 30–31, 32, 33, 41, 53, 58–59; transnational community networks of, 20, 74; urbanization of, 22, 100; violence against, 17. *See also* Charotar microregion; marriage circles, Vohra

Vohras, Anand, 9, 21–22, 28, 90–91, 144n11; dominance among Muslims of, 96; government employment for, 59; Hindu friends of, 121; landowners, 91; mobility of, 121; neighborhoods of, 3, 8, 13, 14–18, 121; population size of, 15; regional orientation of, 125; rural-urban linkages of, 10, 100–105. *See also* Muslims, Anand

Vohras, overseas, 15, 22, 92, 141n5, 147n1; aid to refugees, 121; Anand as anchor for, 126; Anand homes of, 71–74, 92, 121; associations of, 27–28, 77–81; in Australia, 74, 75, 113–14, 141n5, 148n1; collective action among, 77; community organizations of, 74; critique of Hindutva, 71; experiences of return, 86, 148n2; fundraising for relief by, 78, 79–81, 93; investment in Anand, 72, 73, 77; investment patterns of, 71, 90; migration of, 74–77; migration to East Africa, 76–77; myth of homeland for, 88; numbers of, 74–75, 125; permanent residents,

148n3; real estate investments, 81; relations with India, 71, 74, 81–88; relevance of Anand for, 93; relocation to Anand, 14, 70–71; remittances to Anand, 80; reproduction of regional orientations, 125; reunions among, 78; self-organization by, 77; social networks of, 89–90; understanding of community structures, 80–81; in the United Kingdom, 21, 70–81, 89, 148n7; in the United States, 27, 76, 77, 78; villages of origin, 81

women, Muslim: clothing of, 107–8; sexual violence against, 5
women, Vohra: as keepers of kinship networks, 125; as marriage migrants 36; reproduction of regional community, 37; role in marriage systems, 32, 36
WOTRO Science for Global Development programme (Netherlands), 143n8

xenophobia, 83

GLOBAL
SOUTH
ASIA

Padma Kaimal,
K. Sivaramakrishnan,
and Anand A. Yang,
SERIES EDITORS

GLOBAL SOUTH ASIA takes an interdisciplinary approach to the humanities and social sciences in its exploration of how South Asia, through its global influence, is and has been shaping the world.

Adivasi Art and Activism: Curation in a Nationalist Age, Alice Tilche

New Lives in Anand: Building a Muslim Hub in Western India, by Sanderien Verstappen

Mumbai Taximen: Autobiographies and Automobilities in India, by Tarini Bedi

Outcaste Bombay: City Making and the Politics of the Poor, by Juned Shaikh

The Ends of Kinship: Connecting Himalayan Lives between Nepal and New York, by Sienna Craig

Making Kantha, Making Home: Women at Work in Colonial Bengal, by Pika Ghosh

A Secular Need: Islamic Law and State Governance in Contemporary India, by Jeffery A. Redding

Making the Modern Slum: The Power of Capital in Colonial Bombay, by Sheetal Chhabria

History and Collective Memory in South Asia, 1200–2000, by Sumit Guha

Climate Change and the Art of Devotion: Geoaesthetics in the Land of Krishna, 1550–1850, by Sugata Ray

Bhakti and Power: Debating India's Religion of the Heart, edited by John Stratton Hawley, Christian Lee Novetzke, and Swapna Sharma

Marrying for a Future: Transnational Sri Lankan Tamil Marriages in the Shadow of War, by Sidharthan Maunaguru

Gandhi's Search for the Perfect Diet: Eating with the World in Mind, by Nico Slate

Mountain Temples and Temple Mountains: Architecture, Religion, and Nature in the Central Himalayas, by Nachiket Chanchani

Creating the Universe: Depictions of the Cosmos in Himalayan Buddhism, by Eric Huntington

Privileged Minorities: Syrian Christianity, Gender, and Minority Rights in Postcolonial India, by Sonja Thomas

High-Tech Housewives: Indian IT Workers, Gendered Labor, and Transmigration, by Amy Bhatt

Making New Nepal: From Student Activism to Mainstream Politics, by Amanda Thérèse Snellinger

The Rebirth of Bodh Gaya: Buddhism and the Making of a World Heritage Site, by David Geary

Mobilizing Krishna's World: The Writings of Prince Sāvant Singh of Kishangarh, by Heidi Rika Maria Pauwels

Banaras Reconstructed: Architecture and Sacred Space in a Hindu Holy City, by Madhuri Desai

Displaying Time: The Many Temporalities of the Festival of India, by Rebecca M. Brown

The Gender of Caste: Representing Dalits in Print, by Charu Gupta

Sensitive Space: Fragmented Territory at the India-Bangladesh Border, by Jason Cons

The Afterlife of Sai Baba: Competing Visions of a Global Saint, by Karline McLain

A Place for Utopia: Urban Designs from South Asia, by Smriti Srinivas

Lightning Source UK Ltd.
Milton Keynes UK
UKHW011943280722
406528UK00003B/348